Praise for *Loving Creation*

"*Loving Creation* puts biblical themes together in an entirely original and uniquely insightful way, joining theology and ethics in a new vision for the Christian life. Gary Chartier's 'creational love ethic' overcomes several time-worn and troublesome dichotomies: Old Testament vs. New Testament, sacrificial love vs. human flourishing, Protestant love command vs. Catholic natural law, and the neighbor who needs our care vs. the all-sufficient God. Chartier's comprehensive and fair-minded approach makes this an exceptional introduction to key topics in Scripture, theology, and applied ethics. A wonderful springboard for theological discussion and learning!"

—LISA SOWLE CAHILL, J. Donald Monan, S.J.,
Professor of Theology, Boston College

"Chartier offers a *tour d'amour* in ethics. He employs various conceptual tools in the name of love to address specific moral questions that both ancient and contemporary people ask. Taking creation—not just humans or God—as the focus, *Loving Creation* offers an appealing exploration of well-being in our time. Highly recommended!"

—THOMAS JAY OORD, author of *Pluriform Love*
and *The Uncontrolling Love of God*

"*Loving Creation: The Task of the Moral Life* successfully argues for a creational ethic of love and well-being. Chartier masterfully weaves together a wide variety of sources to ground Christian ethics in a theological anthropology that is at once compelling and profound."

—ANDREW KIM, associate professor of theology, Marquette University,
and author of *An Introduction to Catholic Ethics since Vatican II*

"Love matters again. Understanding it as appropriate regard for the well-being of sentient creatures, Chartier calls for renewed attention to this vital topic in Christian ethics by probing issues of significance to everyone—from war and peace to sexuality to property punishment to dispute resolution within the church. Specialists in Christian ethics should read this book because of its contribution to advancing the conversation about love shaped by predecessors like Joseph Fletcher and Paul Ramsey. But engaging with it will also profit many others, including everyone who has sat in classrooms long enough to earn an undergraduate degree. After all, what's not to like about love?"

—DAVID R. LARSON, professor of religion (retired),
Loma Linda University

LOVING CREATION

LOVING CREATION

The Task of the Moral Life

GARY CHARTIER

Fortress Press
Minneapolis

Print ISBN: 978-1-5064-8104-3
eBook ISBN: 978-1-5064-8105-0

For
Brian Hebblethwaite,
Charles Scriven,
Charles W. Teel Jr.,
David R. Larson,
Jack W. Provonsha,
Nicholas Wolterstorff,
Paul Ramsey,
and
Roy Branson

"Ethical rules are not mere accidents of social history. Nor are they arbitrary impositions. They are based on the nature of things as they came from the hand of the Creator. . . . Violation of the ethical rules . . . is a violation of one's own being."

—Jack W. Provonsha, "Creation"

"All valid patterns of moral behavior (ethics) will necessarily reflect the divine creation and can be considered descriptions of it (in contrast with being arbitrary or merely prescriptive)."

—Jack W. Provonsha, "Creation"

"Wherever the Creator is creatively and redemptively at work in the world and its institutions, something sacred is going on. . . . The Creator affirms the world. . . . The Creator has sanctified the whole of what He has made—and is making."

—Jack W. Provonsha, *God Is with Us*

"It is the defender of exceptionless rules who would build a floor under the individual fellow man by minimum faithfulness-rules or canons of loyalty to him that are unexceptionable, while it is the proponent of future possible exceptions who may be placing societal and gross consequence-values uppermost."

—Paul Ramsey, "The Case of the Curious Exception"

"Moral laws . . . are rules of meaning for the word 'love.' . . . The moral laws must exclude certain kinds of behavior—there must be some things which do not count as love."

—Herbert McCabe, *Law, Love and Language*

Contents

Acknowledgments

Writing a book about love seems like a particularly welcome occasion for expressions of gratitude.

I'm pleased by the opportunity to voice my deep appreciation to the usual suspects—A. Ligia Radoias, Aena Prakash, Alexander Lian, Alicia Homer, Andrew Howe, Annette Bryson, Carole Pateman, Charles Teel Jr., Craig R. Kinzer, David B. Hoppe, David Gordon, David R. Larson, Deborah K. Dunn, Donna Carlson, Eddy Palacios, Elaine Claire von Keudell, Elenor L. A. P. L. B. B. Webb, Eva Pascal, Fritz Guy, Gen Mensale, Jeffrey Cassidy, Joel Wilson, John Thomas, Julio C. Muñoz, Kenneth A. Dickey, Lawrence T. Geraty, Maria Zlateva, Melissa Cushman, Michael Orlando, Nabil Abu-Assal, Nicole Regina, Patricia M. Cabrera, Roderick Tracy Long, Roger E. Rustad Jr., Ronel Harvey, Ruth E. E. Burke, Sel J. Hwahng, Sheldon Richman, Stephanie Burns, W. Kent Rogers, Wonil Kim, and Xavier Alasdhair Kenneth Doran—for the usual reasons.

I want enthusiastically to thank Ryan Hemmer at Fortress for his belief in this project. I conceived of this book while completing *Understanding Friendship*, which I'd enthusiastically agreed to publish with Ryan, and I appreciate his willingness to embrace a related book so readily. I am also thankful to Jessica Lockrem and Elvis Ramirez for help throughout this book's production and to David R. Larson, Thomas Jay Oord, Lisa Sowle Cahill, and Andrew Kim for their willingness to endorse it. I also want to underscore my appreciation for David Gordon's rapid and incisive review of the book in draft, which has reduced my risk of embarrassment at multiple points. And Roderick Long deserves my thanks for confirming my freedom to use a small portion of an essay to be published in the *Molinari Review* in this volume.[1]

John Thomas has been an exceptional friend during the twenty-two years I have been associated with what is now the Tom and Vi Zapara School of Business at La Sierra University. I am deeply appreciative of his loyalty, his confidence, and his willingness to welcome and support my scholarly endeavors. Thanks, too, to Lovelyn Razzouk for aiding me on a variety of fronts.

---

1. Gary Chartier, "Love in Dialogue," *Molinari Review* (forthcoming).

Almost thirty years ago, as we stood on the lawn of the Loma Linda University Church, the late Bob Reeves put me on the spot. "Do you believe?" he asked. Awareness of the complexity of our circumstances, of many countervailing considerations and conflicting approaches, prompted me to respond, "I hope." I can't demonstrate that many of the assertions I make here or their various presuppositions are correct, but I can offer what I'd like to think are good reasons for belief and for hope.[2] I want to thank Bob for engaging me so directly and prompting me to think and speak more clearly.

While the notes acknowledge a range of people with whom I have engaged and from whom I have drawn innumerable useful ideas, thanks are due especially to the new classical natural law theorists, orthodox and otherwise, for their development of the theoretical position I seek to explore here. This book is a relatively liberal Protestant appreciation, appropriation, and revision of this important contemporary Aristotelian-Thomist approach to Christian ethics. I am grateful for opportunities to learn from Chris Tollefsen, Germain Grisez, John Finnis, Joseph M. Boyle Jr., Mark C. Murphy, Robert P. George, and Sophie-Grace Chappell.[3] Since discovering *Natural Law and Natural Rights* in the La Sierra University Library three and a half decades ago, I have found Finnis's

2. For the felicitous expression "reason for hope," see Stanley J. Grenz, *Reason for Hope: The Systematic Theology of Wolfhart Pannenberg*, 2d ed. (Grand Rapids: Eerdmans 2005).

3. Thus, what I say throughout reflects—even if in ways the authors might not endorse—my reading of, *e.g.*, Germain Grisez, *The Way of the Lord Jesus* 1: *Christian Moral Principles* (Chicago: Franciscan Herald 1983); Germain Grisez, *The Way of the Lord Jesus* 3: *Difficult Moral Questions* (Quincy, IL: Franciscan 1997); John Finnis, *Natural Law and Natural Rights*, 2d ed. (Oxford: Clarendon-Oxford University Press 2011); John Finnis, *Fundamentals of Ethics* (Oxford: Clarendon-Oxford University Press 1983); John Finnis, *Aquinas: Moral, Political, and Legal Theory* (Oxford: Clarendon-Oxford University Press 1998); John Finnis, Joseph M. Boyle Jr., and Germain Grisez, *Nuclear Deterrence, Morality and Realism* (Oxford: Clarendon-Oxford University Press 1987); Germain Grisez and Russell Shaw, *Beyond the New Morality: The Responsibilities of Freedom*, 3d ed. (Notre Dame, IN: University of Notre Dame Press 1988); Robert P. George, *In Defense of Natural Law* (New York: Oxford University Press 1999); Mark C. Murphy, *Natural Law and Practical Rationality* (Cambridge: Cambridge University Press 2001); and Timothy Chappell (now Sophie-Grace Chappell), *Understanding Human Goods: A Theory of Ethics* (Edinburgh: Edinburgh University Press 1998). My goal here is to articulate a moral position that falls within a recognizably Protestant tradition, emphasizing love, but that is, at the same time, continuous in important ways with first-rate contemporary Catholic moral reflection. Grisez and those with whom he's worked are not oblivious to the relationship between love and right action; Grisez and Shaw speak of what I'm calling the specifications of love in practice as "guidelines for love" (Grisez and Shaw, *Beyond the New Morality* 117), and Grisez regards these specifications (he calls them "modes of responsibility") as responding to the question "What does love really require?" (*Questions* 858). But love is not centrally emphasized in the new classical natural law theorists' presentation of their approach.

elaboration of natural law theory clear, provocative, and systematic, in some contexts liberating and in others thoroughly challenging. He is a person of massive erudition and evident integrity. It is a pleasure to offer my own perspective on a theoretical approach with which he is distinctively identified (a perspective he will surely decline to share at multiple points). Other thinkers in the broad Aristotelian tradition have also been quite helpful to me as I've sought to elaborate an ethic that is simultaneously rooted in creation and focused on love; they include Alasdair MacIntyre, Henry Veatch, Philippa Foot, Richard Kraut, Roderick T. Long, and Stephen R. L. Clark.

I have incurred debts of gratitude to Christian ethicists with theoretical orientations and substantive convictions different in various ways from my own. They include, among others, Gene Outka, Gilbert Meilaender, Herbert McCabe, John Milbank, Keith Ward, Nicholas Wolterstorff, Oliver O'Donovan, Paul Ramsey, Robert Merrihew Adams, Stanley Hauerwas, and Timothy P. Jackson. I have dedicated this book to scholars who have inspired me in a particularly pronounced way—by precept, example, or both—during the decades of reflection that have led to the completion of this book.

Brian Hebblethwaite supervised the inquiry into the nature and limits of friendship I undertook as a doctoral student; at the same time, he modeled a theologically sensitive and essentially creational Anglican via media in ethics. Charles Scriven's creativity, capacity for effective communication, recognition of the importance of peace, sparkling prose style, and willingness to change his mind are all worth emulating. Charles W. Teel Jr. taught me to think theology and politics together, to ask personal and structural questions in tandem, even as he offered warm friendship and pointed challenge.

In the years following our first meeting at the Loma Linda University Ethics Colloquium in Griggs Hall in December 1984, Dave Larson has spent more time reading and talking about my theological and ethical work than anyone else. I never tire of his company or of the opportunity to celebrate his friendship. The work of Jack W. Provonsha, Dave's predecessor as director of Loma Linda University's Center for Christian Bioethics, appealingly exemplified and encouraged an approach to Christian ethics that put creation front and center. Jack reflected on theological and ethical issues with a striking combination of venturesome creativity and profound fidelity to tradition and inspired generations of students to bring the life of the mind and the life of faith together. I have enjoyed learning from his work since I first began reading theology in the early 1980s, and I am honored to conduct the Sabbath School class he led for so many years with so much impact around the world.

Nicholas Wolterstorff never fails to impress. That's true whether one's focus is his breadth of concern and understanding, his perceptiveness, his clarity and vigor of expression, his moral passion, or his personal graciousness. His own emphasis on flourishing—captured, on his view, by biblical talk of *shalom*—as lying at the heart of Christian thinking about ethics and society and his careful parsing of talk about love make acknowledging him here particularly appropriate. I grappled with his *Justice in Love* much too late in the process of writing this book, realizing with appreciation and dismay how frequently my concerns echoed his and how probing his rejoinders would doubtless be in cases in which we disagreed. For decades, his example has helped me understand more clearly what it means to think philosophically as a Christian, and I look forward to continuing to learn from him.

I never knew Paul Ramsey, and I frequently find myself arguing with him. But I continue to be inspired by his dedication to rigor, precision, clarity, and comprehensiveness; his ability to think through the complex facets of a problem; and his defense of covenant fidelity and noncombatant immunity as aspects of love—indeed, by his capacity to see the links between love and a broad range of issues in Christian ethics.

As a scholar and public intellectual, Roy Branson enthusiastically linked moral reflection with literature, history, and the arts. As a teacher, he inspired a generation of students to focus their creative energies on ethics. As a participant in church life, he drew on a distinctive moral vision as a passionate advocate of peace, inclusion, and justice. He was also, in his role as editor of *Spectrum*, the first person to publish scholarly work under my byline. He died much too young, and I'm glad I can honor him and his legacy here.

It is a joy to express my gratitude here. I hope this book will be a testament to the value of the relationships I have highlighted as well as an encouragement to others to enact and celebrate love.

Introduction

The Christian moral life should express love and therefore focus on creation. Appropriate regard for well-being is essential to love in its primary sense, love as an irreducibly ethical category. And well-being is best understood in creational terms. So this book offers an account of love rooted in an understanding of our created well-being.

Putting Love and Creation Together

The emphasis on love in the teachings of Jesus, Saint Paul, and Saint John—as well as later thinkers, including Saint Augustine and Saint Thomas Aquinas—has made it central to multiple strands of Christian moral theology. In the twentieth century, love-centered approaches to ethics were particularly common among Protestants, both liberal and conservative.[1] Paul Ramsey articulated a Christian ethic of care and respect for persons in which love—ultimately expressed in covenant—played a definitive role. Joseph Fletcher's "situation ethics" used the language of love to ground a kind of Christian act-consequentialism. However, despite the importance of love for Christian faith generally, it ceased to play a dominant part in Christian thinking about ethics not long after Ramsey and Fletcher debated their alternative construals of it in the 1960s,[2] even if it continues to attract provocative attention.[3]

---

1. For an influential typology, see William K. Frankena, "Love and Principle in Christian Ethics," *Faith and Philosophy: Philosophical Studies in Religion and Ethics*, ed. Alvin Plantinga (Grand Rapids: Eerdmans 1964) 203–25.
2. Ironically, Gene Outka's *Agape: An Ethical Analysis* (New Haven, CT: Yale University Press 1974), which sought to dissect the use of love in Christian ethics using analytic philosophical tools, may have marked the last major contribution to the debate it attempted in part to interpret and assess. (I mean not to downplay the merits of later books on the topic but only to suggest that those books form part of a later conversation less central, as it seems to me, to the ongoing discussion of method in Christian ethics.)
3. See, *e.g.*, Eric Gregory, *Politics and the Order of Love: An Augustinian Ethic of Democratic Citizenship* (Chicago: University of Chicago Press 2010); Timothy P. Jackson, *Love Disconsoled: Meditations on*

I won't try here to offer an explanation for love's eclipse as a principal motif in Christian, especially Protestant, thinking about the moral life. But I am confident that love deserves renewed attention as a normative and organizational principle for Christian ethical reflection. That's true because of its vital role in the Christian tradition, because of the important place it can and should occupy in Christian theology generally, and because of its capacity to keep moral reflection focused on the issue of creaturely welfares.[4] A focus on love helps to protect Christian ethics from a spiritualization that encourages us to turn away from God's good creation and from the temptation to put our moral actions in the service of purported impersonal values rather than actual creatures.

Creational approaches to ethics, politics, and law are often viewed as static, inflexible, and insensitive to the complexities of the human situation. I want to show here how a creational approach can be open and liberating. Similarly, love-centered interpretations of Christian ethics too often seem to urge *undifferentiated* love and thus to prove alienating and inhospitable to particular relationships and projects, with many of the predictable liabilities of consequentialist or Kantian approaches. Perhaps unsurprisingly, creational and love-centered approaches are often kept at arm's length. It is striking, for instance, that the second edition of a classic twentieth-century American exposition of natural law ethics features only two references to love of creatures—one concerned with spousal love, the other with love of neighbors more generally—in its 627 pages.[5]

Anchoring love in a rich, creation-rooted conception of well-being can allow Christian ethics to remain focused on love while avoiding difficulties associated with alternative love-centered proposals. Similarly, a creational ethic that includes a rich account of well-being and incorporates a limited number of robust specifications of love[6]—ways of loving rather than a profusion of detailed, domain-focused rules—can allow Christian ethics to remain focused on creation while shunning inflexibility and detachment from ordinary human life.

Christian Charity (Cambridge: Cambridge University Press 1999); Timothy P. Jackson, *The Priority of Love: Christian Charity and Social Justice* (Princeton, NJ: Princeton University Press 2009); and Timothy P. Jackson, *Political* Agape: *Christian Love and Liberal Democracy* (Grand Rapids: Eerdmans 2015).

4. See Gary Chartier, *The Analogy of Love: Divine and Human Love at the Center of Christian Theology*, 2d ed. (New York: Griffin 2020).

5. Austin Fagothey, *Right and Reason: Ethics in Theory and Practice*, 2d ed. (St. Louis, MO: Mosby 1959) 333, 365 (per the volume index).

6. Language about specifying love is very much in evidence in the work of both Paul Ramsey and Nicholas Wolterstorff, though I am not consciously aware of having drawn from either of them in this regard.

Loving Creation is intended as a contribution to Christian analytic moral theology. It offers an interpretation of the Christian moral life as ordered by love. The book's title emphasizes its twofold concern with *love* as the activity of the ethical subject and *creation* as the ground of love's focus—well-being. Throughout, *Loving Creation* presupposes and stresses the pluriform quality of love. By emphasizing the ways in which love is differentiated and structured—offering a clear, nonarbitrary basis for regarding love as channeled in particular ways rather than homogeneous—it preserves love's centrality without ignoring the richness and diversity of our relationships and the varied ways in which our lives can go well. By highlighting the degree to which each sentient is irreplaceable and unique, the book seeks to underscore the importance of choosing fairly and without embracing the intent to injure, ever, without embracing interpretations of Christian love as detached, impartial, or impersonal. And it attempts to integrate love thus understood with a theological vision in which love is a constitutive attribute of God.

What Doesn't Count as a Love Ethic?

By linking love and creation as I've done, I'm not seeking to engage in some logical sleight of hand of a sort that could potentially convert any ethic into a love ethic. So it's worth noting some obvious examples of ethics that *aren't* love ethics:

- An ethic of divinely commanded moral requirements that features a set of duties, whether general or situation-specific, arrayed like items on a clothesline, is neither organized around nor focused on love per se.
- A natural law ethic that involves fulfilling the putative demands of human nature—say, by respecting presumed natural *teloi*—without any clear sense of their connection with well-being would be unlikely to count as a love ethic.
- An ethic of prima facie duties that treats the set of requirements on which it focuses as freestanding wouldn't be a love ethic.[7]

---

7. See W. D. Ross, *The Right and the Good* (London: Oxford University Press 1930); and W. D. Ross, *Foundations of Ethics* (Oxford: Clarendon-Oxford University Press 1939). While benevolence is one of the requirements Ross highlights, love doesn't ground the others or constrain their interactions.

- The same would be true of a variety of *particularism*, marked by sensitivity to situation-specific considerations, which might potentially have nothing to do with love.
- To the extent that a moral approach treats putatively impersonal values as carrying independent normative weight, it isn't a love ethic. While impersonal realities can be admired, delighted in, and so forth, they can't be loved in the primary sense with which I am concerned here, since they have no welfare for which an agent could show regard, appropriate or otherwise, and since they are unable to appreciate agents' actions.

Various approaches to ethics not *defined* by love could be cast as *concerned* with love. But there is nothing about the approaches I have listed here that would lead us to expect them to be particularly attentive to or rooted in love.

The Plan of the Book

In this book, I spell out what I take to be the connections between love and creation by underscoring the link between love and well-being, elaborating a creation-rooted conception of well-being, responding to a range of moral issues in light of this conception, and critically examining multiple alternatives to what I'll call a creational love ethic. In some cases, I develop and display the features of such an ethic through a systematic exposition, in others through an extended engagement with particular topics, and in yet others through an illustrative exploration of the significance of this kind of ethic for classic moral injunctions and themes.

In chapter 1, I seek to lay some groundwork for thinking about love, creation, and Christian ethics together. I attempt to show how love serves to shape understandings of divine revelation and providence that unavoidably affect the way we do and understand ethics. And I suggest an interpretation of creaturely love for God that might be consistent with the approach I've elaborated.

I emphasize in chapter 2 that well-being is central to any plausible understanding of love. I elaborate multiple dimensions of well-being but also multiple aspects of love, aspects we can see as specifying what love involves and requires. I highlight ways in which embracing these varied ways of loving leads to a discernible *structure* for love. And I offer an understanding of divine truth and creaturely fallibility that I hope complements my elaboration of a creational love ethic and is consistent with the understanding I've offered of God's relationship with the world.

I go on in chapter 3 to consider a provocative alternative to a creational love ethic—theistic voluntarism, the view of Christian ethics as a matter of obedience to moral requirements freely created by God. I explain why theistic voluntarism is unsatisfactory before going on to scrutinize the idea of personal vocation, which is often cast in voluntarist terms.

While theistic voluntarism provides one Christian alternative to a creational love ethic, it is unsurprising that there are many different ways of understanding Christian ethics concerned with love and thus significantly closer to the one I offer here. In chapter 4, I briefly examine several construals of Christian ethics centered on love. I consider understandings of love as uniquely determined in the moment by the need of the other; as the promotion of aggregate well-being; as covenant-shaped service to the other; and as a distinctive combination of equal and unqualified regard with overflowing generosity. I conclude by looking critically at an alternative that generates an ethic of respect for persons on the basis of what's needed to enable people to exhibit creative love.

I seek in chapter 5 to clarify what love looks like in action by considering two key areas of particular emphasis for Christian ethics. I begin by considering the use of force, explaining how I believe a creational love ethic could address both the isolated person's use of force and the challenge of using force in the context of war. Then, I consider a range of issues related to human eros, building a general account of how love might find expression in erotic interactions before considering moral questions raised in connection with same-sex relationships and divorce.

In the final three chapters of the book, my goal is to continue clarifying the meaning of a creational love ethic by highlighting its significance for our contemporary application of key Christian moral sources. Chapter 6 examines the Decalogue, pointing to ways in which its constituent injunctions might look when viewed through the lens of love. I turn in chapter 7 to the New Testament, showing how love understood creationally can help us frame and apply moral teachings found there. Finally, in chapter 8, I use a creational love ethic to help develop accounts of the seven deadly sins and the seven Christian virtues. I summarize the book's arguments in the conclusion before seeking to point the way toward future conversation.

Love matters. In what follows, I hope to point a perhaps unexpected way toward a genuine life of love concerned with the characteristics and dynamics of creaturely life.

1

Creation and Love

Whatever else it involves, to love is to choose out of appropriate regard for the good (well-being, fulfillment, flourishing, welfare, self-realization, . . .) of the one loved.[1] Choosing in this way can mean *realizing* well-being, *protecting* it, *promoting* it, or *respecting* it.[2] In this chapter, I explain why we might want to view well-being as essential to love, elaborate an understanding of God's love in particular, and reflect on what divine providence and divine revelation might look like in light of this understanding before briefly exploring how we might think about creaturely love for God.

Concern with Well-Being as Essential to Love

If I love you, I may *also* want to spend time with you; I may want your life to be enriched *through my actions*; I may desire to share my life with you. These and other features may be part of love. But at minimum, if I love you, I act (if I can) with appropriate regard for your welfare. The notion of appropriate regard is

1. Nicholas Wolterstorff, *Justice in Love* (Grand Rapids: Eerdmans 2011), argues that, while all aspects of well-being are goods, not all goods are aspects of well-being (15, 76). I think we can understand Wolterstorff as having rightly highlighted that someone can choose wrongly in relation to me without affecting my well-being. But I don't think it follows that someone's choosing wrongly *in relation to me* necessarily wrongs *me*; it can still be the case that I am not wronged unless, at minimum, my well-being is affected. James Griffin, *Well-Being: Its Meaning, Measurement, and Moral Importance* (Oxford: Clarendon-Oxford University Press 1986), plausibly suggests that morality needs to attend to the same kind of well-being with which prudence—which he distinguishes from morality, as I would not—is concerned (64–72).
2. We also talk about love in relation to the desire for connection or union, as also with delighted appreciation. There are interesting family resemblances and other links here, ones I would not wish to obscure or deny, but I will not focus on them in what follows.

built into our notion of love. I can do things for you because you want them, and refusing forcibly to interfere with someone's choices is not infrequently an important part of love for her. But loving you is about something other than doing or giving just whatever you happen to want. It's about concern for your welfare. So, for instance, giving you space to choose is part of loving you because, among other things, developing and exercising your capacity for judgment help to constitute your own well-being.

Just as with other people, so with myself: loving myself means choosing with genuine regard for my own well-being. I can seek to fulfill my own desires—setting off, for instance, on a program of revenge that will likely result in my death and that will leave alienation and destruction in my wake. But doing just what I want, giving myself what I feel like having just because I feel like having it, isn't a way of loving myself. What I want won't necessarily contribute to my fulfillment. In loving myself, just as in loving others, it's important to ask what contributes to my real-world welfare, not just to my acquisition of whatever I happen to desire.

If I love when I choose with appropriate regard for well-being, then love must be love for some particular sentient creature. Well-being is always *some creature's* well-being. There's no such thing as well-being that's distinct from the well-being of every actual moral patient (that is, every morally considerable entity whose welfare can be affected by what some agent does). You can't promote, protect, respect, or realize friendship in the abstract, for instance; every friendship is the friendship of particular human or nonhuman sentients. An aesthetic experience has to be a particular experience; there can't be the experience of seeing the *Mona Lisa* that's not *some creature's* experience of seeing the *Mona Lisa*. Aesthetic experiences are always located in consciousness and so a particular consciousness; and knowledge must at least have the potential to do so, with the result that it must be my knowledge or yours or hers. And so on.

There's a sense in which I can speak of loving, say, a house—a house that helps connect me with generations of ancestors, with childhood memories, with a lost loved one—because I've cathected it, incorporated it into myself. But this is love in a different sense: the house isn't an independent moral subject. It matters to me, but it matters as part of my own identity or as a means to particular experiences, not as an entity with moral standing of its own. I can't have regard for its well-being because it's not a subject and so doesn't actually have well-being. It doesn't have a point of view; it can't appreciate, much less help to realize, any goal. It's not the kind of reality that can flourish. And so others' consideration of the house in their plans makes sense, if it does, out of their regard for *me*.

Love as regard for well-being can include a desire for the benefit of the agent and of others. Recognizing the worth of friendship, for instance, I can desire your friendship as good for me and offer my friendship as good for you (though a friendship, once formed, transcends simple divisions between self and other). But love as desire counts as *love* only if it includes appropriate regard for the well-being of the one desired.

Grounded in Love

God is love. So God's activity of creation both expresses divine love for creatures and seeks to bring about love among creatures and love of creatures toward God. In what follows, I suggest some reasons for speaking of God as love; emphasize that to talk about God as love must mean that creation is real and that creatures are God's partners in love; indicate why we might think of created persons as inherently and, at base, equally loveable; and spell out what might be involved in calling creation "good." Then, I reflect on the dynamics of God's love for and with creation and consider what a love-centered approach might mean for talk of the relationship between nature and grace and the relationship between creation and redemption.

God Is Love

The conviction that God is essentially love deserves extensive development and explication. But, to make a case briefly here, biblical writers speak repeatedly of God's love and of God *as* love. Divine love is at the center of both prophetic declamation and New Testament teaching—notably the teaching of Jesus. It has also figured centrally in the Christian tradition, both in theology and in the experiences of Christian mystics. (It has also, of course, been evident in texts and religious experiences in a variety of non-Christian traditions.) We can see talk of divine love as essential to what we say about divine goodness; without incorporating reference to such love, our talk of divine *goodness* risks being vacuous. If divine goodness is a necessary aspect of who God is, then—presuming love is integral to divine goodness—love, in particular, is an essential divine attribute. And this can seem even more evident if we understand the lives of creatures as in some sense incorporated in the divine life, so that God wills God's own good and the good of creatures inextricably.

Created Partnership in Love

Affirming that God the Creator is love commits us to, among other things, the conviction that creation is *real*. God could *contemplate* a purely imagined world, and divine contemplation could involve a delight we might perhaps regard as a kind of love by courtesy or extension. But, if concern for well-being is essential to love in the primary sense, then, in order to be the object of God's love, any creature must be capable of *having* well-being. Something can have well-being only if it is real—I can't make a fantasy object better or worse off. And something real can have well-being only if it possesses, at least in some sense, the capacity to appreciate and act; there's no such thing as the well-being of a grain of sand. Any creature who is the object of God's love must, then, be real and possess the capacity to appreciate and act. To be able to appreciate and act is to be a partner in love, capable of loving along with God. So the creatures who are the objects of God's love must themselves be partners in love, not only loving God responsively but also mediating God's love to their fellow creatures.

Persons as Loveable

"Are not two sparrows sold for a penny? Yet not one of them will fall to the ground apart from your Father."[3] Persons are objects of love for us and for God because of the irreplaceable uniqueness of each individual life, of each unique individual world, a world that could not drop out of existence without loss.[4] God's love and ours are also fitting because persons exhibit the beauty of sheer, particular existence. God treasures us as products of divine creativity, as partners in loving the world (whether or not we realize this), as friends (again, whether or not we know it), and as sentients incorporated in the divine life.

Irreplaceability and the inherent beauty of particular existence are characteristics of all persons, and they thus render persons fundamentally morally equal in entitlement to moral consideration. I have reason to treasure every other created person as possessing the same characteristics that entitle me to moral consideration by others, so that ignoring or discounting another would make no sense given my valuation of myself and my conviction that others should value me. We welcome, even desire, other persons and seek their well-being for all

3. Matt 10:29.
4. See, *e.g*, Helen Oppenheimer, *The Hope of Happiness: A Sketch for a Christian Humanism* (London: SCM 1983) 77–110, on which I depend at multiple points in this paragraph and elsewhere.

sorts of reasons, just as we may respond instinctively to some with aversion. But, whatever may attract us to or repel us from another person, just as a person, she is rightly an object of love.

The same considerations warrant our declining to attack nonhuman sentients—the sparrows God notices in their uniqueness[5]—and our openness to welcoming them into friendship. The basic characteristics that unite finite persons and render them morally significant similarly entail our loving recognition of these fellow members of "lifekind."[6]

Creation as Good

Genesis 1 repeatedly affirms that God contemplated this or that product of divine creative activity and "saw that it was good."[7] And, the Bible's first chapter declares, God saw that creation as a whole "was very good."[8]

It should come as no surprise that what is made by God, perfect in knowledge and power, should be good. But it is worth emphasizing that Genesis 1 speaks of God's *seeing* that what God has made is good. Perhaps this is just a matter of God's seeing that divine intentions have been realized. But we can also understand it as premised on the assumption that goodness is objective; that it's not, somehow, an arbitrary posit of the divine will; that claims about goodness are correct or incorrect in virtue of how things actually are.

The world God has made is good for both God and sentient creatures.

The world is good for God. (*i*) It is home to sentient creatures who can enter into friendship with God. (*ii*) The impersonal, nonsentient aspects of the world make possible the activities and experiences of these sentient creatures, including their awareness of and responsiveness to God. (*iii*) The sentient and nonsentient aspects of the world are aesthetically excellent and so inherently worth contemplating.

The world is also good for sentient creatures. (*i*) Each sentient creature is good for itself. It can welcome the goods realized in its own life. (*ii*) Sentient creatures can flourish in a variety of ways in and through their interactions with one another. (*iii*) Sentient creatures can flourish in a variety of

5. Cp. Daniel Dombrowski, *Not Even a Sparrow Falls: The Philosophy of Stephen R. L. Clark* (East Lansing: Michigan State University Press 2000).
6. For this expression, see, *e.g*, Stephen R. L. Clark, *Biology and Christian Ethics* (Cambridge: Cambridge University Press 2000) 318.
7. Gen 1:10, 12, 18, 21, 25; cp. 1:4.
8. Gen 1:31.

ways in and through their interactions with nonsentient realities. Nonsentient realities can extend sentient creatures' capacities, offer them sustenance, and enrich their lives by serving as foci of curiosity, sources of insight, occasions for the development and display of various skills, and objects of aesthetic contemplation.

Creation and Love

God's activity in the world is ongoing. This activity can be spoken of as creation or providence. It is creation because it fosters the emergence of what is new, and, whenever what is new occurs, God is present and active. It is providence because it involves God's influence on and interaction with existing creatures. Whether viewed through either lens, this activity is an expression of love.

God creates intending friendship with sentient creatures. Divine-creaturely friendship is good for God and creatures alike, and creative activity designed to effect this good is thus an expression of love for both. There is no creaturely reality from which God is absent. So there is no such thing as seeking the good of creatures apart from God. To talk about the flourishing of creatures in the world without referring to God is ultimately no more than a sometimes useful abstraction. God creates intending that creatures will flourish as they develop all of their created potentials. In this way, God seeks the good of—God loves—the sentient creatures God makes.

God makes creaturely sentients not only so that they can love and be loved by God but also in order for them to love. As creatures seek their own well-being and the well-being of other sentients, they love. And their doing so is a reflection and expression of the loving intention God embraces as Creator, so that God loves in and through them.

At the same time, insofar as creaturely life occurs in a sense within God's own life, the benefits sentients create for themselves and other sentients can be seen as enriching the divine life: God could *envision* these without their occurrence, but their *actual* occurrence in the lives of creatures whom God loves offers something of value to God (even if creatures are unaware that this is the case). Love is in a sense the characteristic activity of the created world because creatures seek their own well-being and the well-being of other sentients on an ongoing basis, even if often quite imperfectly.

Creation is thoroughly lovable, too. Sentient creatures are lovable for their own sakes. Loving them means showing appropriate regard for the various aspects of their flourishing. And, while there is no way to foster the well-being of a nonsentient, which means that it can't be an object of love in the primary sense, it can be thoroughly appreciated for its role in or promotion of the well-being of sentients.

Love, Grace, and Nature

God's loving interaction with the world provides a valuable anchor point for reflection on what Christians sometimes talk about as the relationship between grace and nature, which are too often seen as distinguished in ways that leave open the possibility that grace could be absent from nature.

We can understand "grace" as (*i*) another word for divine love; as (*ii*) a name for the divine activity that reflects, proceeds from, and seeks to foster the embodiment of divine love; or as (*iii*) a label for something given to us in and through that loving activity. "Nature," by contrast, is another word for creation.

Creation flows from and embodies grace. Providence expresses grace. For Christians, the universality and inescapability of grace can be understood as functions of the ongoing activity of God as Creator but also as matters of the work of God as Word and Spirit. As John 1 emphasizes, the *Logos* is "the true light, which enlightens everyone."[9] This does not mean that God the Word provides everyone with infallible knowledge. It does mean, however, that God the Word grounds the order and meaning of the world and fosters growth in openness to and apprehension of God's truth, and so in rational understanding on the part of all rational creatures. God as Spirit blows throughout the creaturely world fostering new life, vitality, and freedom—openness to the future, and therefore openness to discovery.

There is no divine activity that is not loving, so there is no divine activity that is not an instance of grace. There is no creaturely event that occurs independently of divine activity, and so all creaturely events are touched by and grounded in grace. "Grace is everywhere."[10] There can be no such thing as creation without grace, nature without grace, because grace is who and how God the Creator is, and there can be no creation without the presence and activity of the Creator. An ungraced nature is not even a logical possibility if we cannot ultimately conceive of nature other than as creation.

9. John 1:9.
10. George Bernanos, *The Diary of a Country Priest*, trans. Pamela Morris (London: Boriswood 1937) 317. (An ellipsis separates the final word of the sentence from its predecessors in the original printing.) Thanks to Wonil Kim for repeated opportunities to discuss this work.

It's perfectly reasonable, therefore, to speak of "Christologically penetrated orders of creation" *as long as* it's clear that there is never a district of experience and activity from which God—and so God the Word, the *Logos*—is *absent*.[11] The language of penetration might seem to presuppose a freestanding world, the work of the Creator, which might or might not be visited—"penetrated"—by the *Logos*. But to talk in this way would be to treat the relationship between Creator and *Logos* as contingent (as well as to fly quite without warrant in the face of John 1's emphasis on the centrality of the *Logos* in creation).

We might be inclined to resist the idea of the universality of grace on the assumption that it could be understood as placing a divine imprimatur on this or that cultural phenomenon. And we should be alert to the reality of creaturely finitude, fallibility, ignorance, and sin and decline to treat God as endorsing the world's brokenness. We know from direct observation that God's intentions are often not realized in the world. God's grace is too often disregarded or resisted. But God—grounding Creator, shaping *Logos*, pervasively blowing Spirit—is always there.

While grace is everywhere, nature is always nature; creation is always creation. Its capacities are always finite. Divine activity cannot make creatures other than creatures any more than it can make square circles. It cannot, therefore, elevate them beyond the creaturely; their destiny cannot be to be anything other than creatures. Divine activity *can*, however, seek the development of creatures *as creatures*. It can seek to foster their continued growth in flourishing. In short, then, nature is always, essentially, graced, and grace is constantly at work seeking to foster nature's ongoing flourishing and to heal nature's brokenness.

Creation and Redemption

Understanding nature and grace this way helps us think about the integral relationship between creation and redemption.

There are multiple dimensions of the divine activity we label "salvation" or "redemption."[12] But we can helpfully describe the aspects that most clearly impinge on or involve ethics as "development" on the one hand and "healing" or "liberation" on the other.[13] "Development" refers to the unfolding of creation's

---

11. Paul Ramsey, *Deeds and Rules in Christian Ethics* (New York: Scribner 1967) 119.
12. We can distinguish at least seven of these dimensions; see Chartier, *Analogy of Love* 328.
13. For the language of "liberation" and "development" in this context, see Nicholas Wolterstorff, *Until Justice and Peace Embrace* (Grand Rapids: Eerdmans 1983).

potential that is the primary focus of ethical choice, while "healing" and "liberation" encapsulate what God does when helping us to move beyond personal brokenness, institutional constraints, and social fetters. God is always at work to heal and liberate creation. To put it another way, God seeks to enable creation to flourish *as* creation ("development") and therefore to enable creation to move beyond impediments to that flourishing ("healing," "liberation"). God's work fostering the healing and liberation of creation and God's work fostering the ongoing development of it occur in tandem. Sometimes, indeed, they're identical.

Creation is dynamic. Consider the grand sweep of the biblical narrative, in which the human story begins in a garden and climaxes in a city. In this narrative, God's ongoing activity involves the continued enhancement of creaturely life as creaturely life. To emphasize that salvation or redemption is normed by creation is not to imagine God as aiming in any narrow sense at the *restoration* of some past golden age. It is simply a way of stressing that creation is not a kind of second-best alternative to be transcended by redemption: healing and liberation have to do with enabling creation to be itself, which is always God's purpose as Creator.[14]

Love, Providence, and Revelation

Taking God's love seriously means offering an account of God's relationship with the world that doesn't obscure that love in the context of talk about how God acts and so how God communicates with us. A plausible account of divine action will need to begin with the experienced reality of evil. Taking the reality of evil seriously means recognizing that God's will is often not done in the world and conceiving of divine action the world accordingly—as at least ordinarily constrained and mediated. Thinking about divine action in this way means understanding the reception of divine communication with creaturely persons as impeded by their finitude, fallibility, ignorance, and sin.

Providence and Evil

Sometimes, the problem of evil is posed as a tension between the reality of evil and the *goodness* of God. This kind of framing makes it easy for someone who

---

14. I learned to think this way thanks to the work of Al Wolters; see Albert M. Wolters, *Creation Regained: Biblical Basics for a Reformational Worldview*, 2d ed. (Grand Rapids: Eerdmans 2005).

wants to affirm the reality of God in the face of evil to argue for a definition of *goodness* that disconnects it from *moral* goodness, perhaps by identifying divine goodness with a kind of abstract divine perfection. This approach allows its proponents to insist that there is nothing about perfect divine goodness that is even possibly inconsistent with the existence of the kind of world we actually experience. The problem of evil is no problem at all. But this response to the problem of evil isn't available if we understand God as essentially love, if divine perfection and divine goodness necessarily involve perfect love.

Losses like the ones creatures constantly experience seem very difficult to square with divine love on the assumption God exercises "meticulous" providence. Paul Helm puts it this way when clarifying the significance of this view of divine action: "One clear corollary of . . . [belief in] meticulous providence is the banishment from our thinking of 'lucky' events or actions as the operation of Fortune. There is no source of events, however surprising and capricious they may be to us, than the will of Almighty God who 'works all things according to the counsel of his will' (Eph. 1:11)."[15]

This way of putting the matter rules out not only fortune but also physical accidents and creaturely choices contrary to God's intentions. If providence is meticulous, then God is responsible for all events—our choices, natural disasters, diseases, predatory violence by nonhuman creatures, and so forth. And this means that there really *aren't* creatures. Creaturely existence is a sham. Creatures are, in effect, sock puppets because they have no capacity for agency; the divine will lies behind all of their actions. Ironically, then, while this view is often defended by Christians who seek to affirm God's transcendence of creation, by denying the genuine reality of creation, it ultimately becomes a kind of pantheism, collapsing any meaningful distinction between creation and God.

Affirming an understanding of providence as meticulous, or any nearby view, is inconsistent, then, with treating genuine love for creatures as definitive of God. That's in part because it makes God responsible for evil: if no event happens contrary to God's intentions, then that must include evil events. In denying creatures' capacities for genuine agency, the conviction that providence is meticulous also renders creaturely love for God impossible. It treats creaturely actions as entirely determined by God. And love, while it aims at unity, presupposes a duality that divine determination erases. Love comes from a genuine other. The beloved cannot be other than the lover if the lover exhaustively

---

15. Paul Helm, "Providence," *Gospel Coalition*, 2021 <https://www.thegospelcoalition.org/essay/providence/>.

determines the beloved's behavior, including the beloved's response to the lover. If the lover and the beloved are finally indistinguishable, there can be no love between them (though we might want to talk in this case about self-love).

In effect, belief in meticulous providence turns creaturely love of God into divine self-love. Given meticulous providence, when creatures do not love God, this cannot be contrary to God's intentions: their not loving God is itself an expression of those intentions. And, when they *do* love God, they do so as determined, directed by God's will. They love God because God, who determines every aspect of the being of each creature, wills that they do so. Ultimately, then, when they love God, God is loving God's own self through them.

There is nothing shameful about the idea of God's loving God; God is eminently worthy of love. But it is very different from the kind of divine love for creatures often depicted in the Bible and in the Christian theological and spiritual tradition. To envision God as seeking the love of creatures, as Scripture and tradition do, is to underscore the reality that there may be barriers to creatures' responsiveness to God. It is to maintain that creaturely love for God is not *necessary* and that it is not unilaterally up to God whether and how creatures respond. If this were not the case, there would be no point to divine pursuit, divine outreach. (In addition, if the world is finally indistinguishable from God, because everything that happens in it is determined by the divine will, to affirm that its current state is a product of meticulous providence might also seem to suggest a kind of divine masochism.)

To affirm divine love is to insist that creation is in fact real and therefore capable of behaving contrary to God's intentions. It is also to believe not only that creation *can* behave contrary to God's intentions but also that it *does* behave contrary to God's intentions. When sin, destructive accident, natural disaster, or predatory violence takes place, God does not intend them or endorse their occurrence. Whatever else might be involved in the conviction that God is love, it must involve, at minimum, the idea that God does not will injury to any sentient. If God cherishes each sentient and each aspect of the well-being of each sentient, then there will never be any reason for God to attack the well-being of that sentient and so to intend that any other creature attack that sentient or to encourage any other creature to do so or to will that that sentient be injured by any physical process. And God, whose capacities for engagement or attention are unlimited, will actively focus on each sentient and actively foster each sentient's well-being rather than disregarding it.

Alternative Understandings of Divine Action

If divine love means that God does not injure and actively seeks the good of each sentient creature, then the fact that injuries occur means that, when they do, God's intentions are thwarted, God's action is constrained, even while God is conceived of as perfect in power. There are different ways of understanding how the reality that God is perfect in power comports with the reality that divine intentions are not always realized. Perhaps (*i*) to say that God is perfect in power means God has all the power that any reality *could* have, but such power, the greatest conceivable power exercisable by a metaphysically perfect reality, does not include the capacity to determine how created realities behave, even potentially; rather, it is the capacity to exert the maximum possible *influence* on each such reality.

Someone might defend this view on the basis that creation isn't genuine unless those created are real and capable of responding to the Creator's action and that the genuine reality of creatures means that it's not possible even in the abstract for God to override their freedom.[16] Creaturely freedom is not only real but necessary. How we assess this view will depend in part (given the argument I've imagined) on whether we think finite reality does involve, inescapably, freedom in relation to God or whether we think God could in fact override creaturely freedom, whether such freedom is a gift God could retract.

Perhaps, alternatively, (*ii*) to say that God is perfect in power means that, while God has the metaphysical capacity to prevent the injuries that occur by determining what creatures do, there is a decisive reason for God not to do so. A defender of this view might suggest that creaturely freedom is real but contingent, so that the limits on divine action we observe result from factors like God's loving regard for the freedom of creatures and God's intention that the physical world constitute a regular, orderly whole and present a predictable backdrop for creaturely action.[17] Our assessment of this alternative will depend on whether we think these are likely to be sufficient reasons for an unqualifiedly loving God to exercise self-restraint, even when doing so means not preventing horrific injuries, or whether the occurrence of such injuries is better explained on the assumption that, as on (*i*), God cannot act coercively to keep them from happening.

16. See, *e.g.*, David Ray Griffin, *Evil Revisited: Responses and Reconsiderations* (Albany: SUNY 1991).
17. See, *e.g.*, Austin Farrer, *Love Almighty and Ills Unlimited* (London: Collins 1962); and Richard Swinburne, *Providence and the Problem of Evil* (Oxford: Clarendon-Oxford University Press 1998).

If we accept (*i*), then we will understand all divine activity as a matter of noncoercive influence, working in and through the actions of sentient creatures and the dynamics of natural processes. If we accept (*ii*), it might still be the case that all divine activity was, again, noncoercive and mediated.[18] Because a view, whether rooted in (*i*) or (*ii*), that treats all divine activity in this way can be seen as characterizing all such activity as undertaken through mediated and constrained influence on the world, and so as providential rather than miraculous, we can label such a view PROVIDENCE.

While (*ii*) is *compatible* with the view that all divine activity is mediated and constrained, this position leaves room for the possibility that a very limited range of divine actions in the world might instead be *immediate*, bypassing or overriding nonsentient natural processes (even if not free creaturely choices).[19] The range would have to be narrow. So many injuries that we might want God to prevent, even coercively, *do* occur. Since they do, and since on the view under consideration they do because God *chooses* not to prevent them, God who is love

18. For contemporary accounts of particular divine providence as constrained and mediated, see, *e.g.*, Arthur Peacocke, "God's Interaction with the World," *All That Is: A Naturalistic Faith for the Twenty-First Century*, ed. Philip Clayton (Minneapolis: Fortress 2007) 45–7; Arthur Peacocke, *Theology for a Scientific Age: Being and Becoming, Natural and Divine* (Oxford: Blackwell 1990) 159–63; Austin Farrer, *Faith and Speculation: An Essay in Philosophical Theology* (Edinburgh: Clark 1967) 60–7; Austin Farrer, *Saving Belief: A Discussion of Essentials* (London: Hodder 1964) 37–83; Brian Hebblethwaite and Edward Henderson, eds., *Divine Action: Studies Inspired by the Philosophical Theology of Austin Farrer* (Edinburgh: Clark 1990); Brian Hebblethwaite, "Providence and Divine Action," *Religious Studies* 14.2 (1978): 223–36; David Ray Griffin, *A Process Christology* (Lanham, MD: University Press of America 1990) 206–16; Diogenes Allen, *Christian Belief in a Postmodern World: The Full Wealth of Conviction* (Louisville, KY: Westminster John Knox 1989) 165–81; John B. Cobb Jr., "Natural Causality and Divine Action," *God's Activity in the World: The Contemporary Problem*, ed. Owen C. Thomas (Chico, CA: Scholars 1983) 101–16; John R. Lucas, *Freedom and Grace* (London: SPCK 1976); Keith Ward, *Divine Action* (London: Collins 1989) 119–69; Langdon Gilkey, *Reaping the Whirlwind: A Christian Interpretation of History* (New York: Crossroad-Seabury 1976) 303–6; Philip Clayton, *God and Contemporary Science* (Edinburgh: Edinburgh University Press 1997) 188–269; Thomas F. Tracy, ed., *The God Who Acts: Philosophical and Theological Explorations* (University Park, PA: Pennsylvania State University Press 1994); Thomas Jay Oord, *God Can't: How to Believe in God and Love after Tragedy, Abuse, and Other Evils* (Grasmere, ID: SacraSage 2019); and Timothy Gorringe, *God's Theatre: A Theology of Providence* (London: SCM 1991).

19. While (*i*) is incompatible with *creatio ex nihilo* (see Charles Hartshorne, *Omnipotence and Other Theological Mistakes* [Albany: SUNY 1984] 65–96; and David Ray Griffin, "Creation Out of Nothing, Creation Out of Chaos, and the Problem of Evil," *Encountering Evil: Live Options in Theodicy*, ed. Stephen T. Davis, 2d ed. [Louisville, KY: Westminster John Knox 2001] 108–24), a proponent of (*ii*) who was also a proponent of PROVIDENCE could affirm this traditional doctrine as long as she also maintained that there were no instances of bringing anything new into being out of nothing distinct from the creation of the universe itself.

and who thus intends the nonoccurrence of these injuries must have very good reasons not to do so. And these reasons, we might think, must in most cases preclude miraculous divine intervention, given that they are serious enough to preclude this kind of divine action in such a wide range of awful circumstances. We can use the label PROVIDENCE-PLUS for a view that treats most divine activity as providential but that allows for some nonmediated, coercive, miraculous, and so nonprovidential acts.

If we embrace PROVIDENCE, then, while some divine acts or clusters of divine acts in the world will be remarkable, they will all still involve the behaviors of creatures employing their own natural powers. God will act by influencing—noncoercively—how creatures employ these powers. But God will not act by conferring nonnatural powers on creatures or by exercising any sort of influence in the world apart from noncoercive influence on the ways in which creatures use their natural powers. Alternatively, if we embrace PROVIDENCE-PLUS, we will understand *most* divine activity as providential in this way while acknowledging the possibility that some divine acts will be immediate and will involve coercive determination of the behavior of natural processes. This will mean not only influencing these processes in ways that override their integrity but also, potentially, empowering creatures to do things they couldn't otherwise do. In neither case, however, will divine activity involve overriding creatures' capacities to make free choices: it would be very difficult to understand the occurrence of moral evil in the world if preventing creatures from choosing freely were a live option for God.

Mediated Divine Communication

To understand divine action in the world as ordinarily or always a matter of mediated and constrained influence is, in particular, to understand God's *communication* with humanity as constrained. For divine communication is a kind of divine action. If God seeks to convey insights to some human beings through the activities of others, God will interact with these human beings by means of persuasive influence rather than coercive determination. And this means that these human beings may respond more or less aptly to God's persuasion. This may be because of moral or spiritual deficiencies on their part. Or it may be because they lack the background knowledge or cognitive capacity to understand the truths it might be ideal for them to comprehend. In either case, while they may seek sincerely to share the insights God has conveyed (whether or not they recognize that these insights are rooted in God's activity), what they

communicate may be quite unlike the truths God intends human beings ultimately to understand. Just as sin, ignorance, and fallibility explain why, despite
divine influence, people can act in ways that bring about serious injuries, they
also explain why, despite divine influence, people can fail to grasp important
truths about God and God's world and to convey these insights to others.[20] The
point is not that people cannot potentially grasp important truths any more
than that they cannot potentially choose well even in the face of great difficulty.
However, if God cannot guarantee that people will choose rightly, then God
cannot guarantee that they will aptly grasp and communicate important truths.

I have assumed here that, whether PROVIDENCE or PROVIDENCE-PLUS turns
out to be correct, God will communicate with people in persuasive rather than
coercive ways. Someone could maintain that God *wouldn't* do this.

The critic might contend that God *would* override the freedom of the
humans through whom God seeks to communicate, necessitating their behavior, in order to ensure that they conveyed the messages God intended them
to convey perfectly. This sort of contention would raise serious problems for any
attempt to square divine love with the reality of evil in the world.

Reasoning as the imagined critic does appears to presuppose God's willingness to turn creatures into things in order to fulfill divine purposes, and thus to
do evil to bring about good. Because doing evil to achieve good is a purposeful
instance of doing evil, the imagined critic envisions God as doing evil. In this
way, the critic makes it impossible to see God as good without qualification.

To adopt the critic's approach would call into question the assumption,
crucial to making sense of evil in the world, that God really does prize the
individuality and freedom of persons without qualification. On the critic's
view, God could at best be thought to prize persons' individuality and freedom
only sometimes. Thinking of God in this way is hard to square with belief in
God's love for persons. More than that, it's hard to square with God's apparent
decisions not to override the freedom of persons in other cases. In addition,
the assumption that the personal creatures responsible for the biblical documents responded freely—and in light of their finitude, fallibility, ignorance, and
sin—to divine influence seems to make better sense of the actual features of

---

20. See, *e.g*, David Basinger and Randall Basinger, "Inerrancy, Dictation, and the Free Will
Defense," *Evangelical Quarterly* 55.3 (July 1983): 177–80; David Basinger, "Inerrancy and Free
Will: Some Further Thoughts," *Evangelical Quarterly* 58.4 (Oct. 1985): 351–4; and Austin Farrer,
"Infallibility and Historical Revelation," *Interpretation and Belief*, ed. Charles C. Conti (London:
SPCK 1976) 151–64.

those documents than does the view that God meticulously superintended their production by overriding creaturely freedom when necessary.

Alternatively, someone might accept PROVIDENCE-PLUS as I've envisioned it here while suggesting that God engaged in unmediated, coercive action to communicate in unambiguous ways with free persons but that God did so by necessitating the behavior of physical objects and processes. On this view, God might communicate with free persons by causing them to hear audible words in their languages or showing them written texts in their languages.

However, if God did communicate in this way, God's doing so would be quite compatible with failure on the part of those with whom God sought to communicate to understand the meaning of what they had heard or read. God's communicating in this way would also be compatible with decisions by those with whom God sought to communicate to resist recording particular words or phrases because they understood the meanings of these words or phrases but didn't like them: genuinely free persons would, after all, remain free to copy or pass on words other than those God presented.[21]

In any case, it would be a challenge to establish with respect to any text that it had been, as on this hypothesis, miraculously dictated. If, as on PROVIDENCE-PLUS, miracles may occur and may be expected to occur, then it is not unreasonable to think a miracle's occurrence could be confirmed on the basis of strong a priori and a posteriori considerations.[22] But to say that a miracle claim *could* in principle be confirmed is not to say that any given miracle claim *has* been confirmed. And a claim by someone to have received a dictated divine communication would be particularly difficult to confirm in the absence of something like witness testimony.

In addition, biblical texts—most likely to be seen by conservative Jews and Christians as repositories of divine communication—and the papal and conciliar pronouncements taken to be infallible by a subset of conservative Christians are in general not naturally read as *claiming* to be rooted in divine dictation. While we may see divine influence at work in their production, they ordinarily don't give us any reason to think that their authors took themselves to have

21. Thanks to David Gordon for discussion on this point.
22. See, *e.g.*, Richard Swinburne, *The Concept of Miracle* (London: Macmillan 1970); Richard Swinburne, *The Resurrection of God Incarnate* (Oxford: Clarendon-Oxford University Press 2003); N. T. Wright, *The Resurrection of the Son of God* (Minneapolis: Fortress 2003); and William Lane Craig, *Assessing the New Testament Evidence for the Historicity of the Resurrection of Jesus* (Lewiston, NY: Mellen 1989).

received and transmitted dictated words. So only a limited number of texts will even be *candidates* for the status of dictated disclosures.

A further complication arises when words might be taken to have been dictated but when these words have been *recorded* secondhand. Even if a prophet hears and accurately records particular words intended for public transmission, persuasive divine action cannot ensure that the prophet's amanuensis will accurately record what the prophet says.

In the abstract, it's compatible with PROVIDENCE-PLUS to suppose that God worked miracles to dictate some prophetic avowals, ex cathedra papal declarations, and the like. But recall that the reason PROVIDENCE and PROVIDENCE-PLUS seem like plausible accounts of divine action in the world is that evil occurs, that it is not the work of God, and that God does not in many cases prevent it. Even on PROVIDENCE-PLUS, miracles must be expected to be very infrequent. If most divine action, at minimum, is persuasive, then we should not treat miracles as likely in any particular case. We might reasonably expect miracles only in a narrow range of highly significant instances, and we might wonder whether many seeming instances of dictation qualified as putative, much less as credibly confirmed, miracles.[23]

As perfect in knowledge and reason, God would not dictate texts containing false historical, theological, or normative teachings. If someone asserts that she is sharing a dictated divine text and we have reason to believe that it contains inaccurate teachings, we will need to determine which is more likely erroneous: the *assertion* that the teachings actually did arrive by means of divine dictation or the alternative *judgments* we have reached regarding the topics of those teachings.[24] If we were warranted in a given case in accepting particular words as divinely dictated, this would give us good reason to question our judgments. But, to the extent that we lacked credible warrant for the belief that the words *were* dictated, we would be justified in trusting our prior judgments about their accuracy. In this case, it would make sense for us to view these judgments as

23. See, *e.g*, Brian Hebblethwaite, *In Defence of Christianity* (Oxford: Oxford University Press 2005) 104–5; and Brian Hebblethwaite, *The Essence of Christianity: A Fresh Look at the Nicene Creed* (London: SPCK 1996) 80–2, 90–1.

24. Cp. Nicholas Wolterstorff, *Divine Discourse: Philosophical Reflections on the Claim That God Speaks* (Cambridge: Cambridge University Press 1995) 226. Wolterstorff makes a point similar to but not identical with mine, in his case concerned with interpretation. If we take a text to contain a divine communication, we will—because we understand it this way—have good reason to regard it as not communicating a teaching we judge to be erroneous and so to reject any interpretation taking it to be doing so. For Wolterstorff's own caveats regarding this position—organized around the question "Has Scripture become a wax nose?"—see *Discourse* 223–39.

giving us reason precisely to avoid crediting the assumption that the words were divinely dictated or that, if dictated, they had been perfectly recorded.

Human language is necessarily culturally embedded. There is no such thing as language outside history. So there will be significant difficulties with the interpretation and application of any dictated divine text outside the immediate context in which it is dictated. And this limitation on the efficacy of dictation might well make it even more unlikely that text will be dictated in any given case.

As I've emphasized, PROVIDENCE-PLUS acknowledges the possibility of miracles. And there could thus, on this view, be revelatory miracles that didn't involve the dictation of texts. The most obvious of these would be the resurrection of Jesus. However, while on PROVIDENCE-PLUS there could be such miracles, in the absence of dictation (and perhaps even if it occurred), those recording evidence of a miracle would still need to understand and communicate its significance, and their attempts to do so would necessarily be affected by their fallibility, ignorance, and sinfulness.

The point is not that God would not or could not communicate with finite persons. It is, rather, that divine communication can be expected—certainly on PROVIDENCE and at least standardly on PROVIDENCE-PLUS—to take place by means of mediated, noncoercive divine action and that human cognitive, moral, and spiritual limitations will constrain the human appropriation and transmission of any such communication. If we accept PROVIDENCE-PLUS, we will have reason to suppose that some divine communication could be more unequivocal and, in a sense, not limited by the factors that constrain communication effected by mediated, noncoercive divine action. But we will need to acknowledge the a priori unlikelihood of dictation, in particular, and to recognize how few instances of putative divine communication present themselves as involving anything like miraculous dictation.

If we're considering potentially dictated words, we will need to take into account the difficulties involved in confirming that these words are plausibly regarded as actually having been communicated or vouchsafed miraculously. We will also need to take into account prior judgments regarding the claims conveyed by putatively dictated words in the course of assessing claims regarding the divinely dictated status of those words. And we will need to acknowledge that, while possible on PROVIDENCE-PLUS, nonverbal miracles would be described and interpreted by finite, fallible, ignorant, sinful persons.

God seeks constantly to communicate with every creature at every level of being. Our own finitude, fallibility, ignorance, and sinfulness impede our capacities to apprehend what God wills to communicate. The constrained nature of divine providence, which we must affirm in light of God's love and the reality of evil in the world, affects what God's communication in any given case will be like.

Loving God

Jesus identifies love for God as the subject matter of the greatest commandment. It's not clear whether we can love God in the sense of choosing with appropriate regard for the divine well-being. For classical theism, nothing we do could affect God, and benefiting is a kind of affecting. For neoclassical theisms of various sorts, we *can* affect, and so perhaps in some sense benefit, God. But the gap between God and creatures is infinite in either case, and we might be wisest to treat our talk of loving God in the sense of choosing with appropriate regard for well-being as *analogical*. We can, at any rate, orient ourselves aright in relation to God in various ways, and we can speak and talk of this as a kind of love because of its similarities both to love as appropriate regard for well-being and to various other kinds of creaturely love.

We don't engage lovingly with God as we would with a finite self, a potential object of our attention alternative to others. As infinite Creator, God is not in competition with creatures for our attention, much less for any benefits we might confer. Rather, we can affirm God's presence and activity as the background to all finite events—acknowledging that we have to do with God in all circumstances—and learn to read the world as God's creation. We can come to see that we encounter and interact with God in and through every experience we have.

Because God is an infinite being, the divine life in some sense incorporates the lives of all creatures: the good of creatures is thus integrated with the divine good, and our love for creatures just is at the same time love for God. We love creatures, and thus God, well when we can accept the constraints on wise choices inherent in a creational love ethic when we interact with other sentients. In addition, we love God when we own ourselves as God's creatures and thus orient ourselves rightly in relation to God. We do this not only by explicitly affirming and accepting our own creatureliness but also by doing so implicitly, which we do when we engage with the rest of the world in ways appropriate to our creaturely identities and those of the sentients we encounter.

We can love God as we love other creatures not only because in so doing we acknowledge that *we* are creatures and because creaturely well-being is incorporated within the divine well-being but also because in loving other creatures we are joining in *partnership* with God. Just as we can love one another by sharing one another's loves intentionally, we can love God by loving creatures together with God, who loves them infinitely more consistently and comprehensively than we do. (We are also opening ourselves in ways that allow God to love them through our actions as well.) In addition, we love God in and through our love for creatures insofar as our love involves or is rooted in our embrace of excellences in those we love that reflect and in some sense participate in God's own.[25]

God is infinite goodness and beauty, so we can rightly admire and delight in God. We can experience gratitude, treating all of finite reality as, ultimately, God's gift. We can similarly welcome specific gifts of beauty, love, and truth. In seeking to understand God, we may find, again, that our recognition of ourselves as creatures is reconfirmed, and this, too, can be a way of loving God. And we can celebrate God's goodness and greatness in worship—though it is important to remember that God has no need of our flattery, that we worship in order to understand ourselves more clearly as parts of God's good creation.

Loving creatures is not the only way in which we love God, but it is a crucial way in which we do so. In chapter 2, I offer an overview of an ethic of creaturely love rooted in God's good creation.

---

25. See Robert Merrihew Adams, *Finite and Infinite Goods: A Framework for Ethics* (New York: Oxford University Press 1999) 187–98.

2

A Creational Love Ethic

Love is concerned with welfare. Our welfare is given shape and content by creation, by the ways in which we (and other sentients) have been, as it were, put together. In this chapter, I seek briefly to develop an account of the welfare of creatures like ourselves, love's focus. I go on to depict the structure of enacted love by examining several complementary *specifications* of love. Then, I make some observations about moral truth and our apprehension of this kind of truth.

Love and Well-Being

Christians have often emphasized that love should be seen as central to ethics. Doing so is no doubt in significant part a reflection of repeated biblical stresses on love, including New Testament affirmations that seemingly independent moral requirements express and are grounded in love. There are various—complementary, mutually reinforcing—ways of identifying aspects of well-being, each of which is qualitatively distinct from the others and none of which can be reduced to or understood as intended to serve or promote something else. Affirming as I do here that an apt understanding of welfare is rooted in creation is, I will suggest, quite compatible with acknowledging the reality of sin.

Identifying the Elements of Human Well-Being

If love is appropriate regard for well-being, then we need some sense of what well-being amounts to. Even if we're not able to indicate precisely what we're getting at when we say that something is good for ourselves or others, we do have a sense of whether something is or isn't a contributor to a person's welfare.

There are multiple ways of identifying what's good for, and so what it means to love, creatures like us.

(*i*) We can tell ordinarily when a dog, say, is flourishing. "Whether or not a given individual . . . is . . . flourishing *qua* member . . . of . . . [the] plant or animal species . . . to which it . . . belong[s] is in itself a question of fact."[1] The same seems to be true of whether a human person is flourishing as a human person.[2] We can move from the instinctive judgment that a person's life is going well in a particular way to a deeper understanding of what her flourishing actually involves.

To do so, we might start by reflecting on the judgment that things are going well for someone in a given case and then asking just *how* they're going well, just *what it is* in virtue of which they're going well. What makes the judgment that the person is flourishing a correct judgment? It might help to think about a specific feature of a thickly described situation ("the conversation at the café with Samantha about her impending wedding," "reflecting on the factors relevant to deciding whether to tell my mom about the pregnancy"). Doing so could help us to go on to recognize a general feature of the situation, something we might discern in other contexts (*friendship, practical wisdom*). Alternatively, we might simply ask ourselves in the abstract what might lead us to think someone was flourishing. We could begin by imagining particular events or qualities that might occur to us before proceeding to generalize.

When we settle in this way on something that seems at first blush like a dimension of welfare, it will be worth inquiring whether what we've limned is really itself a constituent of flourishing or, rather, a means to the end of fulfillment. To take what may be the most obvious example, we could instinctively judge that someone was flourishing because she'd inherited a large sum of money. But we might conclude after some reflection that the money was not so much an aspect of well-being but, rather, something that made possible the beneficiary's participation in various other kinds of well-being (relaxed time building friendships, contemplation of beautiful objects, space for play, . . .).

We also need to distinguish between our affective and cognitive responses and what it is *to which* we're responding. For something to qualify as a genuine

1. Alasdair MacIntyre, *Dependent Rational Animals: Why Human Beings Need the Virtues* (Chicago: Open Court 1999) 64.
2. Cp. MacIntyre 79; Alasdair MacIntyre, *Ethics in the Conflicts of Modernity* (Cambridge: Cambridge University Press 2016) 24–31, 36, 38–41, 48, 60–1; Owen Flanagan, *The Problem of the Soul: Two Visions of Mind and How to Reconcile Them* (New York: Basic 2002) 272–86; and Philippa Foot, *Natural Goodness* (New York: Oxford University Press 2001) 25–51.

aspect of my well-being, I need to be able *in principle* to appreciate it (whether or not I can be aware of it directly). But that doesn't mean that I will in fact be aware of it; that, if I am aware of it, I will actually recognize it as a good; or that, if I recognize it as a good, my recognition will include or give rise to any sort of affective reaction. Its being a good is dependent not on my recognition or reaction but only on its being something that could potentially elicit my recognition of reaction.

(*ii*) Relatedly, when we recognize that someone's undergone an injury, suffered a loss, failed to receive an expected benefit, or been wronged in some other way, we can ask just what actual or potential aspect of her welfare has been affected.[3] So, if Charla's undergone a concussion during an auto accident and now finds she can't remember certain things, we might note that her *bodily well-being* (in this case, the operation of her brain) has been harmed, as has her ability to use her memory to access *knowledge*. If Jean's partner, Chris, abandons her, we might observe that what's been harmed is her relationship with Chris, a variety of *friendship*. If May's father spitefully hides her toys and won't let her friend Pat come over to join her in enjoying them, he's attacked May's *friendship* with Pat and their opportunity to participate in *play*. If a spinal cord injury keeps Kyle from experiencing arousal and orgasm, we might suggest that what's been harmed is not only his *bodily well-being* but also, more particularly, his capacity for *sensory pleasure*.[4]

(*iii*) Another way of getting at what makes for well-being is to begin with what might be involved in making sense of our choices and the choices of other people.[5] We can offer a series of explanations to others or to ourselves. But at some point, we're likely to stop because it would be unclear how to go on, unclear what information we might offer that would be needed as a further source of justification or clarification.

1. *Why do you want to go to Averi's house?*
   In order to take another look at the painting she just got.
   Why do you want to take another look at the painting she just got?
   Because it's complex, evocative, and beautiful (*aesthetic experience*).
2. *Why are you moving to Hawaii?*

---

3. See Grisez, *Way of the Lord Jesus* 1: 123.
4. Cp. Foot, *Natural Goodness* 43–4.
5. See, *e.g*, Chappell, *Understanding Human Goods* 33–7 (Chappell provides multiple examples of the sort of chain of reasoning I outline here); and Grisez, *Way of the Lord Jesus* 1: 122–5.

I want to live on a cliff where I can smell the sea air, get up with the sun, see the blue sky, and hear tropical birds call.

Are you saying you're going because you want to experience these beautiful things?

Maybe that's part of it (*aesthetic experience*), but I mainly just want to feel more aligned with nature (*harmony with reality*).

3. *Why are you up so early?*

I want to read some more of that novel before I have to leave for work.

Why do you want to read some more of that novel before you have to go to work?

Because I'm worried about whether Doug the botanist will survive the masked ball, so I want to find out what happens to him (*imaginative immersion*).

4. *Why did you rub on that ointment?*

To reduce the discomfort I'm feeling after that scratch (*freedom from physical pain*).

5. *Why are you watching that video?*

So I can learn about late medieval usury laws.

Why do you want to learn about late medieval usury laws?

In order to understand the development of law and economics in Europe more completely (*knowledge*).

6. *Why did you take that pill?*

Because it will help keep my blood pressure under control.

Why do you want to keep your blood pressure under control?

Because doing so will make it less likely that I'll suffer a stroke.

Why do you want to avoid suffering a stroke?

Because doing so will help me to live longer than I otherwise would and to avoid the serious damage to my health a stroke could cause (*life and bodily well-being*).

At least ordinarily, in each case, the questioner has received all the explanation and justification she could reasonably expect: the focus on aesthetic experience, harmony, imaginative immersion, freedom from physical pain, knowledge, or life and bodily well-being makes the speaker's actions perfectly intelligible and in need of no defense.

(*iv*) Cross-cultural inquiry and observation might help to identify aspects of well-being. Suppose we found in many cultures not only desires for food, clothing, and shelter but also choices to engage in and value games (*play*), activities designed to align people with God or the gods (*harmony with reality*), eros, or chocolate consumption, for its own sake (*sensory pleasure*), absorption in stories and care for their characters (*imaginative immersion*), and cultivation of the ability to make good decisions (*practical wisdom*).[6] If we did, we might reasonably conclude that we'd at least found aspects of human experience and activity that were widely experienced and *regarded* as worth pursuing and realizing and that were not *treated* as requiring any further justification. Widespread appreciation of these forms of life wouldn't *demonstrate* that they were worthwhile, but it might suggest that they could be and support judgments regarding their value made on other grounds.[7]

(*v*) It's possible to see the various elements of welfare as heterogeneous, and to some degree, they surely are. However, we can understand them as unified at a deeper level by their status as expressions of *created potentialities*—dimensions of the kinds of creatures we are, dimensions that are capable of development.[8] On this view, we flourish when our capacities are exercised and extended and enlarged. That doesn't mean that we can focus on developing or displaying *all* of our broad potentialities or *all* of the ways in which any particular potentiality might be enriched and amplified. But we can certainly see our flourishing as, precisely, the development of at least some of these potentialities, fostered in full openness to the value of all.

There are many different ways in which our potentialities can develop. To identify them, we can inventory our capacities for choice, judgment, accomplishment, experience, and relationship (we might focus on our own or on those we observe in particular cases or on those that seem to be typical of or conceivable for us) and ask what forms the development of each of these potentialities might take. This ought to give us a sense of the different ways in which things can go well for us, for creatures with our characteristics and in our circumstances.

6. Whether harmony is a good doesn't depend on what the ultimate or comprehensive reality with which it's possible to be in harmony *is*. It matters that we understand ourselves in relation to the rest of reality and situate our own lives in relation to the cosmic story. Thus, the first example of this good I offer involves the pursuit of attunement with the physical world.

7. Cp. Finnis, *Law* 83–5.

8. See, *e.g.*, Henry Veatch, *For an Ontology of Morals* (Evanston, IL: Northwestern University Press 1971) 99–124; and Richard Kraut, *What Is Good and Why: The Ethics of Well-Being* (Cambridge, MA: Harvard University Press 2007) 131–45. Cp. John Dewey, "The Conception of Happiness," *Ethics*, by John Dewey and James Tufts (New York: Holt 1908): "Happiness *consists* in the fulfillment in their appropriate objects (or the anticipation of such fulfillment) of the powers of the self manifested in desires, purposes, efforts" (280; my italics).

Using these various approaches, we can, I think, identify several broad, generic ways of flourishing. A tentative list: aesthetic experience,[9] avoidance of physical pain,[10] friendship,[11] harmony with reality in the widest sense,[12] imaginative immersion,[13] knowledge,[14] life,[15] play,[16] practical wisdom,[17] self-integration,[18] sensory pleasure,[19] and skillful performance.[20]

There can, of course, be disagreements around the edges. But I hope that, reflecting on this list, you find yourself inclined to recognize the things I've listed as, indeed, worth pursuing, respecting, protecting, and realizing. I don't mean to suggest that this list is necessarily exhaustive.[21] Perhaps something that I think belongs under one heading or another is more clearly understood if it's treated separately. Alternatively, perhaps it would be better to collapse some categories

9. See Finnis, *Law* 87–8; Murphy, *Natural Law* 109–11; Chappell, *Understanding Human Goods* 37–8; and Grisez and Shaw, *Beyond the New Morality* 80.

10. See Chappell, *Understanding Human Goods* 38.

11. See Finnis, *Law* 88; Murphy, *Natural Law* 126–31; Chappell, *Understanding Human Goods* 37–8; and Grisez and Shaw, *Beyond the New Morality* 81–2.

12. See Chappell, *Understanding Human Goods* 39; Finnis, *Law* 89–90; Grisez and Shaw, *Beyond the New Morality* 82; and Murphy, *Natural Law* 131–3. Finnis refers here to religion (in scare quotes). I'm fine with this in principle, but I think the formulation for which I've opted might be less question-begging.

13. I have in mind here the good involved in becoming caught up in a fictional narrative, taking up stances regarding the fates of the characters, and so forth—the good in which we want to participate when huddled around a campfire listening to a story. Perhaps this is an aspect of play or aesthetic experience, but it seems to be interestingly different from both. Cp. *The Aesthetic Illusion in Literature and the Arts*, ed. Tomáš Koblížek (London: Bloomsbury 2017).

14. See Chappell, *Understanding Human Goods* 39–40; Finnis, *Law* 59–80, 87; Murphy, *Natural Law* 106–8; and Grisez and Shaw, *Beyond the New Morality* 79–80.

15. See Chappell, *Understanding Human Goods* 39; Finnis, *Law* 86–7; Murphy, *Natural Law* 101–5; Finnis, Boyle, and Grisez, *Nuclear Deterrence* 279, 300, 304–7, 309; Grisez, *Way of the Lord Jesus* 1: 137–8; and Grisez and Shaw, *Beyond the New Morality* 79.

16. See Finnis, *Law* 87; Grisez and Shaw, *Beyond the New Morality* 80; and Murphy, *Natural Law* 111–4. Murphy focuses more narrowly on "excellence in play and work."

17. See Chappell, *Understanding Human Goods* 39; Finnis, *Law* 88–9; and Grisez and Shaw, *Beyond the New Morality* 81. The *activity* of loving is itself part of our own flourishing, since it's a way in which we exercise and so participate in the good of practical wisdom.

18. Grisez and Shaw, *Beyond the New Morality* 81. Cp. Chappell, *Understanding Human Goods* 39 (discussing "harmony" as a good of the soul).

19. See Chappell, *Understanding Human Goods* 38; and Gary Chartier, *Public Practice, Private Law: An Essay on Love, Marriage, and the State* (Cambridge: Cambridge University Press 2016) 115–9.

20. See Grisez, *Way of the Lord Jesus* 1: 124; and Murphy, *Natural Law* 111–4. Cp. Chappell, *Understanding Human Goods* 41–3 (discussing the good of "achievement").

21. See Finnis, *Law* 59–99; Chappell, *Understanding Human Goods* 33–45; and Murphy, *Natural Law* 96–138.

I've proposed. There's nothing magic about the list. But I hope you'll conclude that, at least in general, it resonates with your experience and judgment.

Qualitative Differences

The various aspects of what's good for us are not reducible to any single underlying or generic good. They're not valuable as means to anything else. These aspects of well-being are *different*.[22] This is true in at least two senses.

The broad categories themselves are different: friendship isn't the same thing as play, and knowledge isn't the same thing as sensory pleasure. (Perhaps what I've called imaginative immersion is part of, is a certain kind of, aesthetic experience.) And because the broad categories are different, there's no way to *equate* them, no way to turn one into a variant of another. In addition, the individual *instances* of the various categories are distinct: two friendships differ from each other in many ways; one aesthetic experience isn't a perfect substitute for another; when one life disappears, another can't simply take its place.

Because of the qualitative differences among categories of goods and among individual goods, each *particular* good has to be treated as distinctively worthwhile, too. Every friendship is different from every other friendship. And friendships, aesthetic experiences, instances of play, instances of knowledge, and so forth are all different from one another. Because they're qualitatively different, particular goods can't, in general, be ranked or otherwise compared quantitatively. And the absence of a common yardstick means that there's no way of aggregating the various qualitatively different goods produced by a given actual or potential choice, and so of choosing among different options on the basis of some quantitative comparison of the goods they embody.

---

22. See, *e.g*, Owen J. Flanagan, "Ethics Naturalized: Ethics as Human Ecology," *Mind and Morals: Essays in Cognitive Science and Ethics*, ed. Larry May, Marilyn Friedman, and Andy Clark (Cambridge, MA: Bradford-MIT Press 1996) 22; Alasdair MacIntyre, *After Virtue: A Study in Moral Theory*, 2d ed. (Notre Dame, IN: University of Notre Dame Press 1984) 198–9; Hilary Putnam, "Dewey's Central Insight," *Pragmatism as a Way of Life: The Lasting Legacy of William James and John Dewey*, by Hilary Putnam and Ruth Anna Putnam (Cambridge, MA: Harvard University Press 2017) 286–8; Bernard Williams, "A Critique of Utilitarianism," *Utilitarianism: For and Against*, by J. J. C. Smart and Bernard Williams (Cambridge: Cambridge University Press 1973) 80, 144–5; Gary Chartier and Jere L. Fox, "Incommensurable Goods," *Edward Elgar Research Handbook on Natural Law Theory*, ed. Jonathan Crowe and Constance Lee (Cheltenham, UK: Elgar 2019) 252–65; Finnis, *Fundamentals* 86–90; Finnis, *Law* 111–8; and Murphy, *Natural Law* 182–7. Cp. Dewey, "Conception" 275–7; and John Dewey, *Human Nature and Conduct: An Introduction to Social Psychology* (New York: Modern Library-Random 1922) 216–22.

Are the Goods Really Basic?

Consider a possible objection to what I've said. The various basic aspects of well-being aren't, the objector might say, *really* qualitatively different. They might seem to be. But they can all be unified. We can, on this view, compare, rank, and aggregate the goods actually or potentially on offer in any situation if we recognize that the various aspects of well-being are really instances of or means to some single master good. Perhaps this master good is itself one of the dimensions of welfare I've already enumerated. Or perhaps it's something separate and distinct, like *happiness*.

No one of the various aspects of well-being seems like a good candidate for the role of the essence embodied by any of the others. Friendship isn't a species of aesthetic experience. Knowledge isn't an aspect of play. Bodily well-being isn't a kind of sensory pleasure. The basic goods present themselves as clearly different from each other. So, for someone who wants to find a putatively rational way of comparing, ranking, and aggregating them, a more fruitful line of attack might be to understand them as promoting something that is distinguishable from all of them.

Perhaps all of the nominally distinct goods are really good because they produce welfare—understood not as I ordinarily view it here, as one label for the whole array of basic goods, but, rather, as a single quantity identical with happiness or some specific kind of sensory pleasure. If what makes the various goods good is the fact that they generate welfare, we needn't be concerned with the particular goods themselves; rather, we should focus on the welfare produced by participating or attempting to participate in them. Because, on this view, welfare is homogeneous, we can compare the desirability of various actual or potential states of affairs by measuring the amount of welfare they involve.

One way of thinking about happiness is to understand it as, roughly, a sensory signal that tells one that things are going well in one's life.[23] From a slightly different angle, we might think of it as a condition of being satisfied with some state of affairs—an evaluative reaction, a judgment that something is worthwhile. But, either way, the production of happiness doesn't seem to be the reason we do or should participate in the various basic goods.

Presuming one's psyche is healthy and one's perceptions accurate, the occurrence of happiness understood as a sensory signal of value just means that one

---

23. *Happiness* is sometimes used as a synonym for *flourishing*. But this isn't how the term is commonly employed in English today.

is participating in one or more genuine goods in suitable ways. So we're getting things backward if we think of ourselves as participating in the diverse forms of well-being in order to produce happiness viewed this way. Participating in the goods isn't a way of promoting or producing happiness any more than driving a train along a track is a way of promoting or producing a crossing alert. And participating in the goods isn't justified by the occurrence of happiness any more than the movement of a train is justified by the sound of its whistle. Signals matter because of what they signal.

Suppose we think of happiness as the condition of being satisfied, as an evaluative judgment rather than as a sensation. An attempt to view generating happiness as the goal of seeking the various goods encounters the kind of problem I've already noted if we think this way instead. When I make an evaluative judgment, I'm concerned with whatever it is I'm evaluating. The judgment itself isn't my focus; the evaluation is an assessment of the reality on which I'm focused. If I'm happy in virtue of how an afternoon with an old friend is developing, it's my interaction with the friend that matters; the interaction is what my happiness is *about*. I only have reason to want to assess the interaction as satisfactory if it really is satisfactory. And my goal in pursuing a given good is my participation in the good itself, not, per se, the experience of making the judgment that pursuing it has been worthwhile.

Instead of happiness, perhaps we might focus on sensory pleasure. It's clear that the various goods aren't *identical* with sensory pleasure. But perhaps the individual goods are important just because they *produce* sensory pleasure. However, one thing that complicates the attempt to treat participating in the various goods as if doing so were about pleasure is that participating in the goods (ignore the special case of sensory pleasure itself) doesn't actually yield some sort of straightforwardly physical pleasure in the way that chocolate consumption or erotic stimulation might.

I don't play a game of soccer, for instance, so I'll feel particular sensations. (Muscle aches and the feeling of sweat running down my body don't seem terribly pleasurable in any case.) The point of playing a game of soccer is to play the game, to play it well, and (often) to enrich my connection with my fellow players. It may also be to provide an appealing experience for any spectators and to connect with them. In and through my actions, I seek to realize the goods of play (for myself and the players and, in a different sense, the audience), skillful performance, and, perhaps, friendship. (In addition, I may seek to earn income by playing, with the idea that the income will help me participate directly or indirectly in various genuine goods.)

I can say that I "feel pleasure" because of the realization of these goods, but what I experience is in fact a complex emotional reaction featuring both sensory and cognitive elements. It's a conscious affective register of my awareness that I'm doing or that I've done something valuable. So I'm not actually *seeking* this kind of pleasure, per se, when I play soccer any more than I'm seeking happiness-as-satisfaction when I do so. Rather, I'm seeking to participate in the goods of which this kind of pleasure is a signal. And I recognize that the game would be worth playing even if—because I'm depressed, say—I'm not actually feeling that signal.

The game is not a complex mechanism for producing affective states. If it were, I could bypass the activity of playing it entirely. I could hook myself up to a machine that gave me the subjective experience of playing it and that yielded the associated emotional reactions.[24] No doubt having the simulated experience of playing the game would be a good deal easier than actually playing. But I could choose to have the experience by connecting myself to the machine only if I'd failed to see that the purpose of playing the game was playing the game (with the various ramifications and dimensions I noted earlier), not the production of this or that subjective state.

The affective reactions associated with my experiences of various goods differ qualitatively. The pleasure associated with my experience of friendship with Nabil isn't the same as the pleasure associated with my experience of friendship with Aena. The pleasure associated with my experience of friendship with Ligia isn't the same as the pleasure associated with my experience of playing soccer. The pleasure associated with my experience of playing soccer isn't the same as the pleasure associated with my experience of contemplating an elegantly designed building. So even if, as I deny, the point of participating in this or that good were the production of particular feelings, the pleasures produced by my actions wouldn't be homogeneous and couldn't, therefore, be treated as forming a singular quantity capable of being measured and maximized.

The same kind of analysis seems to apply if we focus on preferences rather than affective reactions. I can always ask of something I prefer, "But is it worth preferring?" Preferences don't *make* things worthwhile. Ordinarily, when I prefer something, I do so because I take it to be valuable (though of course I can be mistaken). I may seek as preferred-by-me, but, if I ask whether I would be wise to prefer it, I can't simply advert to my preference. My preferring something

24. See Robert Nozick, *Anarchy, State and Utopia* (New York: Basic 2013) 42–5; and Finnis, *Fundamentals* 38–41.

can give it a place of importance in my order of priorities, and thus render it particularly significant for my choices, but I ordinarily don't, and can't reasonably, regard something as worth preferring in the first place if I don't treat it as valuable.[25] And, again, my preferences for different goods may plausibly be seen as qualitatively different.

The various categories of welfare and their individual instances don't reduce to some one substrate that's common to all of them. Similarly, the point of the basic goods isn't the production of happiness or pleasure (or, I'm confident, anything comparable). As a result, the value of seeking to realize a given good can't be measured by its contribution to the generation of happiness or pleasure. The basic goods really do seem to be basic.

Sinfulness and Creational Flourishing

To understand human flourishing as rooted in creation, as what makes for the well-being of those created in the way we have been, doesn't require us to understand creation as perfect or to ignore the inadequacies of and the effects of brokenness on humanness as we experience it.

No creature is capable of being perfect in the sense that it's unsurpassable. For any finite reality, there could be another finite reality that exceeded it in one or more valuable ways (ways valuable to the creature herself or to others). Similarly, for any finite creature, there could be another creature of its own general kind that exceeded it, again, in one or more valuable ways. These are unavoidable features of creatureliness. And any sentient creature capable of moral choice could grow morally and spiritually in one way or another.

In addition, every creature capable of moral choice sometimes experiences the desire to act contrary to love and sometimes does, in fact, do so: finite agents sin. For instance, insecurity rooted in human developmental processes—an inherent concomitant of finitude, vulnerability, and ignorance—can prompt self-protective and self-assertive impulses that can lead to sinful choices. And sinning has ongoing ramifications. Dispositions to self-preservation, which can become occasions for sinful—aggressive and dominating—behavior, can

25. To be sure, in the course of a more general nihilism or subjectivism, I might simply treat my own preferences as products of arbitrary willing on my part or as surd results of my biological constitution or of the social influences to which I've been subjected. I wouldn't presume to essay a refutation of nihilism or subjectivism here; I gesture in the direction of the kind of response I'd be inclined to offer in *Understanding Friendship: On the Moral, Political, and Spiritual Meaning of Love* (Minneapolis: Fortress 2022) 59–60.

be inherited. Sinning humans can influence their contemporaries and their descendants alike by the examples they set, the stories they tell, and the substances they consume. And they can do so by altering the physical environments within which they act and the social environments they form. The disposition to make particular bad choices and to orient oneself wrongly in relation to God can thus be transmitted intergenerationally.[26]

The attempt to root an account of flourishing in creation might be misunderstood as calling us to return to the pristine condition of an unspoiled world, with perfect human nature identified with the nature of the humans inhabiting that world. Current understandings of how the world works and how its current conditions have come into being make it hard to embrace an understanding of human nature as the nature of unspoiled persons. If we want to talk about creational flourishing, we have to focus on creation as it actually is now and what we can discern its actual potential to be. We have to ask about *our* well-being given the characteristics and dispositions we have. That does *not*, I emphasize, mean regarding all of the features of the humanness we experience as desirable. We can definitely acknowledge the results of and propensity for wrongdoing and alienation from God that we experience as well as the importance of enhancing our capacities, protecting ourselves from disease, and so forth. We don't have to accept anything like the status quo. But, in reflecting carefully on creaturely well-being, we have to recognize that there's no way of vaulting over or tunneling under the present so that we can make our way to a perfect past in which human flourishing is perfectly on display. Instead, we have no choice but to examine sentient creatures as they are now and ask what makes for the flourishing of *these* creatures.

Specifying Love

Love has a concrete character. It means choosing in particular ways. These are not alternatives to love, free-floating demands that bear no relation to love. Nor are they subordinate to love, generalizations about what love might sometimes mean—as if they were, say, rules of thumb that could, under the right

---

26. For thoughtful attempts to connect existing knowledge of human nature with a theological account of sin, see, *e.g.*, Wolfhart Pannenberg, *Anthropology in Theological Perspective*, trans. Matthew J. O'Connell (Philadelphia: Westminster 1985) 80–153; and Diogenes Allen, *Theology for a Troubled Believer: An Introduction to the Christian Faith* (Louisville, KY: Westminster John Knox 2010) 183–95.

circumstances, be overridden by direct appeals to love. Instead, they are *specifications* of love. Together, they constitute the particular *shape* love takes. I'll refer to these ways of loving as RECOGNITION, THE GOLDEN RULE, THE PAULINE PRINCIPLE, COMMITMENT, and EFFICIENCY. Choosing in accordance with these specifications of love is a way of participating in the good of practical wisdom.

I begin by explaining the difference between choosing to love in these ways on the one hand and rule-consequentialist approaches to moral judgment on the other.[27] (Christian love has often been understood in broadly consequentialist terms. And, when many people think about general rules, they think of the rule-consequentialist variety.) I go on to explain and ground the specifications of love. Then, I explain why we can see them as genuinely exceptionless.

Specifications of Love and General Rules

One common way of thinking about general principles in relation to an ethic of love is to understand these principles as rules for specific kinds of human activity derived in roughly the same way as the sorts of rules embraced by rule-consequentialists.[28]

Consequentialism urges us to bring about as much good as possible in the world. According to the basic form of consequentialism, act-consequentialism, each time I choose, I should perform the action I reasonably expect to bring about the most net good (adjusted for the probability of its occurrence). There are serious difficulties with the consequentialist program, beginning with the notion of "the most net good." But even those who think of consequentialism as viable often suppose that while each of us really should bring about as much good as possible, *act*-consequentialism in particular can't serve as a useful guide to decision-making. Some ethicists argue, therefore, for various still-consequentialist alternatives like rule-consequentialism. On a common rule-consequentialist view, one considers possible rules on the basis of their operability—their simplicity and comprehensibility—and chooses the set of readily operable and mutually compatible rules that, among all such sets, can be expected to bring about the most net good (again, adjusted for the probability of each outcome's occurrence).[29]

---

27. As a matter of convenience, I will ordinarily not differentiate between rule- and practice-consequentialism, since the distinction isn't of particular importance here.

28. Frankena, "Love and Principle" 212–4.

29. Two standard accounts of rule-consequentialism are Richard B. Brandt, *A Theory of the Good and the Right* (Oxford: Clarendon-Oxford University Press 1979); and John C. Harsanyi, "Morality

A worry about rule-consequentialism that is internal to consequentialism is that, if one follows the rules uncompromisingly, there will be individual cases, perhaps many, in which one's actions are *not* the ones that would be required by act-consequentialism, not the ones that would, in fact, yield the most net good.[30] There seems to be something curious, at least, about following a rule on the basis that, if everyone obeyed it, better consequences would follow than if they obeyed any alternative rule, when, in fact, many people *aren't* adhering to the rule. This sort of worry naturally arises when an ethic of love is interpreted in roughly rule-consequentialist terms. Such an ethic might be thought to require "the most loving action" in any situation. In this case, "the most loving action" would mean, typically, not the act arising from the strongest loving feelings or the most deeply held loving attitude but the most beneficent act, understood in much the same way as a utilitarian would understand a welfare-maximizing act (except, perhaps, on some interpretations, that the agent's own welfare would be ignored). But, in the nature of the case, an ethic of general rules will direct one to perform acts that don't qualify as the most loving (in the relevant sense). And this seems at odds with embracing an ethic of love. Those inclined to understand an ethic of love in consequentialist terms might be tempted, therefore, to understand such an ethic in specifically *act*-consequentialist terms.

A creational love ethic is quite different from an act- or rule-consequentialist love ethic. But it shares the suspicion with which proponents of act-consequentialist understandings of Christian love might view rule-consequentialist versions. A creational love ethic insists that each *act*, rather than each *kind of act*, be directly consistent with love.[31] It embraces continuity of character and relationship, however, in a way that act-consequentialist readings of Christian love arguably can't. That's because (*i*) it acknowledges a range of distinctions that don't figure in consequentialist reasoning. It emphasizes the qualitative differences among the various ways in which lives can go well. Thus, (*ii*) it doesn't assume—indeed, it denies—that the good can be maximized. (*iii*) It also recognizes the qualitative differences among our different relationships with the

---

and the Theory of Rational Behaviour," *Utilitarianism and Beyond*, ed. Amartya Sen and Bernard Williams (Cambridge: Cambridge University Press 1982) 39–62. An influential contemporary treatment is Brad Hooker, *Ideal Code, Real World: A Rule-Consequentialist Theory of Morality* (Oxford: Clarendon-Oxford University Press 2000). Cp. Derek Parfit, *On What Matters*, 3 vols. (New York: Oxford University Press 2011–7).

30. See, *e.g.*, J. J. C. Smart, "An Outline of a System of Utilitarian Ethics," Smart and Williams, *Utilitarianism* 10–2.

31. Cp. Ramsey, *Deeds* 131n10.

various aspects of flourishing. Where consequentialism focuses on producing or promoting (what it takes to be) the overall good, a creational love ethic acknowledges that producing or promoting a (particular) good is different from realizing it in one's choice. There's a difference between fostering the formation of friendships and participating in an actual friendship. A creational love ethic also acknowledges the importance of respecting particular goods—not attacking or otherwise interfering with them—and protecting them. And (*iv*) it recognizes that the various dimensions of love itself yield substantial coherence in the moral life.[32]

The various specifications of love do not serve to trump love. In no case does adhering to one of these specifications of love mean following a general rule in virtue of which one is permitted or required to do something inconsistent with love in an individual case. Rather, they make clear what it *means* to love well in particular circumstances, given that there are common features that unite those circumstances.[33] There is no circumstance in which it is *not* loving to embrace THE GOLDEN RULE or THE PAULINE PRINCIPLE, for instance. At the same time, the specifications of love are not confiningly narrow rules but generic principles that allow in many cases for flexibility and a broad range of choices.

Love by Choosing What Matters

RECOGNITION. This specification of love can be summed up as "Love. Really love." It's important to *recognize* what truly makes for welfare and act accordingly. I'm not really doing something *for* you if what I do doesn't protect, respect, promote, or realize your well-being. So this requirement says: when you choose, for yourself or in order to affect someone else's life, choose in order to respect, protect, promote, or realize *an actual good*, a real aspect of flourishing, fulfillment, welfare, well-being. Choose with an authentic benefit in mind.

---

32. It also differs from some interpretations of Christian love in regarding the agent's own well-being as meriting moral consideration. But this distinction isn't directly relevant to the distinction between a creational love ethic and Christian consequentialism, since consequentialism in general treats the agent's well-being as of direct moral relevance, and a Christian appropriation of consequentialism need not disagree on this point.
33. Cp. Ramsey, *Deeds* 104–44. Ramsey would hardly endorse all I've said here.

Love Consistently

THE GOLDEN RULE. Whatever the differences among moral patients, all of them are valuable as irreplaceable subjects. They have in common their capacity to flourish, and they welcome or have welcomed their own flourishing. Denying moral consideration to any creature meeting this minimum standard seems arbitrary, not least because I wouldn't want to be excluded from moral consideration as long as I met it myself. As a result, "intelligence and reasonableness can find no basis in the mere fact that A is A and is not B (that I am I and am not you) for evaluating his (our) well being differentially."[34]

This specification of love as fair treatment finds expression in two familiar forms in the Bible: "You shall love your neighbor as yourself"[35] and "Do to others as you would have them do to you."[36] Each of the principal biblical formulations captures the idea of the basic equality of moral status. In both, the agent's love for herself is *presupposed* and not treated as somehow unreasonable or illegitimate. Thus, THE GOLDEN RULE is not a requirement of self-forgetful benevolence but, rather, a requirement of equality, of nonarbitrariness, of fairness.

"On these two commandments hang all the law and the prophets,"[37] the First Gospel affirms with respect to the first formulation in tandem with the injunction to "love the Lord your God with all your heart, and with all your soul, and with all your mind."[38] It makes a comparable claim regarding the second formulation: "This is the law and the prophets."[39] Similarly, Saint Paul says, "The whole law is summed up in a single commandment, 'You shall love your neighbor as yourself'"[40] and, more elaborately:

Owe no one anything, except to love one another; for the one who loves another has fulfilled the law. The commandments, "You shall not commit adultery; You shall not murder; You shall not steal; You shall not

---

34. Finnis, *Law* 107. Cp. Finnis, *Aquinas*: "The basic goods are good for any human being, . . . [so] I must have a reason for preferring their instantiation in my own or my friends' existence" (140).
35. Lev 19:18; Matt 22:39; Mark 12:31, 33.
36. Matt 7:12; Luke 6:31.
37. Matt 22:40. The Markan version features no reference to the law and the prophets but maintains that "there is no other commandment greater than these" (Mark 12:31).
38. Matt 22:37.
39. Matt 7:12.
40. Gal 5:14.

covet"; and any other commandment, are summed up in this word, "Love your neighbor as yourself." Love does no wrong to a neighbor; therefore, love is the fulfilling of the law.[41]

Both Pauline treatments make the same claim as Matthew 7:12: that fairness captures the meaning of the law. (The separate dominical injunction to love God is not addressed.[42]) It's clear that THE GOLDEN RULE itself can ground positive responsibilities of care for others. But fulfilling a negative duty in a way that involves no active thought or behavior can itself be a kind of love, as is clear from the affirmation that negative prohibitions, like the one on stealing, are summed up in the injunction to love.

Both forms of THE GOLDEN RULE are characterized as encapsulating the law. So it is interesting and perhaps a bit disappointing that the two often seem to be read differently. Both emphasize persons' basic equality in moral status. But "Do to others as you would have them do to you" is sometimes interpreted as a pragmatic way of getting what one wants.[43] There doesn't seem to be any obvious reason to read it as carrying this meaning primarily, as if it meant "Choose what to do in light of the behavior you hope to elicit from others." This formulation of THE GOLDEN RULE makes no particular reference to one's hopes regarding the actual outcome of one's behavior or its tendency to influence the behavior of others. Its meaning, rather, should be taken to be essentially the same as that of "Love your neighbor as yourself." It directs one, that is, to treat others as equals, to treat others no differently from the way in which one would be willing to be treated oneself. Following this injunction may, indeed, prompt good behavior from others disposed to play tit for tat.[44] But that's a convenient side effect of following THE GOLDEN RULE, not its point.

Talk about reciprocity in an ethical context can mean multiple things. I engage in predictive or strategic reciprocity when I behave in a certain way in order to elicit desired behavior from others. On the other hand, I engage in normative reciprocity when I behave in a certain way as a matter of fairness to others who have *already* behaved in that way, embracing the explicitly moral

---

41. Rom 13:8–10.

42. Love for God is mentioned affirmingly in 1 Cor (2:9; 8:3). Love for Christ figures in 1 Cor 16:22 and 2 Cor 2:8 and also in the deutero-Pauline Eph 6:24. In none of these cases does it seem like the object of a command.

43. See, *e.g.*, John P. Meier, *A Marginal Jew* 4: *Law and Love* (New Haven, CT: Yale University Press 2009) 553.

44. Cp. Robert Axelrod, *The Evolution of Cooperation*, rev. ed. (New York: Basic 2006).

judgment that "one good turn deserves another."[45] Embracing this latter kind of reciprocity is one implication of following THE GOLDEN RULE. Concern with this or any other kind of reciprocity does not exhaust the meaning of THE GOLDEN RULE, not least because this specification of love is the basis of love for enemies and for the nonreciprocating vulnerable. But reciprocity in this moral sense is one aspect of the meaning of this specification of love.

As I will seek to show, THE GOLDEN RULE can help to ground and render intelligible moral requirements drawn from the Decalogue, the New Testament, and later Christian teaching. Other specifications of love provide additional support for a number of the Decalogue's commandments, with the Sixth Commandment, in particular, articulating a prohibition of murder that can be most effectively spelled out with reference to THE PAULINE PRINCIPLE as well as THE GOLDEN RULE.[46] But THE GOLDEN RULE plays a central role throughout.

A straightforward way to apply THE GOLDEN RULE in practice is to think in terms of avoiding arbitrary distinctions among those affected by your actions. There are two kinds of arbitrariness that are worth avoiding.

There's the arbitrariness we show when we distinguish among those affected by our actions for reasons unrelated to the basic aspects of well-being. It makes sense to pick capable athletes for sports teams (here, we choose in order to foster the realization of the goods of play and skillful performance) or gifted painters for art prizes (here, we choose with an eye to skillful performance and aesthetic experience). On the other hand, it makes no sense to pick athletes on the basis of ethnicity or citizenship or to reward artists on the basis of gender or political ideology—to treat people differently in light of characteristics that have nothing to do with the basic goods. When I choose in this way, I'm pointlessly ignoring actual well-being; I'm declining an opportunity to show appropriate regard for well-being, to love.

There's also the arbitrariness we show when we distinguish inconsistently among those affected by our actions. We can test our actions for consistency by asking about our willingness to adhere to a standard applicable to everyone who's similarly situated. If I'd be willing to accept a standard that permitted someone other than myself to choose in a given way in a particular set of circumstances when that person's choice might affect my loved ones and me, then I'm acting consistently if I choose in this way in relevantly similar circumstances.

---

45. Finnis, *Aquinas* 140.
46. Throughout, I refer to the constituents of the Decalogue using the numbering employed in Reformed circles and in the Septuagint.

On the other hand, if I make exceptions for myself, my friends, my family members, my fellow citizens, it's hard to see my actions as compatible with adherence to THE GOLDEN RULE. When I choose inconsistently, I'm not acknowledging that everyone is equal in fundamental moral status, that everyone is uniquely and irreplaceably lovable.

Love by Refusing to Will Injury

THE PAULINE PRINCIPLE.[47] Love does not purposefully injure anyone. Thus, it does not will injury *as a means* of bringing about some good, whether real (like life and bodily well-being or knowledge) or imagined (like self-assertion or the humiliation of an adversary).[48]

The classic biblical statement pointing the way to this specification of love is Saint Paul's rhetorical question in the Letter to the Romans: "And why not say (as some people slander us by saying that we say), 'Let us do evil so that good may come'?" His response to this question is unequivocal: "Their condemnation is deserved!"[49] So we can call the specification of love that is inconsistent with injuring purposefully—with selecting evil as a purpose directly or making it part of one's purpose by willing it as a means to an end—THE PAULINE PRINCIPLE.

Sometimes, doing things that in fact effect injuries to basic aspects of well-being can be consistent with love. But a choice that injures unintentionally is importantly different from choosing purposefully to injure any basic aspect of well-being. Basic aspects of welfare are genuinely valuable; they're really good for us. To choose to attack, to injure, a basic aspect of flourishing is to choose

---

47. This label was, I believe, introduced by Alan Donagan, *The Theory of Morality* (Chicago: University of Chicago Press 1977) 31, 149. Other uses of the phrase, with different meanings, preceded Donagan's. See, *e.g.*, Augustus Neander, *History of the Planting and Training of the Christian Church by the Apostles*, trans. J. E. Ryland (London: Bohn 1851) 2: 157; Michael Baumgarten, *The Acts of the Apostles; or, The History of the Church in the Apostolic Age*, trans. A. J. W. Morrison (Edinburgh: Clark 1854) 2: 97; and Ferdinand Christian Baur, *The Church History of the First Three Centuries*, trans. Allan Menzies, 3d ed. (London: Williams 1878) 1: 101.

48. See Finnis, *Law* 118–25; Finnis, *Fundamentals* 75, 109–35; Murphy, *Natural Law* 204–7 (cp. 198–201); Grisez and Shaw, *Beyond the New Morality* 121, 129–39; and Grisez, *Way of the Lord Jesus* 1: 215–6. Finnis formulates this requirement as "Do not choose directly against any basic human good" (*Fundamentals* 75), and I follow him in treating instrumental and directly hostile attacks on well-being under the same heading. Given the plausible assumption that any act must be for something taken (whether or not accurately) to be worthwhile, he observes that even what we might think of as a direct attack on a given aspect of well-being rooted in hostility must itself be undertaken in pursuit of some purported good, "even if only . . . self-expression and self-integration" (*Law* 119).

49. Rom 3:8.

in a manner counter to love, either denying the value of the aspect of welfare you're attacking *or* treating it as less important than or simply as a means to the production or realization of some other dimension of welfare.

However, the various dimensions of well-being are qualitatively different, so there's no way of ranking them quantitatively. In addition, no category is qualitatively superior to another; no category is, as it were, ordered to the service of another. So attacking one aspect of well-being for the benefit of another can't be justified on the view that the one you're attacking is less important than or is otherwise supposed to serve the one on behalf of which you're attacking it. And what it makes sense to say about categories or aspects of flourishing also makes sense to say about individual instances, too.

It is never consistent with love, therefore, to seek to kill one person—to attack the good of life and bodily well-being—in the interest of another person. More broadly, I don't love well by purposefully injuring one aspect of well-being (my own or someone else's) for the sake of another aspect of well-being (again, my own or someone else's). The constituents of well-being are all genuinely and irreducibly lovable. Love includes regard for every aspect of everyone's flourishing. Thus, THE PAULINE PRINCIPLE grounds the most important (not the only) human rights protections—against, for instance, murdering, maiming, or torturing.[50] These activities are never consistent with love.

Love by Being Focused, Being Determined, and Diving Deep

COMMITMENT. We should make commitments—choices or resolutions to invest ourselves in particular goods despite potential external and internal challenges—and ordinarily, within limits set by the other specifications of love in action and by the practice of commitment-making itself, fulfill them. Making and keeping commitments is an important way of loving ourselves and others.[51]

So, for instance, Jacob commits himself to engaging in fourteen years of work for Laban in order to marry Rachel. He makes an agreement with Laban; but, separately, he must be sufficiently determined and self-invested to persist in his work for Laban in order to receive Laban's approval for his marriage to the woman he loves.[52] Ruth resolves that she will accompany Naomi to her

---

50. Cp. Finnis, *Law* 225.
51. See Gary Chartier, *The Logic of Commitment* (New York: Routledge 2018). I draw on *Logic of Commitment*, and so indirectly on the various sources on which I rely there, throughout this section.
52. Gen 29:16–30.

ancestral home.[53] Despite their likely appeal, Daniel determines "not [to] defile himself with the royal rations of food and wine."[54] In Isaiah, the Servant of the Lord declares, "I have set my face like flint"—determining to move forward despite adversity and inner resistance.[55] And Luke tells us, perhaps echoing Isaiah 50, that Jesus "set his face to go to Jerusalem"[56]—determined to confront what awaited him there.

There are many complementary reasons for making and keeping commitments. We encounter a wide range of possibilities. There are multiple goods we could realize in our own lives and help others to realize in theirs. We will be able to participate in some goods and to facilitate others' participation in some goods only if we commit to diving deep, to investing ourselves extensively and intensively in particular goods—think, for instance, of professions that require substantial preparation, of friendships, of marriages, of parental relationships. Even as regards short-term goals, it will often be important to stay focused despite distractions, temptations to sloth, and so forth. I need to be able to count on myself to finish working on a book chapter during a given morning, say, rather than reading a novel or calling a friend. Commitments help us love by giving various goods focused attention.

Commitments also enable us to plan rationally. Sometimes, to love others or ourselves, we need to plan. And, when we do, we can see that the various goods we might pursue, protect, respect, or realize don't present themselves in any sort of order. Because they're qualitatively different, we can see that there's no automatic, necessary way of making trade-offs among them. In order to plan, we need to establish priorities, approaches to conflicts, ways of enabling ourselves to make rational calculations when such calculations are required. And (though not all our priorities are or need be objects of commitments) we can do these things precisely by making commitments.

> If we have decided to build a highway through the desert, . . . we can use cost-benefit computations to select among materials and methods of leveling and road-building. But it was not, and could not rationally have been, cost-benefit computations which guided our prior commitment to the level of economic activity (trade) and personal mobility which calls

53. Ruth 1:18.
54. Dan 1:8.
55. Isa 50:7.
56. Luke 9:51.

for highways of this sort. We know that the building and use of highways of this sort involves the death of tens of thousands of persons, and the horrible injury of hundreds of thousands more, each year. But we have not made any computation which shows that the goods participated in and attained by that level of trade and mobility exceed, outweigh, are proportionately greater, than the goods destroyed and damaged by that level, or any level, of deaths and injuries. Nor, on the other hand, could any computation yield the conclusion that the deaths and injuries are an evil which objectively outweighs, exceeds, etc., the good of mobility, etc. . . . The justification, and equally the critique, of any basic commitment [in light of which a choice like this might be assessed] must be in terms of the requirements of practical reasonableness, which give positive direction even though they do not include any principle of optimizing . . . , and even though they permit indefinitely many different commitments (as well as, also, excluding indefinitely many other possible commitments!).[57]

In addition to making and keeping commitments in order to enable myself to invest deeply in particular projects and to plan in the face of diverse possibilities, I will have good reason to develop the *habit* of commitment keeping, since I can achieve my goals more effectively this way. Each time I keep one commitment, I make it more likely that I will succeed in keeping others. I will protect myself from acting on impulse, which may (though it need not) lead me in less-than-desirable directions. Keeping commitments can also be a source of efficiency in decision-making, since doing so can make it unnecessary for me to assess some potential options.

My public success in adhering to my plans tells other people that they can rely on me and thus prompts them to cooperate with me. But I make it more likely that I will adhere to publicly visible commitments if I also adhere sincerely to less-visible ones. Because sticking to what I've decided to do can be difficult, seeing that I've accomplished the difficult task of keeping a commitment can make me more confident in myself and thus more effective generally. And my success in keeping commitments can elicit affirming and so supportive reactions from others, reactions that help me keep future commitments and also, again, boost my confidence.

57. Finnis, *Fundamentals* 91–2.

Keeping commitments helps to ensure that I have a coherent identity, that my life hangs together over time. By contrast, I rupture myself if I disregard my commitments. By abandoning a commitment, I write a certain kind of failure into my story and make it definitive of who I am. Making a commitment can be a way of helping me to be loyal and to self-invest, while abandoning a commitment will impede my capacity to do so. That's true both because I will have less confidence in my ability to keep commitments and because I will have helped to sediment a habit of disregarding commitments, with the result that I may be less reliable in the future.

If I continue to be the same person from moment to moment, even though some features of my existence change, I have reason to hold the various elements of my life together with an eye to my well-being as a person whose needs, concerns, and projects persist. There's something fundamentally incoherent about making commitments and planning to keep them in the face of adversity only to treat them subsequently as dispensable. The same basic reasons I have to take commitments seriously at the time I make a given plan for the future obtain when I later consider abandoning the plan. If it didn't make sense for me to treat commitments lightly then, it doesn't make sense for me to do so now. I can't expect myself to adhere to the plans I make now if I choose in a way that makes me the kind of person who disregards past plans.

"Basic commitments shape our response to, our participation in, basic values—in the form of choices of career, of marriage, of forms of education, of preference for wealth as against leisure or liturgy."[58] One need not make commitments. But they make it possible for us to love ourselves and others in ways that would be unlikely or impossible without them.

Just because we have good reason to keep commitments, it doesn't follow that they can't be modified or retracted. Whether it's consistent with love to alter or abjure particular commitments will depend on one's actual intentions when one made them, on the assumptions underlying them, on whether they create tensions with independently valid moral constraints, on limitations one has built into them, and on the occurrence or nonoccurrence of relevant facts. However, while there are certainly times when changing or abandoning commitments is perfectly sensible, one can't simply release oneself from them at will. To think one could would be to misunderstand or disregard the importance of adhering to our commitments as a way of loving.

58. Finnis 91.

Love by Counting the Cost

EFFICIENCY. We love others and ourselves in part by pursuing our goals with an eye to the effectiveness of the means we employ to achieve them.[59] Consider some questions Jesus poses and his answers:

> For which of you, intending to build a tower, does not first sit down and estimate the cost, to see whether he has enough to complete it? Otherwise, when he has laid a foundation and is not able to finish, all who see it will begin to ridicule him, saying, "This fellow began to build and was not able to finish." Or what king, going out to wage war against another king, will not sit down first and consider whether he is able with ten thousand to oppose the one who comes against him with twenty thousand? If he cannot, then, while the other is still far away, he sends a delegation and asks for the terms of peace.[60]

Counting the cost means taking care to be aware of both good and bad outcomes that might flow from a given choice. Just because, for instance, I am attached to the use of a given surgical technique, it doesn't follow that this technique is the most effective and risk-free in a given case, and I choose unlovingly if I fail to be attentive to its likely results.

Taking consequences and costs seriously also means pursuing our goals without waste—without allowing sloth or susceptibility to distraction to lead to pointless detours and needless expenditures (whether financial, emotional, or otherwise). It's quite possible, however, to pursue multiple targets at once: I might, say, make a business trip to Berkeley while also staying over to see friends in San Francisco, something that might seem wasteful (given the extra expenditures involved) if whatever I hoped to accomplish by means of the business trip were mistakenly seen as my only reason for traveling to the Bay Area. Still, where I do have a specific goal in view and I pursue it ineffectively without good reason, I act unlovingly toward myself and toward others to the extent that they and I might benefit had I opted for a more focused approach.

---

59. See Finnis, *Law* 111–8; Finnis, *Fundamentals* 75; and Murphy, *Natural Law* 207–8.
60. Luke 14:28–32. This passage figures prominently in Paul Ramsey's moral reflection; thanks to Adam Edward Hollowell, *Power and Purpose: Paul Ramsey and Contemporary Christian Political Theology* (Grand Rapids: Eerdmans 2015) 72–8, for citing, highlighting, and analyzing Ramsey's use of it.

This doesn't mean that a typical decision can necessarily be made on the basis of a cost-benefit analysis.[61] That's true for several reasons. (*a*) Decisions need to be consistent with all of the specifications of love, not only this one. (*b*) Costs and benefits can be commensurated only on the basis of prior commitments; commensurating them is possible not just as such but only once relevant commitments have been made. (*c*) Even after such commitments are made, not all goods affected by one's choices will likely have been rendered commensurable. After all, one might simply have focused, quite reasonably, on *some* of the goods in play but not all, and one may find in a given case that one does not have clear preferences or that one otherwise sees no need to commit to particular priorities. It's also possible that, in a particular situation, one has committed oneself unreasonably because of a given commitment's inconsistency with the other specifications of love. But EFFICIENCY calls us to love by taking into account the commitments we've made and the priorities we've embraced and to attend to the predictable outcomes of our choices in light of those commitments and priorities.

Generic Love?

The creational love ethic I've begun to elaborate here involves the idea that there are *generic* moral truths—ones that, in virtue of the way we've been created, apply in all circumstances. Defending *particularism*, some people are skeptical about this idea, suggesting that we need to be sensitive to the unique configuration of goods implicated in each situation in which we find ourselves and to see those goods as relevant in distinctive ways because of how they're related to one another in each situation.[62] No factor will necessarily play the same role from situation to situation. We might be able to generalize from situation to situation, given that morally relevant considerations are often germane in similar ways in different situations. But, if so, we're simply reasoning inductively; there's nothing about the nature of normativity or moral judgment in virtue of which this needs to be or consistently will be the case.

A moral judgment regarding how one should choose in a given situation depends on a variety of factors in play in that situation. But it doesn't follow that

61. See Finnis, *Law* 112–8.
62. This view is articulated from a Christian perspective by Keith Ward, *Ethics and Christianity* (London: Allen 1970) 139–54. The most extensive and careful defense of particularism has been offered by Jonathan Dancy. See Jonathan Dancy, *Moral Reasons* (Oxford: Blackwell 1993); and Jonathan Dancy, *Ethics without Principles* (Oxford: Clarendon-Oxford University Press 2004).

the relevance to moral judgment of a given factor could always, in principle, be different in different situations.

Clearly, *some* factors are relevant in situationally specific ways. Suppose that I have agreed to make a presentation to our company's leadership team promoting a new product line. Changed circumstances or newly discovered ones may affect my duty to keep the promise I've made. Perhaps I discover that the product line poses serious safety risks to consumers and needs to be redesigned from the ground up. Suppose I'm bedridden, weak, and inarticulate the day of the slated presentation. Or suppose I discover that it will be very beneficial to your career if you're able to make the presentation, as you'll be invited to do if I'm unavailable. In these and innumerable other circumstances, it might be perfectly reasonable for me to bow out of making the presentation and perhaps even unreasonable of me *not* to bow out.

But I can readily assess the relevance of these factors in light of the underlying considerations that make promises binding in the first place.[63] In general, it's unreasonable of me to break a promise because doing so is unfair, inconsistent with love in the form of THE GOLDEN RULE. But not fulfilling a promise in the kinds of cases I've envisioned could be perfectly consistent with THE GOLDEN RULE.

While I can sensibly decide not to perform as I've promised to do in light of THE GOLDEN RULE, this specification of love, indicating who and how I should love, remains just as salient when it permits as when it precludes my change in plans. It wouldn't make sense to say that while "This action is inconsistent with THE GOLDEN RULE" was decisively relevant in one case, it might not be in another. There are good reasons, generic reasons, consistently applicable reasons, to avoid violating THE GOLDEN RULE. As a result, to ignore a choice's inconsistency with THE GOLDEN RULE would be to make an error in reasoning no matter what other considerations one might be taking into account.

The same is true of THE PAULINE PRINCIPLE. The fact that a choice is a choice to attack a basic aspect of well-being is always decisive, whatever other considerations are in play. It is never reasonable to torture, to injure any sentient purposefully or instrumentally, and so forth: and THE PAULINE PRINCIPLE grounds these strict prohibitions.

The specifications of love are consistently and definitively relevant no matter what other considerations are in play. The conclusive relevance of these

---

63. See Finnis, *Law* 298–314; and T. M. Scanlon, *What We Owe to Each Other* (Cambridge, MA: Harvard University Press 1998) 295–327.

ways of loving is apparent in virtue of the considerations in light of which, say, THE GOLDEN RULE and THE PAULINE PRINCIPLE *count* as specifications of love in the first place.[64] Arbitrary disregard is always arbitrary disregard, a purposeful attack on a basic aspect of well-being is always a purposeful attack on a basic aspect of well-being, and so forth. We can see why ignoring THE GOLDEN RULE or THE PAULINE PRINCIPLE couldn't make sense in view of the particular factors that make each a specification of love. The decisiveness of these specifications of love doesn't need to be spelled out in the first place by referring to a range of situational details; rather, these specifications of love can be seen to be warranted independently of those details, given certain generic features of the environments in which we choose. And, if that's the case, they will be applicable in particular situations independently of various details evident in those situations, details of kinds that don't figure in their justification or interpretation. The application of these principles will vary with the specific characteristics of each situation because the principles apply to particular kinds of situations and not others, and we can't tell whether a given situation is of the relevant kind without seeking carefully to understand it. But those details don't change the generic applicability of these specifications of love to situations that do turn out to have the relevant features. Love is particular insofar as it attends carefully to each situation. But it is generic insofar as it recognizes the commonalities that obtain across seemingly diverse situations—so that that love never, for instance, involves treating anyone arbitrarily or intending to injure a basic aspect of anyone's well-being.

Structuring Love

Love rooted in and responsive to creation exhibits a predictable structure. That structure reflects the aspects of well-being and the directive effect of the various specifications of love. In what follows, I elaborate an understanding of love's structure. Then, I explain how the creational love ethic I am developing here points beyond sharp divisions, often presupposed by appeals to *agape*, between self and other. A common Christian conception of love, one noticeably different from the one reflected in the specifications of love I've elaborated, is rooted in the sense that the New Testament speaks of love as *agape*,

64. Cp. Christopher O. Tollefsen, "McDowell's Moral Realism and the Secondary Quality Analogy," *Disputatio* 1.8 (May 2000): 29–42.

with a distinctive meaning not paralleled elsewhere. I conclude by indicating why we might want to question this exegetical move as a basis for a love ethic.

Circles of Love

One way to think about love's structure is as involving a set of circles, the smaller ones nested within the largest while sometimes located within, sometimes overlapping with, each other. These circles help to depict love's different foci. We can speak about love as everything from devotion, of a kind that creatures like us can offer to a very limited number of people, to an open respect with which each moral agent can treat every sentient creature. Most of our relationships can't and shouldn't exhibit the characteristics of Jacob's love for Rachel or Hosea's love for Gomer. But they can all be relationships marked by love.

(*i*) *Universal love.* The largest circle is the circle of universal love—the kind of love we can and should show to everyone. This sort of love is negative; it is the variety reflected in (at least) the final six commands of the Decalogue.

Jesus and Saint Paul both indicate that the law (and Saint Paul makes clear that he has provisions of the Decalogue in mind) is summed up in THE GOLDEN RULE.[65] While a great deal is sometimes made of the purported difference between positive and negative formulations of this specification of love, the last five prescriptions contained in the Decalogue are framed in negative terms: don't murder, don't steal, don't commit adultery, don't give false testimony against anyone, and don't covet things that belong to others. And it is on four of these five that Saint Paul focuses when suggesting that love sums up the law.

These commandments can be obeyed with respect to every created sentient quite straightforwardly. I can avoid killing everyone, avoid stealing from everyone, and so forth. If THE GOLDEN RULE concerns, expresses, is a form of love and if the Decalogue is grounded and encapsulated in THE GOLDEN RULE so that the Decalogue itself is best understood as a matter of love, then we can speak of *universal* love as a matter of something like adhering to these negative commandments. The Decalogue's negative commandments don't exhaust the meaning of love. But, unlike other sorts of love, the love embodied in these prohibitions can be shown to everyone.

Most of the time, the morally mature person does not, need not, stop to reflect consciously on whether to adhere to a universal moral prohibition.

65. Matt 7:12; 22:40; Gal 5:14; Rom 13:8–10.

That's part of what it means to be morally mature. Sometimes, it may be helpful to think empathically about a person one might be tempted to injure. On the other hand, one may often have no clear picture of such a person and thus no capacity to respond emotionally to her. Think about the decision not to pump a carcinogen into a river providing drinking water to unsuspecting townspeople or to avoid stealing from a faceless business or its insurers. One can engage in universal love without concrete interpersonal awareness, helpful as this may often be in prompting loving behavior.

Relationships in which prohibitions on aggressive interference with others' lives are respected are relationships marked by peace. Peace is not equivalent to the full-orbed flourishing First Testament writers sometimes call *shalom*. But it creates the space in which people can grow, explore, experiment, and interact. Peace is the absence of sustained, systematic violence—the most important barrier to our discerning, forming, sustaining, and enhancing myriad kinds of welfare by talking, playing, working, worshipping, trading, and contemplating together. And so peace makes possible not only the realization of goods in particular interactions but also the voluntary, nonviolent, extended social cooperation that facilitates *shalom* in multiple ways, enabling *shalom* to emerge from the bottom up.

(*ii*) *Mutual love with strangers.* Our cooperative activities often link us with friends, but they also connect us not infrequently with strangers—in a pickup basketball game at a neighborhood park, in a casual erotic interaction, in a momentary exchange at a retail counter. In addition to the negative requirements that make up the kind of love we owe to everyone, we need to give more to those with whom we are connected in these and other ways. They are aware of us, and we are aware of them, as particular persons, so it will often be inconsistent with love for us not to *acknowledge* their particular personhood in one way or another, to let them know that we see and value them.

In addition, we will often have other responsibilities to them. Just what we need to give them will be largely determined by THE GOLDEN RULE. Sometimes, our responsibilities will flow from explicit promises, sometimes from mutually shared and endorsed background assumptions, sometimes from the silent invitations we issue to others—through what we do and the way in which we say things—to rely on us. In any case, it will be unfair to ignore their reasonable expectations. So we will need to pay what we've promised, play fairly, and so forth. Sometimes, strangers will become friends; in other cases, we will never see them again. Either way, our relationships with them, even if very brief indeed, will need to offer the focused love of fair treatment.

(*iii*) *Love of enemies.* I will explore our relationships with enemies in greater detail in chapter 7. Here, I want simply to emphasize that enemies are at least frequently not strangers, either because those we already know become enemies or because we find ourselves personally connected with others because of our conflicts with them. Our love for them should reflect, at least, RECOGNITION, THE GOLDEN RULE, and THE PAULINE PRINCIPLE. These specifications of love preclude retribution and other varieties of injustice and potentially prompt transformative, healing engagement.

(*iv*) *Love for the vulnerable.* Another kind of focused love is love for vulnerable people.[66] (None of us is invulnerable, but some vulnerabilities are particularly pronounced.) One might love vulnerable people by donating to a refugee assistance or economic development or education program, counseling a depressed student, brightening the day of an evidently dejected fellow shopper or retail clerk with a kind word, buying lunch for a homeless person or directing her to a shelter, changing a tire for an elderly person . . . A baseline for one's love for vulnerable others is set by THE GOLDEN RULE; COMMITMENT may play a further role in some instances, shaping one's self-investment in an ongoing relationship with those served by a given nonprofit, a given economically insecure person, or a given nonhuman animal.

(*v*) *Love for those associated with particular causes and institutions.* We are connected in a variety of ways with various groups of people. We may or may not know them personally. Even if we don't, we share attachments, and perhaps commitments, with them. Those who patronize or work at or display their creations at an art museum, those who participate in a pressure group or benefit from its work, the members of a nonprofit musical ensemble or of the ensemble's audience, employees or students at the college one attended, the members of the church one attends, the scientists who make up a research group whose work one values—any of these might claim one's loyalty. One might give time, money, or influence to support them. Sometimes loving those linked with a cause or institution will be a matter of assisting them on a whim. In other cases, one's love will be channeled by promises, morally significant because of THE GOLDEN RULE, which will also figure in our judgments about whether it's consistent with love to

66. For some reasonable guidance, see, *e.g*, Onora O'Neill, *Towards Justice and Virtue: A Constructive Account of Practical Reasoning* (Cambridge: Cambridge University Press 1996) 195–200; Scanlon, *What We Owe* 224; Luke T. Johnson, *Sharing Possessions: Mandate and Symbol of Faith* (Philadelphia: Fortress 1981) 132–9; Finnis, *Law* 173–7; David Schmidtz, "Separateness, Suffering, and Moral Theory," *Person, Polis, Planet: Essays in Applied Philosophy* (New York: Oxford University Press 2008) 145–64; and Liam Murphy, *Moral Demands in Nonideal Theory* (New York: Oxford University Press 2000).

aid a given cause or institution in the first place. In yet other instances, one will have made commitments, whether separate from or supportive of promises. Causes and institutions may be of limited importance in some people's lives, but they may prove central and identity-constitutive for others.

(*vi*) *Love as intimate connection.* Various close relationships enrich our lives and claim our loyalty and our attention. Those in this circle include friends who are simply friends as well as those one has chosen as friends while also engaging with them in other capacities; this latter subset may include colleagues, some family members, some fellow volunteers and hobbyists . . . Relationships with friends—marked by openness, intimacy, loyalty, and shared experience—are solidified by promises, invitations to reliance, and personal self-investments. Their moral status is thus a function of THE GOLDEN RULE and COMMITMENT as well as of the acknowledgment, consistent with RECOGNITION, of the worth of friendship.

(*vii*) *Love as devotion.* The inmost circle will include those to whom we are devoted. Perhaps these are most likely to be spouses, lovers, children, parents, siblings, our closest friends . . . (There is nothing inherently exhaustive about this list.) At least some of these will likely be those whom the *Didache* says "you shall love more than your own life."[67] Love within this circle is channeled in virtue of THE GOLDEN RULE insofar as we have made promises and, through our behavior, invited reliance. This specification of love is particularly relevant to parent-child relationships, since children's distinct vulnerability to parents yields particular obligations on the part of the parents that at least initially and perhaps permanently are grounded not in mutuality but, rather, in the recognition of vulnerability.[68] Devoted love is also given focus in virtue of COMMITMENT: our self-investment in relationships with and care for particular others can be established and sustained by means of our (implicit and explicit) resolutions.

Love takes shape. It assumes a structure. And this means that it is focused and differentiated. It is an act of love when I rescue an enemy from a burning building, as also when I decline to take the first step toward adulterously disrupting the marriage of a complete stranger. Love is always appropriate regard for well-being in one form or another, but just what that form is depends on the specifications of love. Those specifications yield a structure that features diverse kinds of relationships, from the impersonal to the casual to the intimate to the devoted.

67. *Didache* 2:7, trans. Matthew B. Riddle, *Ante-Nicene Fathers* 7, ed. Alexander Roberts, James Donaldson, and A. Cleveland Coxe (Buffalo, NY: Christian Literature 1885) <http://www.newadvent.org/fathers/0714.htm> (rev. and ed. Kevin Knight).
68. Cp. Robert E. Goodin, *Protecting the Vulnerable: A Reanalysis of Our Social Responsibilities* (Chicago: University of Chicago Press 1985).

Loving Self and Other

While I have elaborated what I take to be love's structure in a way that emphasizes our love for others, when we love others, we also love ourselves. And, when we choose against love for others by disregarding the specifications of love, we choose *not* to love ourselves and, indeed, injure ourselves. This is true for several reasons, including these:[69]

(*i*) Practical wisdom is an aspect of each agent's well-being. To choose in accordance with love is to affirm and respect the good of practical wisdom and so to affirm and respect one's own good. Conversely, to choose in a way that disregards one or more of the specifications of love is to injure oneself—in particular, to interfere with one's exercise of the good of practical wisdom and perhaps to inhibit one's long-term capacity to participate in this good. Choosing well with respect to others is thus also choosing well with respect to oneself, while choosing, in a manner inconsistent with love, to behave in a way that will injure others is thus choosing (even if not intentionally) to injure oneself.

(*ii*) Some goods we seek to realize in our lives can be essentially *common*. Think about friendship with some key instances of play (you can't play real-world soccer or tennis by yourself). To injure these goods in one's own life or in the lives of others with whom one is participating in them is thus to injure oneself and others simultaneously, while we enrich both ourselves and others by enhancing these goods.

(*iii*) Relatedly, we can identify (even if imperfectly) with some others—lovers, friends, and children, for instance—so that their goods become ours and they themselves are integrated to some degree into who we understand ourselves to be. Again, to injure these others is to injure ourselves, while to benefit them is to benefit ourselves.

(*iv*) We are social creatures. We live interdependent lives in multiple ways, drawing on others for language, for emotional nurture, for information, and for a vast array of goods and services. When we choose in a manner contrary to love, we can and often do disrupt the social connections on which we ourselves

---

69. I've gained useful insights from Roderick Long and Sheldon Richman about moving beyond the unhelpful idea of a necessary dichotomy between self and other. Worth consulting in this connection is Talbot Brewer, *The Retrieval of Ethics* (New York: Oxford University Press 2009) 192–235. Brewer calls our attention to insights from classical authors that can help us love and move beyond "modern dualism about the good" (192). He particularly highlights the importance of exercising virtue for its own sake as serving the agent's good by integrating the self and preserving the centrality of reason.

depend. By contrast, when we choose to love, we can nurture and strengthen those connections.[70]

Social institutions can reduce or eliminate conflicts of interest when they serve to align each agent's pursuit of her own goals with others' efforts to realize theirs. This is a contingent matter—institutions can encourage us to treat each other as adversaries or even as objects of predation. But institutions like justly ordered markets can help to foster *shalom* by precluding the use of force and fostering interactions to which persuasion is basic and in which we help strangers to meet their goals in and through the same actions that also help us to meet our own. Here the relationship is contingent and causal rather than constitutive, but it can reliably link the well-being of one with that of others nonetheless.

The Meaning of *Agape*

The creational love ethic I have begun to elaborate here can seem to be in tension with a common understanding of love in Christian ethics. This understanding is often seen as based on the Greek New Testament and on the meaning of the word often used for "love" there—*agape*. This kind of love, on a familiar interpretation, gives no independent weight to the agent's well-being, interests, or projects. It is heedless, self-sacrificial, and unfocused. However, while the Bible does, indeed, call for love, while it treats love as the heart of Christian ethics, it does not provide anything like unequivocal, straightforward support for the approach to ethics and spirituality often derived from this interpretation.

Interestingly, despite the centrality this approach is often seen as having in the moral vision of Jesus, the form *agape* itself appears only once in Matthew and Luke and never in Mark, suggesting that it did not necessarily seem natural to render Aramaic sayings of Jesus in Greek using this word.[71] The Fourth Gospel (with seven usages) and the Epistles employ the word more frequently.[72]

---

70. I've tried to address this broad range of issues in *A Good Life in the Market: An Introduction to Business Ethics* (Great Barrington, MA: AIER 2019) 39–46; and *Flourishing Lives: Exploring Natural Law Liberalism* (Cambridge: Cambridge University Press 2019) 9–11.

71. James Barr, "Words for Love in Biblical Greek," *The Glory of Christ in the New Testament: Studies in Christology in Memory of George Bradford Caird*, ed. L. D. Hurst and N. T. Wright (Oxford: Clarendon-Oxford University Press 1987) 18. I draw on Barr throughout this section.

72. Barr 18.

The idea that there is a special, biblical meaning of *agape* has sometimes involved the notion that the Septuagint initiated a distinctive theological use of this word, which was then picked up by the New Testament writers. However, as far as we can tell, it is used in the Septuagint because it was, by the time that translation came into being, a "general all-purpose word for love."[73] It was anything but a special coinage designed to capture a distinctive idea (as, say, of spontaneous and unqualified beneficence).[74]

Agape is not the only noun form in the relevant word family. And other forms, other members of the family, are very much in evidence in the Septuagint. So far from being a remarkable de novo creation, this word (even if—and we don't know that this is the case—it first actually appears in the Septuagint) "is no more than a nominalization of those same relations and emotions which in verb form were expressed by ἀγαπᾷν; no one has argued that this noun said something different about love from what the verb said."[75] And, if the New Testament authors had intended to take over from the Septuagint a special sense of *agape* as the master variety of love, it seems unlikely that they would have used *philein* to mean "to love" more frequently (relative to size) than the Septuagint's translators had done.[76]

In the Septuagint, members of the *agape* family are used to refer to mutual erotic love,[77] Amnon's uncontrolled lust for Tamar,[78] Gomer's partners in adultery,[79] or attachment to false oaths.[80] *Eros*,[81] by contrast, seems to have a

73. Barr 11. It also appears that the translators of the Septuagint were inclined to try to use consistent equivalences between particular Greek and particular Hebrew words. As a result, having opted to use a given Greek word for a particular Hebrew word at a key point, they typically continued to use the same Greek word for that Hebrew word at other points, even if the two might have been less equivalent at those other points. This seems to have been what happened with respect to biblical talk of love (Barr 7–8; cp. 11, 17).

74. Barr 7.

75. Barr 8.

76. Barr 14 (offering multiple examples), 18. It's curious that *philia* is not used positively in the New Testament.

77. Barr 10.

78. 2 Sam 13:1; Barr, "Words for Love" 12.

79. Hos 3:1; Barr, "Words for Love" 12. This passage uses a member of the *agape* family to call Hosea to love Gomer, and his love for her has often been highlighted as a particularly striking example of generous, loyal, accepting love. But it seems likely that the root meaning is not in any way limited to something like unconditional or other-centered love, given that Gomer's lovers are themselves identified using a member of the *agape* family.

80. Zech 8:17; Barr, "Words for Love" 12.

81. I italicize *eros* to make clear that I'm alluding to a Greek word here. When I refer to the realm of erotic feelings and activities, I will use "eros" without italics.

rather narrower semantic range;[82] however, *agape* is used as a parallel for *eros*, for instance,[83] and is employed, quite apart from the setting of poetic parallelism, to point to erotic attitudes.[84] The Septuagint translators use forms of *agape* and *philia* for the same Hebrew word in a given passage, presumably as a means of elegant variation—thus treating the two as semantically equivalent on occasion.[85]

The words of Jesus were presumably uttered in Aramaic, so *he* wasn't concerned with making special points using Greek words for love. Thus, it is unsurprising that the evangelists might have taken different paths to translating sayings that came to them in Aramaic. For instance, "people who 'love' the front seats in the synagogue or at dinner have ἀγαπᾶν in Luke but φιλεῖν in Matthew."[86] And, while we can be less sure about what lies behind sayings in the Fourth Gospel, it's not unreasonable to think that, when Jesus asks Peter if he loves him in John 21, the evangelist represents him as employing ἀγαπᾷς and φιλεῖς as equivalent in significance.[87] It is particularly striking to find words in the *agape* family used to say that "people loved darkness," that Demas was "in love with this present world," and that Balaam "loved the wages of doing wrong."[88]

James Barr observes that, in using the word-study approach to make sense of *agape*,[89] Ceslas Spicq

> seems to be influenced throughout by the conviction that the word . . .
> *must be* the proper and peculiar designator of a special kind of love, its
> proper name as it were, so that the study of this word will surely reveal
> the contours of this special kind of love. Again and again the evidence

82. Barr, "Words for Love" 11.
83. Barr 10.
84. Barr 12.
85. Barr 15.
86. Barr 12.
87. Barr 15.
88. John 3:19; 2 Tim 4:10; 2 Pet 2:15. Barr ("Words for Love" 4) notes these passages, emphasizing that Anders Nygren recognized that *agape* was not always used with the meaning on which he sought to focus in *Agape and Eros*, trans. Philip S. Watson (London: SPCK 1953) (this is the edition Barr cites), but instead saw himself as identifying an ideal type. However, Barr observes, "though Nygren acknowledged this [variation in meaning], it cannot be said that his recognition of it and its implications was adequate in detail or in profundity" ("Words for Love" 4n4).
89. He cites Ceslas Spicq, *Agapè: Prolégomènes a une étude de théologie néo-testamentaire* (Louvain, Belgium: Nauwelaerts 1955); and Ceslas Spicq, *Agapè dans le Nouveau Testament*, 3 vols. (Paris: Gabalda 1958–9) (the reference form, orthography, and details are mine).

suggests that this is not so, and Spicq half acknowledges this, but then he starts off again on the same track, convinced that the meanings of this word will somehow lead us to a deeper knowledge of this peculiar kind of love.[90]

While words in the *agape* family can be used to denote "good" and "bad" varieties of love, the noun form in particular, *agape*, is used in the New Testament only for the good varieties.[91] But that doesn't mean that it expresses just the good ones we might talk about using expressions like "unconditional love," "love of the other as other," "selfless generosity," or "self-giving love." Rather, something like the ambiguities and ranges of meaning that are evident when contemporary speakers of English use *love* are apparent here. New Testament usage simply doesn't seem to involve a consistent, narrow meaning. Ironically, "ἀγάπη, ἀγαπᾶν in actual biblical Greek did not always signify *agape*" in what has become a popular theological sense.[92] Whatever the merits of this theological sense, it can't justifiably be treated as the exclusive or primary biblical sense.

Creation, Love, and Truth

An ethic of love is often assumed to be one that is sensitively responsive to changing realities, perhaps as a result unpredictable and inconstant. An ethic of creation is sometimes thought to be static, even stagnant. But neither stereotype is quite correct.

Creation is dynamic. It has a history, and it's constantly growing and changing. That's true of particular living creatures. It's also true of societies made up of such creatures. As a result, what is actually the case at any given time shifts, as does our understanding of what is the case. People's capacities for inquiry and judgment may change over generations as different social and environmental complexities bring different strengths into play. And, even if our capacities remain the same, various kinds of experiences, various sorts of intellectual encounters, may be required to enable us to discern a basic good, a given instance of a basic good one already recognizes, or a particular specification of love or to discern just what love presupposes in a given kind of case. (An obvious

90. Barr, "Words for Love" 5.
91. Barr 12.
92. Barr 4.

example here is the developing recognition that everyone, and not merely each member of one's own community, deserves respect as an irreplaceable divine creation.) This kind of historical development doesn't involve any change in what is true about what it means to live a life of love. Rather, it involves a change in our *awareness* of what is true, in our *knowledge* of the creation and of the meaning of love.

There is always a gap between, if you will, what God knows and what we know.[93] And one of the things that God knows and we generally don't know is *whether* we don't know about this or that in the first place. We find it easy to be arrogant, and we are deeply attached to our beliefs about what is the case. As a result, we find it easy to insist that someone who challenges one of our deeply held beliefs is a relativist or a subjectivist, someone who thinks the truth is simply up to her, or a historicist, someone who thinks that truth itself is changing. But this needn't be the case at all. To challenge deeply held beliefs can—and, indeed, should—be a reflection of the conviction that there really is a way the world is independent of us, independent of our biases and prejudices and background assumptions, that there are things, infinitely many things, that God knows and we don't.[94] To challenge established beliefs need not be any sort of expression of nihilism; it can, rather, be an attempt to enable us to get, in one sense, a little closer to knowing what God knows (even though we'll always be infinitely distant from divine omniscience).

Even though the deep character of love is constant, there can sometimes be changes in what we ought to do. For instance, it's possible, though it seems unlikely, that the natures of the sentient persons on our planet might shift sufficiently so that something that isn't now an aspect of *our* flourishing might qualify as an aspect of the flourishing of later created persons. (The reverse probably wouldn't be true.[95]) And in this case, there would be an important change in what love looked like in their lives as compared to its form in ours. Whatever might happen as regards the emergence of new aspects of welfare, we know that the social, institutional, and environmental circumstances of intelligent creatures on this planet have shifted over time and will likely continue to shift. This means that living out the various ways of loving and responsiveness to the same basic goods will have looked, and doubtless will look, interestingly

93. Thanks to Fritz Guy for introducing me to this way of putting the matter.
94. I owe this point to Stephen R. L. Clark.
95. I draw appreciatively in this paragraph on Chappell, *Understanding Human Goods* 44–5.

different at different times, even as THE GOLDEN RULE, THE PAULINE PRINCIPLE, and love's other specifications continue to obtain.

When changes in nature or social circumstance occur, it can seem as if the historicist is right. But it's important to see that the *underlying* truths about love remain the same: *For a creature like that, flourishing will necessarily look like this. Act in pursuit of genuine goods. Don't discriminate arbitrarily among those affected by your actions. Don't treat an aspect of well-being as if it weren't an aspect of well-being.* And so forth. Something it would be wrong to do in a given situation will always be wrong in a relevantly similar situation. But whether there *is* a relevantly similar situation will depend on the natures of the creatures involved and their historical and environmental circumstances. And whether we *understand* those natures and circumstances correctly will depend on a range of factors: the possibilities for understanding presented by our families, cultures, and institutions; our own intellectual and emotional responsiveness to unexpected potential discoveries; our engagement with relevant arguments and arguers; and, ultimately, whether we've responded to divine persuasion, exercised in and through all of these and, no doubt, various other factors as well.

I might, for instance, discover that what has always seemed to me like an unquestionable argument for a given moral position has been decisively refuted. I might see reason to question the credibility of an authority figure responsible for telling me to accept a certain moral position as an expression of love. So I might suppose that two men couldn't possibly participate in a fruitful, flourishing marriage before encountering neighbors who make it impossible for me to retain this belief. I might believe potentially procreative erotic activity was deeply risky and should thus be avoided; but I might change my mind once safe forms of contraception became available. The truth doesn't change, but our knowledge of it does, and so does the relevance of particular truths to our conditions.

While, on the robustly realist view I have outlined, what counts as love is appropriate regard for well-being and what counts as our well-being is a function of how we've been created, an alternative Christian view treats moral requirements as contingently created by God. I look critically at this view, along with the sometimes associated notion of vocation, in chapter 3.

3

Love, Voluntarism,
and Vocation

The moral life is a life of love grounded in creation. But one common understanding of ethics, *theistic voluntarism* (from *voluntas*, "will"), treats the moral
life as instead a matter of obedience to particular or general moral requirements created contingently, *ex nihilo*, by God.[1] In this chapter, I look critically
at theistic voluntarism, explaining why it is both unattractive and unsuccessful,
before turning to the idea of vocation. A vocation is a responsibility or range of
responsibilities assigned (literally or metaphorically) to a specific person.[2] I consider the idea of vocation here because of its frequent association with theistic

1. For critiques of voluntarism, see, *e.g*, Oliver O'Donovan, *Resurrection and Moral Order: An Outline
for Evangelical Ethics* (Leicester: IVP 1986) 16–8, 31–52; Grisez, *Way of the Lord Jesus* 1: 101–2; and
Finnis, *Law* 342–3. I do not mean for a moment to suggest that O'Donovan, Grisez, or Finnis
would agree with what I say in this chapter.
2. The idea of vocation is often taken to refer to a set of duties that can't be derived from but
that might coexist with general moral requirements. However, as Adams, *Finite and Infinite Goods*
297–300, observes (critically), it would be possible to articulate a consequentialist understanding
of vocation: act-consequentialism, at any rate, could generate a person- and situation-specific
duty at each point of choice for each person. A position that treats the moral life as shaped by
moment-by-moment divine directives would, similarly, offer little basis for distinguishing between
the realm of vocation and the rest of the moral life: in effect, every aspect of the moral life could
be understood as vocational. See Karl Barth, *Ethics*, ed. Dietrich Braun, trans. Geoffrey W. Bromiley (New York: Seabury 1981) 76–81. (I'm interested here in the position rather than in the
question of whether Barth's personal view in his later work was identical with the one he took in
this 1928–9 book.) Similarly, moral particularism—*e.g*, Ward, *Ethics* 141–54; and Dancy, *Ethics
without Principles*—according to which there are no generic moral requirements and one must wisely
take all relevant considerations into account in each situation, effectively turns all requirements into
vocational ones. As I note below, a creational love ethic might sometimes ground something like
a vocation in generic requirements; but whether what such an ethic affirms is close enough to the
notion of a vocation as traditionally conceived to merit the name is, at any rate, open to question.

voluntarism; a vocation need not be rooted in a contingently created moral requirement or a set of such requirements, but it will often be understood as grounded in this way. I believe the idea of vocation is potentially fruitful and interesting, but it can't readily be incorporated within a creational love ethic. A life lived in accordance with such an ethic can, however, offer a number of the goods a vocation might be prized for making available.

Moral Requirements as Contingent Creations

Theistic voluntarism understands rightness and wrongness as created contingently by God—as tags arbitrarily attached to created activities. On what I'll call a *comprehensive* voluntarist view, God also contingently creates what we might call *values*, including the goodness or badness of activities, relationships, or capacities. The view that right and wrong, good and bad, are fiat divine creations is troubling in much the same way as the view, also embraced by some voluntarists, that mathematical and logical truths are fiat creations.

There is considerable tension between comprehensive voluntarism and belief in divine goodness and love. This kind of voluntarism offers us no understanding of why God should create moral requirements in the first place, and creating them (or anything else) seems entirely unnecessary on comprehensive voluntarist premises. Voluntarism leaves us with no sense of why we should obey contingently created moral requirements: neither divine power nor divine love nor gratitude to God provides any warrant for obedience if one is a comprehensive voluntarist. And a hybrid variety of voluntarism, in accordance with which rightness and wrongness are contingent divine creations but goodness and badness aren't, encounters many of the same difficulties as comprehensive voluntarism.[3]

Voluntarism and Meaning

Theistic voluntarism renders talk of divine goodness vacuous. As C. S. Lewis observes, "If good is to be *defined* as what God commands, then the goodness of God Himself is emptied of meaning and the commands of an omnipotent fiend would have the same claim on us as those of the 'righteous Lord.'"[4]

3. For an earlier assessment of voluntarism, see Chartier, *Analogy of Love* 189–204.
4. C. S. Lewis, "The Poison of Subjectivism," *Christian Reflections*, ed. Walter Hooper (Grand Rapids: Eerdmans 1967) 79.

Love and Created Normativity

Lewis's point seems to hold whether goodness is understood as love or as any other recognizable moral excellence. But I want to focus here on goodness as love.

As I've emphasized, while love can take different forms, I'm concerned in this book with love understood as appropriate regard for well-being. To love creatures is at least to be concerned with whatever is good *for* them. However, if what's valuable for a creature is determined by a contingent divine assignment of value, then there will be no independent account of welfare (well-being, flourishing, fulfillment, self-realization), since there will be no independent sense in which something is, in fact, good for someone. But, and here's Lewis's point made with more focus on love in particular, if God simply *decided* what counted as good for a creature—as when Karl Barth says, "The good *is* what is commanded me"[5] or "The truth of the good *is always* a concrete individual command"[6]—then anything God did would count as loving. There would be no way of making sense of God's loving someone in the sense of seeking or fostering or cherishing or protecting her welfare or well-being. The claim that God loves someone would turn out to be an uninteresting tautology. What's good is what God says is good, so whatever God does in relation to someone will be an instance of God's loving that person. "God loves David" will turn out to be consistent with "God does anything at all."[7]

To avoid this problem, we need to say, rather, with Lewis, that "the good is uncreated; it never could have been otherwise; it has in it no shadow of contingency. . . . God is not merely good, but goodness; goodness is not merely divine, but God."[8] What counts as good for a creature is a function of how that creature has been created. Given the actual characteristics of a creature, it's no more arbitrary to say that X or Y is good for that creature than to state the solution to a problem in mathematics. God determines what moral requirements we

5. Barth, *Ethics* 55 (my italics).
6. Barth 76 (my italics).
7. One might try to argue that moral requirements weren't contingent divine creations but that they were necessitated by something other than what was inherently good for creatures. By making putative moral requirements independent of creaturely welfare, this approach would raise questions about divine love and so divine goodness. Assuming that moral goodness is real and that love is integral to God's nature, we can reasonably expect moral requirements to be necessary, not fiat creations; and we can expect them to be concerned with the well-being of creatures. Thanks to David Gordon for a discussion on this point.
8. Lewis, "Poison of Subjectivism" 80.

confront, but God does so by making a particular kind of world; goodness and badness, rightness and wrongness, are what they are just because of the kind of world God has made.

Contingently Created Requirements as Unintelligible

On a voluntarist view, it seems as if created requirements themselves would be finally unintelligible. If nothing is *inherently* worthwhile to God or to any creature (as would be the case if values were free, contingent, divine creations), then there would be no reason for God to do one thing rather than another, including create a given requirement. God's action in creating any given requirement would seem to be a pointless exercise of will for the sake of will.

Contingently Created Requirements as Unnecessary

If nothing were inherently worthwhile *for us*, then no created requirement would be more conducive to our well-being than any other. There would be no reason for God to create any requirements. And the creation of such requirements would thus represent an unnecessary imposition on the autonomy of those subjected to the requirements.

Why Obey Contingent Requirements?

A theistic voluntarist view makes it difficult to see why anyone should obey moral requirements understood as the voluntarist understands them. In raising this question (and repeating it again in the following section), my goal is not, I emphasize, to encourage us to respond impiously and dismissively to our infinite and perfectly good Creator. It is, rather, to highlight difficulties internal to voluntarism.

Divine *power* surely wouldn't give anyone good reason to obey contingently created moral requirements. Fear of divine power seems like the wrong *sort* of reason to, for instance, avoid murder. Presuming I'm not a sociopath, it would be odd to say that I decline to murder you just because God can be expected to sanction me if I do so. In any case, if what *made* putative moral requirements binding were sheer, arbitrary divine *power*, then it's not clear why there would be anything unreasonable about ignoring them. It would likely be *prudent* to adhere to them, but there would be no deep objection to ignoring them. It might even seem admirable to oppose one's own will, even if fruitlessly, to naked divine power, since God, on this understanding, wouldn't be good but would be instead something like the supreme exemplar of moral nihilism.

The suggestion that we should adhere to contingently created moral requirements because God is perfectly loving won't do, either. On the comprehensive voluntarist view, talk of divine love is contentless, since whatever God does is loving. So the affirmation of divine love in this case wouldn't give us any particular reason to obey divinely created requirements.

Perhaps, it might be argued, we should adhere to contingently created moral requirements out of gratitude to God for creating, loving, and healing us. But there are several problems with this approach.

For instance, it's not clear how gratitude could ground obedience to *all* of the requirements contingently created by God. One response might be that unqualified gratitude, with a resultant willingness to do whatever God asks us to do, is the only possible response, given our dependence on God for existence itself and for salvation. After all, someone might say, if you saved my temporal, bodily life, I would owe you a great deal, just as I owe my parents a great deal for bringing me into existence.

What we are ordinarily thought to owe those who initiate and save our lives is, ordinarily, to benefit them or, sometimes, to make something valuable of our own lives. But, given that the divinely created requirements that gratitude is supposed to induce us to obey are contingent, not rooted in any independent fact of the matter about what is good for us or others (on the voluntarist view, there is no such fact), we're not benefiting any creature or, therefore, God by adhering to them. And, given that judgments about well-being are arbitrary, as they would be on the comprehensive voluntarist view, they could make it the case that we could benefit others or make something of our lives by doing anything. (If judgments about well-being *aren't* arbitrary, it will make sense for God to intend that we do things only if they *do* involve our making something valuable of our lives, and this will be incompatible with many contingently created requirements.) In addition, a parent or lifesaver who, because of the substantial debt of gratitude we owed her, insisted on choosing how we were to live our lives would ordinarily seem to be controlling and manipulative and so worth resisting.

Gratitude does not, then, I think, provide a satisfactory justification for embracing obedience to a comprehensive set of contingently created requirements. But there are other difficulties with the appeal to gratitude. We might ask, for instance, whether gratitude was a matter of motivation alone, an impulse that might arise in us in response to some perceived good, or whether it was a matter of obligation.

In the former case, there would be nothing objectionable about not feeling gratitude, and, if we felt it, there would be nothing objectionable about not acting on it. Gratitude would be just a particular response, a taste, like an appreciation for vanilla or mint-and-chip ice cream. Its occurrence would just be an interesting natural fact; it wouldn't have any particular normative significance, any claim on our loyalty.

On the other hand, if someone maintains that gratitude *is* an obligation, the obvious question would be what the source of this obligation might be. It couldn't be a contingent divine creation if a putative obligation to follow contingently created moral requirements is what needs to be explained. There might perhaps be only one objective moral requirement: to be grateful. All other requirements might be derivatives of this one insofar as a duty of gratitude meant a duty to follow contingently created moral requirements. (These requirements would be limited insofar as they couldn't obligate anyone to disregard whatever obligations flowed from the duty of gratitude.) But in this case, the duty of gratitude would seem like a *surd*. As soon as we began to articulate *reasons* for this duty, they might well begin to yield more constraints on the content of morality.

Suppose, for instance, that we treated this duty as rooted in some account of well-being. It might seem odd, at minimum, if there were no *other* elements of well-being apart from the element or elements underlying the duty of gratitude. And the more we had to say about other elements of well-being, the harder it would likely be to see gratitude as a freestanding obligation. This would increasingly limit what the contingently created moral requirements we were expected to obey because of gratitude could reasonably involve. In whatever way a duty of gratitude flowed from an understanding of the human good, other obligations might do so as well. And the duty of gratitude would provide no justification for ignoring these or treating them as overridden by contingently created requirements.

A related difficulty is that gratitude *presupposes* that some things are good, are aspects of well-being. It does so because, to be grateful, *I* must take something done by another to be good for me or for some creature or group of creatures with whose well-being I am especially concerned.[9] In addition, the person to

---

9. That someone has done something I *want* is insufficient to show that gratitude is warranted, since what I want might not contribute to my well-being; it might, indeed, be harmful.

whom I am grateful must intend my good in acting in a way that evokes gratitude. And I must take her to have acted in this way.[10]

If my being grateful presupposes the occurrence of something objectively
good, then it does not seem as if a contingently created moral requirement can
(on the gratitude-based view of obligation) lie at the root of valuation. Otherwise, *whatever* God did could occasion gratitude, since God could *decide* that
something was valuable to me. And, in this case—to parallel a point I made
earlier—gratitude would provide no independent basis for obligation (since, on
the envisioned view, God could do anything at all and decide that it merited
gratitude), and we'd be back where we started, with a need to explain obligation
(including the obligation of gratitude).

Hybrid Voluntarism

I've focused here mainly on comprehensive voluntarism, the idea that what
makes any normative claim—any claim about what we have reason to choose,
believe, or feel—*true* is that God has decided that it will be true. The truth
maker for any such claim is, on the comprehensive voluntarist view, a purely
contingent divine creation. This is, I think, the standard variety of voluntarism.
But the many difficulties associated with it might make a hybrid version of voluntarism attractive.

On the sort of version I have in mind, what's good and bad, and so what's
good and bad *for us*, is an objective matter of fact, not a contingent divine creation.[11] However, what counts as right or wrong remains a function of free
divine decision. This approach lacks some of the liabilities associated with treating welfare as arbitrary. However, it's still problematic.

Some of the same puzzles about reasons for accepting contingently created requirements that beset comprehensive voluntarism would apply to hybrid
voluntarism. Certainly divine power and gratitude wouldn't provide decisive
reasons for obeying these requirements.

A further problem arises if the voluntarist thinks, as she might, that all
instances of rightness and wrongness, and not merely *moral* rightness and
wrongness, have been contingently created by God. Suppose, that is, that what's

---

10. If you do something that turns out to benefit me but which you did or which I believe you did
for a quite different reason, my gratitude will ordinarily be muted at best.

11. An excellent statement of such a position is Adams, *Finite and Infinite Goods* 13–128, 231–76.
My goal in this brief discussion is not to engage with the intricacies of Adams's sophisticated and
complex view.

right and wrong in the arena of judgment—of sound practices of gathering information, assessing knowledge, and gauging the relationships among ideas (epistemology and logic)—were divine creations.[12] In this case, adhering to norms of judgment would require some sort of justification just like adhering to moral norms.

However, the practice of justification is just the practice of giving good, ideally decisive, reasons. What would be needed in this case would be, precisely, good reasons for obeying divinely created requirements for sound judgments regarding what we believe and how ideas are related. But assessing something as a good reason and integrating good reasons in a chain of argumentation would be, precisely, instances of adhering to norms of judgment, the activity in need of defense.

A voluntarist account of norms of judgment seems like a nonstarter. But, once reasoning in general is accepted as objective, as inherent in the way things are and not a contingent divine creation, we might wonder why moral rightness and wrongness should be treated as any less capable of independent objectivity than logical or epistemological (or mathematical or aesthetic) rightness and wrongness.[13]

Even if we conclude that we don't have to reject a voluntarist account of rightness and wrongness on the basis of parity among various sorts of norms, it seems as if there are perfectly good reasons to embrace the various specifications of love as directives for wise judgment regarding conduct and character. And these specifications flow from human goods and the human situation, together with basic requirements of reasoning. They don't seem very much like contingently created requirements. Their existence and normative weight can apparently be understood without reference to any special exercise of divine will.

The voluntarist might deny this, claiming that the specifications of love are contingent divine creations. But I think the burden of justification would rest with the voluntarist, given that these ways of loving and their reason-giving force don't appear to be contingent divine creations.

The voluntarist might grant that the specifications of love were independently objective, not products of free divine decisions, while maintaining that there were supplementary moral requirements that were freely created by God.

12. Descartes evidently believed that the truths of mathematics were contingent divine creations.
13. Arguments for parity among various sorts of normative judgments have been offered by, *e.g.*, Nathan Nobis, "Truth in Ethics and Epistemology: A Defense of Normative Realism" (PhD diss., University of Rochester 2004); and Terence Cuneo, *The Normative Web: An Argument for Moral Realism* (New York: Oxford University Press 2007).

They couldn't, presumably, prescribe choices inconsistent with the specifications of love. But the voluntarist might suggest that they established, or could establish, limits on choice more extensive than those derived from the specifications of love.

We might wonder, as we might wonder about the prescriptions embraced by proponents of comprehensive voluntarism, why God would create these supplemental requirements in the first place. After all, they don't flow from the created character of humanness and the dynamics of the human situation: if they did, there would be reason to acknowledge them without God's choosing to make them obligatory. And, again, given their arbitrariness, we might wonder exactly why anyone should adhere to them. In addition, if there *were* decisive reasons for people to adhere to them, creating them would seem problematically restrictive, constraining choice and autonomy unnecessarily and thus, arguably, to this extent, not loving.

We unavoidably risk turning our Creator into a domineering tyrant when we speak of God as "the commanding will."[14] To be sure, divine choice and intention lie behind the contingent structures of reality and so at the root of who and how we are. And since who and how we are determine what it means for us to flourish and since what it means for us to flourish determines what will qualify as consistent or inconsistent with love, as right or wrong, divine choice and intention ground right and wrong.

The moral order—like the mathematical, the logical, the epistemological, the aesthetic—is what it is because of the way things are. God couldn't create a requirement in virtue of which murder was required for the same reason God couldn't make it true that $1 + 1 = 6$. God's creative work lies behind all the moral truths that hold in our world. But it does so precisely in virtue of divine creative activity's role in shaping the existence and character of the way things are.

Vocation

The idea of a vocation is the idea of a task or set of tasks that is distinctively *mine*. It can be understood as offering a very personal directive about the focus of our love.[15] A vocation might be a responsibility to marry someone in particular; to

14. Oliver O'Donovan, *The Ways of Judgment* (Grand Rapids: Eerdmans 2008) 190.
15. See Adams, *Finite and Infinite Goods* 302.

take up a particular kind of work; to study a particular subject; or to move to, return to, or remain in a particular geographic location.

If moral requirements aren't contingent divine creations, if these requirements flow from the nature of created reality, then, if a vocation is understood as a moral requirement, a vocational obligation can't be a contingent divine creation, either. But in this case, there probably aren't vocations as traditionally understood.[16] On an alternative account, vocational obligations are grounded in the unique features of particular situations, but there are problems associated with the view of obligation underlying this sort of account, as I noted in chapter 2. The idea of vocation is appealing. But a creational love ethic can affirm much of what makes the idea of vocation attractive without running into the difficulties associated with that idea.

Why Someone Might Want a Vocation

The notion of vocation is powerful and evocative. Several factors, I think, render this idea especially appealing.[17] Someone who believes that she has a vocation might think some or all of the following thoughts.

(*i*) My vocation offers me a kind of reassurance regarding the distinctive value of my role in history. Even if it's small, even minuscule, it's irreplaceable. I need not fear that I will simply vanish into the immensity of the cosmos. By following my vocation, I'm making a genuine, divinely selected contribution to history.

(*ii*) God has given me the specific vocation I've received not just because I am a moral agent but also because I am *me*. The fact that I have a vocation reassures me that my particular gifts—talents, skills, circumstances, and opportunities alike—matter because they make possible my contribution.

16. See, *e.g.*, Adams 252–317; Ward, *Ethics* 141–54; Keith Ward, *The Christian Idea of God: A Philosophical Foundation for Faith* (Cambridge: Cambridge University Press 2017) 171; Oliver O'Donovan, *Ethics as Theology* 2: *Finding and Seeking* (Grand Rapids: Eerdmans 2014) 222–30; Lawrence A. Blum, *Moral Perception and Particularity* (Cambridge: Cambridge University Press 1994) 104–23, 167–9; Germain Grisez and Russell Shaw, *Personal Vocation: God Calls Everyone by Name* (Huntington, IN: Our Sunday Visitor 2003); and David L. Norton, "Education for Self-Knowledge and Worthy Living," *Ethical Issues in Contemporary Society*, ed. John Howie and George Schedler (Carbondale: Southern Illinois University Press 1995) 155–76.

17. While I don't for a second hold Bob Adams responsible for anything I say about vocation in this book—and while he will find various things with which to disagree—I couldn't have written this section, in particular, without the influence of ch. 7 of his Wilde Lectures, which I reread repeatedly, or of the later, published version (Adams, *Finite and Infinite Goods* 292–317).

(*iii*) Because my vocation is particular to me, I know it fits who I am and will thus be personally fulfilling, even if living it out sometimes proves difficult.

(*iv*) Because I have a vocation, I can escape the *anomie* that seems typical of most lives in our society: my vocation frees me from the agony of choice. General moral principles often leave options on the table. If I had to make major decisions simply in light of those principles, I would need to decide on my own what might work for me. By contrast, when I have a vocation, I don't have to spend time wondering about what to do: at least in general terms, I know where I should go.

(*v*) Because I have a vocation, I can feel secure. If God has assigned a particular task to me, then, when things don't seem to be working out, I can remain confident that they will, believing that God wouldn't have given me a duty that will end in ultimate failure and defeat. And I can also be sure that the *meaning* of my life is ensured because I am following God's directive, whether or not things turn out in just the way I want or expect.

(*vi*) Even if I avoid purposefully injuring any aspect of the well-being of any sentient, I will unavoidably neglect some goods (in my own life or the lives of others) to their detriment while actively seeking to realize or to promote others. Doing so can seem arbitrary, unwarranted. I can worry that I have selected the wrong goods to focus on, the wrong ones to disregard. But the conviction that I have a vocation can help to address this worry. For my vocation is, precisely, a good or set of goods God has entrusted to me, assigning these goods rather than others to me and assigning them to me rather than anyone else. So, when I prefer some goods to others, I'm fulfilling my vocation. I'm *responsible for* my vocation, not for everything in the world.

The notion of vocation is existentially attractive, then. And a Christian understanding of ethics and of our place in the world can and should seek to meet the concerns that lie at the root of this notion. But a creation-based ethic must cast things a bit differently from a voluntarist one.

Vocation and a Creational Love Ethic

If voluntarism were correct, God could simply call you (*vocation* is roughly synonymous with *call*) to occupy a particular place in history—deciding, say, that you should become a plumber or a pastor, an actor or a xylophonist.[18] God

---

18. A vocation need not be occupational. One might have a vocation to be a parent and partner while selecting occupations pragmatically to support this vocation. So the occupational vocations are here purely for exemplary purposes.

might voice a call to you in part by equipping and situating you in such a way that you would drift naturally into the occupation God has chosen for you, or by causing a burning desire to grow in your heart to engage in that occupation, or through a process of guided vocational discernment. However you discerned your vocation, you would act wrongly if you disregarded it. However, if voluntarism is a nonstarter, that's true with respect to individual vocations as much as with respect to general rules.

Alternatively, we might think of a vocation as creationally rooted. A vocation might be a task that is distinctly mine—not because God has created a unique moral requirement in virtue of which I must assume this task but, rather, because the unique features of my situation generate a particular set of requirements applicable only to me. If this account is particularist in nature, every obligation for every person is vocational (though we might want to speak this way only about major life choices) because every person chooses in light of a unique set of conditions from moment to moment, necessarily taking account of a particular configuration of relevant reasons.

We don't need, as I suggested in chapter 2, to embrace particularism. So, as with voluntarism, if particularism isn't a compelling account of requirements in general, it can't provide a suitable grounding for putatively vocational requirements. However, a particularist account of vocation isn't the only possible creational account. For instance, someone might suggest that an account of vocation could be articulated using the resources provided by a creational love ethic: perhaps there's a unique task we could describe as my vocation, a task rendered unique by the specifications of love, which rule out all other tasks.

That's possible in the abstract: the various specifications of love might combine in such a way that just one option with respect to an important aspect of one's life or just one narrow range of options was consistent with love. It's possible, but it doesn't seem likely. For me to have a specific vocation with regard to a given aspect of my life, most options related to that aspect would need to be ruled out. However, when I act in a manner that is consistent with THE GOLDEN RULE, THE PAULINE PRINCIPLE, and the other ways of loving, I'm not doing anything wrong.[19] And, if you think about choosing in accordance with these

---

19. A certain kind of Augustinianism might say that I *am* doing something wrong just because my motives are, ex hypothesi, shot through with original sin. Even if this is the case, it follows not that the content of the requirements isn't exhaustive of my responsibilities but only that I am not fulfilling those requirements in the appropriate spirit.

specifications of love, it seems clear that doing so is often likely to leave multiple options on the table, even as it excludes others.[20] There are many options I can pursue while declining to violate THE PAULINE PRINCIPLE by purposefully or instrumentally injuring any aspects of well-being. Similarly, there are many options I can pursue while declining to violate EFFICIENCY by seeking my various goals at pointless cost. And so forth.

It won't normally make sense to say that pursuing a particular option will yield the "best" results. If I choose in accordance with the specifications of love, I will have limited myself to a set of possible choices which, because they are consistent with these requirements, are better than the alternatives. Nonetheless, there will likely be many of these.

Different choices can realize (or promote, respect, or protect) different authentic goods. So there's no sense to be made of the idea that a particular vocational choice will embody the most good. The various goods that will be realized in and produced by the choices I make, consistent with love, in fulfillment of (say) a particular occupational or marital choice are qualitatively different. There's no general way of comparing various vocational options in light of the goods they will realize or produce.

And that assumes that, at the time I'm choosing, there are right answers to questions about what these goods *will be*. However, to the extent that the occurrence of particular goods depends on the future interactions of a wide variety of free creatures, there won't be such correct answers at the time I'm choosing. From my choice to become a filmmaker or a carpenter, multiple possible goods could flow. The goods that flow from my choice are not brought into being once I've made the relevant choice; they take time to arrive on the scene. The goods, then, are not only qualitatively different so that they can't be objectively ranked or combined; they're also ontically and epistemically indeterminate. A given vocational choice won't *necessarily* realize particular goods (though in a given case, it might be that the realization of particular goods is probable), which means that it can't be compared with alternatives in view of the goods it will necessarily bring into being.

20. Cp. Finnis, *Fundamentals* 92.

A Creational Love Ethic Can Capture (Some of) What Makes the Idea of Vocation Appealing

Despite these difficulties with casting the idea of vocation in creational terms, a creational love ethic can embody a number of the features that make the idea so attractive.

The notion of vocation is appealing because we are situated in particular places in history and society. And a creational love ethic can acknowledge this reality appreciatively. For such an ethic, one aspect of the way in which we are created is our capacity to learn from and respond to other creatures. And this means that we will be shaped (even though not overridingly determined) by our historical circumstances. We will confront opportunities and possibilities and challenges that would be absent elsewhere. Someone who comes of age in Vichy France will need to consider options very different from those that present themselves to someone traveling with her parents to settle in Nebraska in 1880. Circumstantial factors like these unavoidably function as constraints on our choices. A creational love ethic can readily acknowledge the significance of these constraints.

To talk about a vocation is to envision a task or set of tasks that *fits* who a person is. And a creational love ethic can readily acknowledge that not only our opportunities but also our abilities, skills, convictions, and dispositions point us in particular directions. I might potentially be a journalist, a literary critic, a lawyer, or a clinical psychologist. But I can be neither a ballet dancer (lacking as I do both the interests and the capacities required for athletic excellence) nor a Roman senator (because I'm not a Roman aristocrat and because the Roman Senate no longer exists) nor a big game hunter (given my belief that killing sentients for sport is wrong and my lack of various physical skills, as well as my lack of interest in a peripatetic lifestyle). It might make sense for someone to choose the disciplined focus involved in celibate ministry, but my own passion for intimate connection would make that sort of ministry a very poor fit for me and would leave me constantly wrestling with temptation. As I develop, the education I've received, the experiences I've had, and the relationships in which I've participated all narrow my options.

These factors, including interests, abilities, beliefs, circumstances, attitudes, dispositions, and preferences, can be morally significant in various ways. For instance, they can effectively rule out certain options not just in virtue of what I'd prefer but also as a matter of fairness to others. Taking on responsibilities—as a worker, partner, parent, or volunteer—by which I'm not personally engaged can render it persistently attractive for me to shirk or shift these responsibilities. In some cases, doing so may be perfectly consistent with THE GOLDEN RULE. In others, however, it will be profoundly unfair to those I have invited to rely on me. It will often, similarly, clash with love in the form of THE GOLDEN RULE for me to commit to pursuing a certain path if my abilities are such that I will constantly struggle to reach my goals with limited prospects of success. In so doing, I will waste other people's time, invite their reliance without warrant, and avoid doing things I could do well. Lack of interest or ability may also tempt me to engage in behavior inconsistent with love in the form of EFFICIENCY. Thus, even in the absence of a vocation in the narrow sense, acting in accordance with the specifications of love will mean narrowing the choices I consider in light of my abilities and desires.

A creational love ethic can likewise affirm the identity-constitutive character of particular tasks. Even if we *choose* these tasks, even if they are not imposed on us externally, they will characteristically emerge from our identities. Absent a vocation as traditionally understood, a creational love ethic can also acknowledge the link between my identity and my path in life. In addition, undertaking a given path will further constrain the paths along which my identity develops. And my pursuit of a given path may itself come to shape, even to be part of, my identity. Thus, there will increasingly be a fit between what I do and who I am.

A vocation as characteristically understood involves an obligation that is in some sense particular to me. As I have already suggested, a number of moral requirements are generic. They may be generic because (per THE PAULINE PRIN-CIPLE), when some situational features obtain, particular requirements unavoidably arise (*Don't purposefully cause the death of a sentient*, say). They may also be at least *relatively* generic because (per THE GOLDEN RULE) there are ways of being that are predictably consistent or inconsistent with love because of reliably evident dynamics of human social interaction. (It is, for instance, perfectly appropriate not to keep promises on some occasions, so that the obligation to keep promises isn't exceptionless; but failing to keep a promise without a good reason is never justified.) Were there vocations as traditionally conceived, by contrast, they would be much more specific.

A creational love ethic is an ethic of freedom and is thus consistent with the embrace of multiple options. But it also allows one to move beyond the anxiety associated with confronting many possibilities by making promises and commitments and accepting duties in virtue of which the range of one's choices consistent with love is focused.

As I've noted, a creational love ethic can offer focus in part by considering the ways in which circumstances, passions, and skills prove to be relevant in light of the specifications of love. However, in a stable, flourishing society, love will frequently leave many options on the table, while to believe that I have a vocation is to be convinced that a particular task is mine in a way that others are not. A creational love ethic leaves open the possibility that one might have just this sort of relationship to a particular task.

That's because, within the constraints set by the specifications of love, one might reasonably choose to invest oneself in a given task and to sustain and solidify one's self-investment by committing oneself. In this case, one has *assumed* an obligation grounded in COMMITMENT. This specification of love might also have been salient even before one's decision to take on a particular task; it might have functioned *negatively* by ruling out some possibilities in virtue of earlier commitments. In addition, however, it can also serve to narrow the object of one's love (at least in a particular district of activity) with laser-like focus.

Commitment-based focus isn't phenomenologically identical with vocation, for one will always be aware of one's own *choice* as a factor in the establishment of a special obligation. On the other hand, a vocation can come to one as an invitation, not a demand, and accepting an invitation is a *choice*.[21] In addition, the choice to make a commitment will have been constrained and motivated by just the sorts of particular, circumstantial features that someone who supposed there were vocations in the traditional sense might see as grounding or signaling a vocation (or both). And, when the constraints are significant (as when I experience a passion for astronomy entirely unlike my attraction to any other field), the phenomenological gap between chosen commitment and accepted vocation may be quite limited.

Another aspect of vocation as ordinarily understood is its role as a source of personal fulfillment. For a creational love ethic, commitments are intimately connected with fulfillment and can thus help to offer something else of value often sought in connection with a vocation. Choices consistent with a creational love ethic will be fulfilling not only because one can quite reasonably take what one knows about one's gifts, circumstances, and dispositions into account when making them but also because commitments, by ordering one's priorities, help to determine just what will *be* fulfilling. One can achieve fulfillment precisely by embracing with gusto the goods to which one has committed oneself.

Even if not in just the same way as a vocation, the specifications of love can ground particularized responsibilities. They can do so because specific positive responsibilities flow from THE GOLDEN RULE and COMMITMENT. A creational

21. Adams, *Finite and Infinite Goods* 301–4.

love ethic also narrows our responsibilities, avoiding the imposition of crushing universal demands, by embodying a clear distinction between the injuries we intend and those we don't. Not focusing on particular goods may lead to various injuries. But, as long as one doesn't intend those injuries and so disregard THE PAULINE PRINCIPLE and as long as one's neglect is consistent with COMMITMENT and THE GOLDEN RULE, one does not act wrongly in not focusing on them. A creational love ethic can thus explain how one's responsibility can be fitted to one's capacities.

This account of the moral life can acknowledge the reality of the factors that make the traditional idea of vocation attractive while also leaving each moral agent free to choose in a manner consistent with love within a range of options, each with its own unique potential contribution to her own well-being and the flourishing of others. Some agents will choose vocation-like foci, while others will opt for greater flexibility.

A creational love ethic differs from an understanding of moral requirements, whether as general or as specific and vocational, as contingent divine creations—also at the root of some, though not all, talk about vocation—because it involves an importantly different understanding of what such requirements are at a deep level. Such an ethic is also different from a range of other Christian accounts of ethics concerned not so much with the metaphysics of moral requirements but with the *contents* of those requirements, accounts, like the one I offer here, centered on love. In chapter 4, I will bring several such approaches into conversation with the creational love ethic I've been elaborating.

4

Loving Alternatives

A creational love ethic contrasts, sometimes sharply, with a range of other approaches to Christian ethics that also center on love. I examine several of these approaches in this chapter. I hope that doing so will contribute to the clarification and development of the approach to Christian ethics I am exploring here as well as of other strands of Christian moral reflection.

I begin by considering two variants of situation ethics, each explicitly focused on love: an ethic of loving responsiveness to the need of the other in the moment and an avowedly Christian variety of consequentialism. Then, I go on to consider a sample of love-oriented approaches to Christian ethics more inclined to stress continuities in our experience and action and more clearly associated with particular thinkers: the agapisms of Paul Ramsey and Timothy Jackson together with Jack Provonsha's appeal to *agape* as an indirect source of moral norms.[1]

Love as Immediate Response

One way of loving situationally is simply to respond with love to whomever one happens to encounter.[2] Loving might thus in principle mean almost anything:

---

1. The sample is by no means exhaustive, of course, given the attention love received in twentieth-century Christian ethics; for a classic overview, see Outka, *Agape*. I have learned from and interacted with Wolterstorff, *Justice in Love*, at multiple points, but examining Wolterstorff's approach in a focused way in this chapter could certainly have made sense.

2. This sort of position is often associated with the ethical reflections of Leo Tolstoy. For some related but non-Tolstoyan approaches, see, *e.g*, Zygmunt Bauman, *Postmodern Ethics* (Cambridge, MA: Blackwell 1993); and Knud Ejler Løgstrup, *The Ethical Demand* (Notre Dame, IN: University of Notre Dame Press 1997).

comforting a crying child, interposing oneself between an attacker and a victim, buying lunch for a homeless person . . . What matters, on this view, is that we respond to the needs of the particular other we meet in each new moment.

This view doesn't make room for consistent, ongoing engagement in particular projects. Redirecting one's focus to anyone who crosses one's path will be profoundly disruptive to such projects. Each encounter will set one on a course to one's next encounter as one careens through life unable to concentrate on any activity or goal.

Love in the moment is often encouraged as a matter of imitating Jesus, but it is hard to square with the picture of Jesus we actually find in the Gospels, much less with the idea that Jesus worked quietly in the family carpenter shop in Nazareth for decades. It also fails to acknowledge the value of continuity of character and identity, including the value of consistent relationships, projects, and instances of self-investment. It envisions a life whipsawed unpredictably in innumerable directions by successive encounters. From the standpoint of a *creational* love ethic, in particular, it seems oblivious to the reality of the diverse aspects of well-being, which invite participation marked by genuine focus.

It is similarly oblivious to the specifications of love that form part of such an ethic, which permit and can require focus. Certainly, THE GOLDEN RULE doesn't ordinarily call one to swerve hither and yon on an ongoing basis. It will often be consistent with this norm of fairness to maintain stable, reliable patterns of action even when confronted by unexpected circumstances. This won't always be the case: one may be drawn out of one's planned pattern of behavior by an emergency.[3] But choosing fairly doesn't mean changing course constantly; and making promises to or otherwise inviting reliance by others may make it unnecessary or even wrong to disappoint their expectations by swerving. Similarly, COMMITMENT may completely preclude altering course in many cases. And EFFICIENCY might sometimes do so as well when departing from one's plans proves unnecessarily wasteful.

These specifications of love don't interpose some other standard in place of love, preventing one from doing what love actually requires. Instead, they specify what love looks like, set its objects, and determine its methods. Adhering to them will mean loving in a way that is considerably more intensive and reliable than moment-by-moment love. It will often positively preclude the kind of distracted inconstancy that will frequently mark attempts to enact this kind of

---

3. See George, *Defense of Natural Law* 95, 98.

love. But it will not, for this reason, be a deficient kind of love. It will instead reflect the real meaning of love.

Love as Promotion of Good Consequences

Another variant of situation ethics applies the same uniform, very general moral requirement to every situation. On this view, each of us in each moment should, as Joseph Fletcher urges, seek to bring about "the greatest amount of neighbor welfare for the largest number of neighbors possible."[4]

Whatever the abstract appeal of love thus construed, the various basic goods, basic aspects of well-being, involved in all of the states of affairs that might result from any given choice are qualitatively different. That's true of both general categories of welfare (aesthetic experience, friendship, . . .) and individual goods (the experience of viewing *Arrangement in Grey and Black No. 1*, the experience of viewing *Number 3, 1949: Tiger*, . . .). The categories are incommensurable, the individual goods nonfungible. This means that there's no general application of the notion of "the greatest amount of welfare" for any group of people (or other sentients). Welfare isn't a unified quantity that can be maximized. Absent commitments establishing relevant metrics, there simply is no way objectively to aggregate the benefits realized in or produced by a given action in a way that would allow the different options to be ranked.

That doesn't mean that there's no way to choose among options or, indeed, to rank them. We can rank options by sifting them in light of the specifications of love. We can rule out those that don't involve love because they don't involve the attempt to realize or promote actual goods (directly or indirectly) and so violate RECOGNITION. We can rule out the options that involve purposefully or instrumentally injuring some sentient's well-being and so violate THE PAULINE PRINCIPLE. We can rule out the options that involve arbitrary preferences among those affected and so violate THE GOLDEN RULE. We can rule out the options that involve achieving the same results at a greater cost than alternatives and so violate EFFICIENCY. We can rule out those that conflict with our prior resolutions and that would therefore violate COMMITMENT. In addition, earlier resolutions may have established priorities in virtue of which otherwise loving options can be ordered and thus narrow our options further. And, we can recognize the logical

---

4. Joseph Fletcher, *Situation Ethics: The New Morality* (Philadelphia: Westminster 1966) 95.

priority of options which involve just the same goods as others but which also involve additional goods.[5]

Options that are left on the table by these requirements can reasonably be described as "more loving" than the alternatives because they involve loving more wisely than those alternatives, even though there is in general no way of aggregating the good realized in or produced by each alternative. These options are more loving because they are more fully consistent with the specifications of love than the alternatives, not because they produce "more good" understood in quantitative terms.[6]

While THE GOLDEN RULE, for instance, allows for a significant amount of situational flexibility, an ethic of love is not per se a situational ethic. Rejecting the possibility of aggregating goods or ranking aggregates of goods, it resists the consequentialism of Fletcher's version of situation ethics. And it recognizes that various features of our choices can be decisively salient as regards the consistency of those choices with love across a broad range of circumstances and that these features can be specified generically rather than situationally. It thus affirms continuity and focus as key elements of a life of love.

Love as Covenantal Obedience

Paul Ramsey advances a very nuanced and sophisticated understanding of love as the foundation of Christian ethics.[7] He elaborates this account of love impressively, in a broad range of contexts, most notably in connection with the ethics of war and biomedical ethics.[8]

Ramsey's ethic is rooted in what he understands as the command of God to love, with divine love as both an inspiration and a model expressed particularly

---

5. See, e.g., Finnis, *Fundamentals* 90–4.

6. See, e.g., Grisez, *Way of the Lord Jesus* 1: 150–1.

7. Covenant is only one theme in Ramsey's work, but it became increasingly important over time. The title I've selected for this part of chapter 4 is a riff on "Obedient Covenant Love," the title of the chapter concerned with Ramsey in Jeffrey S. Siker, *Scripture and Ethics: Twentieth-Century Portraits* (New York: Oxford University Press 1997).

8. Ramsey's ideas and forms of expression develop over the multiple decades of his writing career. For one window on his intellectual development, see Adam Edward Hollowell, "Revising *Basic Christian Ethics*: Rethinking Paul Ramsey's Early Contributions to Moral Theology," *Studies in Christian Ethics* 23.3 (2010): 267–83. The evidence regarding the ways in which Ramsey could have revised his first book is not sufficient to illuminate all of the shifts in his thought, but it provides interesting insights into multiple aspects of his understanding of Christian ethics.

in the teaching and practice of Jesus.[9] Ramsey draws on love throughout his arguments regarding particular issues. He articulates a consistent ethic of love while emphasizing how love constrains as well as encourages particular choices. For Ramsey, love requires not only that we use force to defend the victims of injustice but also that we refuse to use force deliberately against noncombatants.[10] It limits medical interventions even as it encourages them. Ramsey elaborates the limitations love imposes with an emphasis on covenant faithfulness to particular persons and communities. As his thought develops, he vigorously resists the idea that it is ever acceptable to treat someone as simply a receptacle of well-being to be taken into account in some sort of consequentialist calculation. Love for the neighbor rules out injuring that person as a means to some end: it embodies its own constraints.[11]

Ramsey consistently affirmed a moral asymmetry between self and other at the ground level of ethics that is both unappealing and hard to defend. He qualified the practical implications of this view and advanced a richer understanding of human moral identity, as he began to stress the significance of covenant for moral life, though he didn't emphasize in tandem with his stress on covenant the significance of a substantive understanding of well-being for love. He increasingly moved beyond even a nuanced rule-consequentialism as a depiction of what love requires, and the spirit of his approach, as well as his careful analyses, can continue to inform our thinking about the role of love in Christian ethics.

9. On Ramsey's use of the Bible to ground his moral vision, see Siker, *Scripture and Ethics* 80–97.
10. See, *e.g.*, Paul Ramsey, *War and the Christian Conscience: How Shall Modern War Be Conducted Justly?* (Durham, NC: Duke University Press 1961) 34–59; Paul Ramsey, *The Just War: Force and Political Responsibility* (Lanham, MD: Rowman 2002) 405, 421, 428–9, 449, 502, 509; and Paul Ramsey, *Speak Up for Just War or Pacifism: A Critique of the United Methodist Bishops' Pastoral Letter* In Defence of Creation (Eugene, OR: Wipf 2016) 72, 84, 197.
11. Ramsey's substantial general works in Christian ethics are *Basic Christian Ethics* (New York: Scribner 1950); *Deeds*; and *Nine Modern Moralists* (Englewood Cliffs, NJ: Prentice-Hall 1962). His treatments of war, sex, and biomedical ethics offer additional insights into his developing theoretical stance, as do his various articles, notably Paul Ramsey, "The Case of the Curious Exception," *Norm and Context in Christian Ethics*, ed. Gene H. Outka and Paul Ramsey (New York: Scribner 1968) 67–135. His work is helpfully sampled in *The Essential Paul Ramsey: A Collection*, ed. William Werpehowski and Stephen D. Crocco (New Haven, CT: Yale University Press 1994). I am thankful to the editors not only for the work they've invested in selecting and editing the elements of this collection but also for their introduction, which has both improved my understanding of Ramsey's ideas and pointed me to useful texts.

Love and Asymmetry

A deeply problematic aspect of Ramsey's early work (never, to my knowledge, definitively disavowed, even if later qualified) is his defense of what he labels "a radically unselfish love."[12] His defense of this kind of love is allied with an essentially asymmetric conception of the moral life in which the moral agent's own good merits no ground-level role in her own deliberation. She may care for herself for the benefit of others but not with an eye to her own welfare viewed as independently valuable.

While "self-sacrificial love" is offered as a prophylactic against the effects of instinctive arbitrary self-preference, asymmetry (which need not, for Ramsey, entail self-sacrifice) is not justified primarily in this way.[13] Instead, it appears to be obligatory, for Ramsey, as a matter of imitating divine righteousness and obeying the commands of Jesus.[14] There is also, he thinks, a conceptual point to be emphasized: "The word 'love' is surely [!] not deserving of use for the self's relation to itself; and what makes the term inappropriate for use in this connection is its univocal meaning no matter what adjectives are attached to it; namely, love is a bond of life with life by which one person affirms the being and well-being of another."[15]

Though Ramsey recognizes that involvement in relationships and social institutions complicates the picture considerably, he seems to suppose that Leo Tolstoy is right in urging what I've called love as immediate response in the one-to-one case.[16] That's because, in effect, there is no basis for choosing anything other than the good of the other when there is only a single other to be considered.

He refuses to root "Christian love" in "the infinite, inherent value of human personality" because "such a doctrine would logically lead to subtracting from obligation as much as the just claims of self require."[17] Unsurprisingly, then, he suggests that Henry Sidgwick's utilitarian maxim be recast as "Each man is morally bound to regard the good of any other individual as more than his own."[18]

12. Ramsey, *Basic Christian Ethics* 160.
13. Ramsey 189.
14. See, *e.g.,* Ramsey, *Moralists* 133.
15. Ramsey 135. This semantic appeal seems question-begging, not least because educated speakers of English *do* speak of "self-love" and "loving oneself."
16. Ramsey, *Basic Christian Ethics* 158.
17. Ramsey 94.
18. Ramsey 163. Echoing Sidgwick, Ramsey goes on to note some relevant situational qualifiers.

He maintains that "ethical humanism is grounded on the infinite inherent value of human personality in general" but that his own understanding of Christian love "proceeds on the inherently more Christian principle of infinite preference for the neighbor's welfare."[19] He observes that "ideally a Christian agent gives no express consideration to whether he participates in, or is a mutual recipient of[,] the good he does."[20] And *agape*, he suggests, "has ceased altogether from preferring some people to others for one's own personal welfare."[21] Thus, "everything may now be thrown away in an heroic act of self-sacrifice without a single limiting exception made on account of the remaining legitimacy of self-love or autonomous duties to the self or the inherent claims of 'humanity' wherever it may be found."[22]

The agent may justifiably seek her own good only when doing so promotes, fosters, enables, or constitutes the good of others. So "the ethics of 'enlightened unselfishness' defines duties to the self vocationally in terms of duties to others."[23] Ramsey characterizes "Christian love" as "unclaiming" while acknowledging that out of concern for the other, the loving Christian might "be obliged to fulfill the claims of neighbor by first or at the same time performing certain duties to the self."[24]

Ramsey found increasing opportunity to acknowledge self-affirmation on the part of the moral agent throughout his career, emphasizing the significance of a robust self as a source of care for others and the value *for the unjust person* of a victim's willingness to resist injustice.[25] Recognizing our rootedness in covenants also frees us to perform our tasks and find our identities and purposes within the terms of covenantal responsibility in ways that ensure continuity of character and the capacity of self-investment while freeing us from the demand—at least in important districts of life—to justify particular actions in other-regarding terms. Nonetheless, the presupposed asymmetry remains an element of Ramsey's account of Christian ethics.

19. Ramsey 219.
20. Ramsey 187.
21. Ramsey 165.
22. Ramsey 162.
23. Ramsey 160.
24. Ramsey 158.
25. Paul Ramsey, *Christian Ethics and the Sit-In* (New York: Association Press 1961) 119–22. Thanks to William Werpehowski and Stephen D. Crocco, introduction to *Ramsey* xii, for calling my attention to this stance on Ramsey's part and alerting me to the chapter in which it finds expression.

While this sort of approach might be understood as an explication of some biblical themes, it ignores the fact that THE GOLDEN RULE in its various formulations presupposes and arguably reinforces the moral standing of the self. It also bypasses the broad range of biblical narratives and teachings which presuppose the moral standing of the agent and which neither depict nor encourage self-disregard. It tends to resist the search for a rational ground for ethics and the attempt to achieve consistency in the context of moral judgment. In so doing, it disregards the positive cases that can be made for various forms of THE GOLDEN RULE, forms that assume the equal moral standing of persons and their irreplaceable value. It seeks to ground ethics in contingently created requirements—a doubtful procedure given the liabilities of voluntarism—or on the imitation of divine action depicted in biblical narratives. And it is deeply alienating, requiring the agent to detach herself from her own projects except insofar as they can be justified by appeals to the well-being of others; one's own value, then, is purely instrumental. One is naturally prompted to wonder, *If I am here for the benefit of others, what are the others for?*[26]

Concern for the well-being of particular others is not, as a general matter, served by encouraging them to love others without regard for themselves. In practical terms, their own well-being is likely to be ignored much of the time by others. So if the Christian ethicist seeks to love them in the course of her pastoral or scholarly work or her social interactions, she can foster their well-being effectively precisely by *not* encouraging them to disregard their own flourishing.

There might, indeed, be reason to practice stepping outside ourselves in order to avoid ignoring others—as a kind of ascetic discipline. And, as I will suggest subsequently, the creational specifications of love might well call someone to engage in what could understandably, if finally unhelpfully, be described as self-sacrificial action. But one can recognize both of these truths without the alienating denial of one's own irreplaceable worth and the aptness of concern with one's own projects.

Love in and as Covenant

While, in his earliest work, Ramsey seems to offer a view of love that resembles act-consequentialism, a kind of immediate love, love in the moment, he increasingly recognizes that a love concerned with the well-being of the other must be

---

26. Without focusing particularly on Ramsey, Wolterstorff (*Justice in Love* 94–6) notes a variety of criticisms of this kind of asymmetric view in Christian ethics.

a constant, reliable love. What the other needs in a variety of settings is, precisely, constancy. And that's true whether the other is a partner in marriage or a fellow participant in the life of a political community.[27] Sometimes, a covenant may be consensual and mutual. (In an earlier era, *covenant* and *contract* overlapped substantially in meaning.) In other contexts, perhaps Ramsey has in mind more a structured and persisting relationship, whether consent is involved or not.[28]

For Ramsey, the notion of covenant, with its stability and seriousness, seems to incorporate the idea of a promise but also some of what I'm talking about when referring to commitment. Human covenants are nested within and modeled on God's covenant with humanity.[29] And they provide us with continuity of character and invitations to invest in particular projects. They change our moral situation so that we cannot reasonably ask what love requires in the moment but must rather consider our long-term obligations.[30] And Ramsey deploys the idea of covenant in a way that clearly serves to qualify what will have been for many readers a natural reading of his earlier work, as when he writes this: "When Christ comes he will ask whether there is any faith and love in the earth, not whether there is any practice of 'the principle of benevolence,' i.e. doing good."[31] Covenant provides a way for Ramsey to move closer to what I think of as a creational ethic, as when he objects to Fletcher's "incessant 'doing good'"[32] and emphasizes the importance of acting in various ways for, in effect, the sake of the goods immediately realized rather than in order benevolently to produce some future good.[33] But his position would have been

27. See, *e.g.*, Paul Ramsey, "Elements of a Biblical Political Theory," *Journal of Religion* 29.4 (1949): 258–83; Paul Ramsey, "The Biblical Norm of Righteousness," *Interpretation* 24.4 (Oct. 1970): 419–29; and Ramsey, *Deeds* 35, 137, 142. Siker (*Scripture and Ethics* 85–91) offers a useful overview of Ramsey's treatment of the biblical language of covenant.

28. Thus the claim in Paul Ramsey's *Fabricated Man: The Ethics of Genetic Control* (New Haven, CT: Yale University Press 1970) that we are "created in covenant" (38, 88), which I take to mean "created *already* in covenant." Thanks to Siker (*Scripture and Ethics* 85) for calling this formulation to my attention. The same idea seems to be in play when Ramsey says that "we [were] 'enmeshed' when out of nothing God created his covenant folk" (*Deeds* 163). By contrast, when Ramsey writes that "the biblical covenant view of marriage, which lies behind our marriage law, affirms the will's competence to bind itself from one moment to another throughout all change" (*Man* 45), he seems clearly to treat consent as integral to the idea of covenant, as when he refers to "covenant-consent" (*Deeds* 87; cp. 142).

29. Cp. Ramsey, *Deeds* 46, 127, 163.

30. See, *e.g.*, Ramsey 163, 185.

31. Ramsey 109.

32. Ramsey 187.

33. Ramsey 186–7, 190–2.

strengthened at just this point had he focused on and spelled out a substantive conception of the human good.

The Substance of Well-Being

While he refers to "the welfare of others,"[34] "the welfare of the neighbor,"[35] "the well-being of the other,"[36] and "the well-being of the person,"[37] Ramsey can appear inattentive to what actually constitutes the good for, the welfare or well-being of, human beings.[38] He seems to have been influenced, at least at first, by his teacher H. Richard Niebuhr, who maintained (unhelpfully, as it seems to me) that "Christians must ask not so much 'What is good?' as they should ask 'Whose good??'"[39] He suggests that "Christian ethics differs from utilitarianism in the primacy each assigns and the answers given to the problem *Whose* good? This question utilitarianism answers in fashion derivative from a prior question, *What* is the good? while for Christian ethics there can be no more fundamental question than, *Whose?*"[40]

Perhaps this is not unrelated to Ramsey's resistance in his early work to linking love with creation:

Man's ethical and religious orientation focuses on the Christ, necessarily turning away from the old Law, away also from the sovereign dictates of natural conscience. . . . No looking back in time toward God's activity in creation, no delving deep into rational human nature or the human heart (which in fact he believed inscrutable) fulfills Jeremiah's expectations, but looking toward that person from whom men may learn something they do not already know from capacities within themselves. Whether in the old Law or the new covenant, God manifests his will in something objectively given to which man must conform rather than something conformable

34. Ramsey, *Basic Christian Ethics* 164.
35. Ramsey 44.
36. Ramsey, *Moralists* 134 (cp. 135, 138, 143).
37. Ramsey 210.
38. Wolterstorff (*Justice in Love* 22) observes that this is a feature of the thought of all the twentieth-century figures he regards as agapists.
39. H. Richard Niebuhr, "The Relationship between Theological and Philosophical Ethics" (unpublished lecture), box 35, "Papers, 1935–1943," Paul Ramsey Papers, David M. Rubenstein Rare Book and Manuscript Library, Duke University, 11–2, qtd. and para. D. Stephen Long, *Tragedy, Tradition, Transformism: The Ethics of Paul Ramsey* (Boulder, CO: Westview 1993) 17.
40. Ramsey, *Basic Christian Ethics* 242.

to man. Christian ethics is an ethics of perfection which cuts [!] man to fit the pattern, not the pattern to fit man; how, then, can any part of its fundamental content be drawn from man?[41]

Clearly, the early Ramsey would have been inclined to avoid cashing well-being in creational terms or, if he did understand well-being creationally, to avoid treating well-being thus understood as playing any sort of foundational role in ethics. This seems less likely to be the case, however, for the later Ramsey, who can ask (with a positive answer fairly clearly implied) "whether Christian ethics does not require also an ethics located under the doctrines of creation and man."[42] An openness to a creation-rooted ethic might, indeed, mean an openness to a creation-rooted understanding of well-being,[43] which could then give content and shape to love.[44]

From Holy Consequentialism to Covenant

While he subsequently embraces an understanding of incommensurability in virtue of which the idea of aggregate welfare seems likely to prove indefensible, it is perhaps unsurprising that Ramsey initially seems to reason very much like a consequentialist.[45] Perhaps at first he would have distinguished his view from consequentialism only insofar as the agent's well-being wasn't supposed to figure in her calculations. So, in his earlier work, he could urge the pursuit of "maximum general welfare."[46] Similarly, he could maintain that "the most effective possible means, judicial or military, violent or nonviolent" should be employed to resist injustice "when the needs of more than one neighbor come into view."[47]

41. Ramsey 85.
42. Ramsey, *Deeds* 72.
43. Also potentially standing in the way of Ramsey's reception of a creational ethic is what appears to be his endorsement of voluntarism; see, *e.g.*, Ramsey, *Basic Christian Ethics* 1; and Ramsey, *Deeds* 57, 163.
44. Cp. Finnis's discussion of Kant's lack of a substantive conception of welfare: Finnis, *Fundamentals* 121–4.
45. See Paul Ramsey, "Incommensurability and Indeterminancy in Moral Choice," *Doing Evil to Achieve Good: Moral Choice in Conflict Situations*, ed. Richard A. McCormick and Paul Ramsey (Chicago: Loyola University Press 1978) 69–144.
46. Ramsey, *Basic Christian Ethics* 358. Interestingly, in *Deeds*, he attributes the identification of "maximum welfare" as an appropriate ethical criterion to "a Proponent of 'the New Morality'" with whose views he clearly isn't sympathetic (238).
47. Ramsey, *Basic Christian Ethics* 165.

Given his early penchant for something like consequentialism, Ramsey's initial work was easy to read as pointing in the same direction as Fletcher's. But Ramsey found himself very much at odds with Fletcher and inclined to defend a conception of the moral life as featuring a conception of love as ordered by a range of covenants and by rules that captured generic features of moral experience. Increasingly, he went on to stress the importance of exemplifying divine faithfulness in our interactions with others. If what the neighbor needs—he said, in effect—is continuity, reliability, faithful love, then we cannot truly love the neighbor in the absence of covenant faithfulness. Truly to love is precisely *not* to ask what love demands moment by moment, in act-consequentialist fashion. It is to ask, instead, what *persons*, with extended lives and projects and expectations, truly need.

Ramsey's developing emphasis on covenant substantially enriched his account of the moral life. However, explicit recognition of a full panoply of diverse goods might have made it easier to talk about a range of relationships and would have helped to make his case against consequentialism more decisive.

Residual Consequentialism

While Ramsey increasingly recognizes the independent value of faithfulness and of regard for persons who cannot be treated as means to our ends in spelling out the meaning of love, he is still inclined to view with sympathy what are essentially rule-consequentialist justifications for some exceptionless rules.[48] He seems inclined to argue that it's our cognitive or affective limitations that should often dispose us to follow a given rule even when, absent those limitations, it might sometimes make sense for us to violate it.[49]

In the broadest sense, we can regard at least some of the rules of a legal system or a comparable institution as enjoying a kind of consequentialist justification (as long as we recognize that objective aggregation and maximization are impossible). And it makes sense to say that a legal system's decision makers should treat its rules as exceptionless even if they are ultimately warranted on the basis of their effects. That is not, as I emphasize in chapter 6, a reason for ordinary moral actors always to do so. Unlike a subset of legal rules, the specifications of love aren't justified in consequentialist terms; and the exceptionless

---

48. See, *e.g.*, Ramsey, *Deeds* 5, 133–44. But cp. 131n10 (making clear that there are some acts that are always wrong in virtue of their generic characteristics).
49. See Ramsey, "Case" 109, 112–20.

rules that flow from love are rooted in love in the form of THE PAULINE PRINCIPLE in particular. And this specification of love doesn't provide subsidiary rules with any sort of consequentialist justification, either.

Refining Ramsey's Ethic of Love

Ramsey's stress on continuity and the consistent application of principle in the moral life certainly points toward an understanding of love appropriate for those with created capacities, dispositions, and circumstances like ours. But his work might have benefited from an extended treatment of substantive aspects of human well-being.

Ramsey recognized the reality of diverse and, indeed, incommensurable goods, but these do not occupy central roles in his early theoretical works.[50] He focused on love as care, as benevolence, stressing the importance of some features of personal life accordingly, including the capacity to choose and relationships he understood as covenantal. Benevolence needs content, however. And the varied importance of qualitatively distinct goods, including knowledge, friendship, aesthetic experience, and play (along with the others, like life and practical wisdom, that did claim Ramsey's attention), can provide that content. They can also help to give texture to the various relationships Ramsey sought to comprehend under the umbrella of "covenant."

We should decline to follow Ramsey with respect to the asymmetry of self and other, and we might wish to enhance our understanding of love by giving greater emphasis to substantive aspects of well-being. But we will have good reason to emulate Ramsey in seeing love as central to Christian ethics; in recognizing that love's concrete meaning in particular situations rightly limits global, broadly consequentialist accounts of loving action; and in acknowledging constraints that love itself imposes on the pursuit of valued ends.

---

50. See Ramsey, "Incommensurability." Ramsey acknowledges a plurality of incommensurable basic (e.g., 91) goods (including moral integrity and life), but he does not attempt to elaborate anything like a complete list. He endorses (see 89, 98) the notion that there might be qualitative distinctions among these goods. (Presumably, if the goods are incommensurable, this *means* that they're qualitatively distinct, but perhaps he's emphasizing the nonfungibility of individual instances of a given variety of good.)

Love as Prophetic Generosity

Timothy Jackson has advanced a rich understanding of Christian love.[51] Jackson seems to me to be attempting to discern a particular trajectory, a particular way of loving, that is articulated in various ways in the Bible and the Christian tradition and for which he's happy to use the term *agape*. A creational love ethic can provide rationales different from Jackson's for some but not all of the features of *agape* as Jackson conceives of it. If we reject the sharp dichotomy between the good of the self and the good of the other, we often won't find talk of self-sacrifice clear or helpful; nonetheless, a creational love ethic can affirm and sometimes require potentially costly generosity.

A Distinctive Vision

Jackson advances "no sustained theory of *agape*, judging the subject unconducive to such treatment."[52] But he suggests that *agape* as a norm of relationship with the (creaturely) other embodies three key elements: "(1) unconditional willing of the good for the other, (2) equal regard for the well-being of the other, and (3) *passionate* service open to self-sacrifice for the sake of the other."[53] He is clear that he regards other goods (he instances aesthetic experience and happiness) as worth pursuing.[54] But *agape* should structure our participation and our attempts to foster others' participation in these goods: it is "the 'root of all virtue,' a metavalue."[55] It is thus a vital precondition for multiple kinds of social relations, "prior but not antithetical to contemporary notions of merit, demerit, and contract."[56]

As I understand Jackson, he hopes we will respond to this elaboration of *agape* with a shock of recognition, finding that we resonate with what he has said and realizing that it captures something centrally important about our moral experience and aspirations. He seems to want to view love of the kind

---

51. See Jackson, *Love*; Jackson, *Priority*; and Jackson, *Political* Agape.
52. Jackson, *Priority* 7.
53. Jackson, *Political* Agape 41 (my italics). Cp. Jackson, *Love* 15; and Jackson, *Priority* 10. (In *Love*, these features are described with a focus on "others," while, in his subsequent treatments of *agape*, Jackson slightly alters the phrasing of his descriptions of its elements, rendering all in the singular.)
54. Jackson, *Priority* 10.
55. Jackson 13.
56. Jackson, *Political* Agape ix–x.

with which he is concerned as divinely commanded and as "a participation in the very life of God."[57] He roots "human equality in our sharing the image of God, the need or ability to receive agapic love, rather than in rationality or self-conscious volition."[58] And he clearly thinks it's reasonable to seek the support of the Bible—especially the narratives of God's relationship with Israel and of the public ministry of Jesus[59]—in identifying the features of *agape* he highlights:

> The first feature is suggested by the steadfastness of God's covenant with Israel and the graciousness of God's gift of the Messiah; the second feature reflects the inclusiveness and attentiveness of Jesus's practice of neighbor-love; and the third feature follows, at a respectful distance, the example of Golgotha/Calvary. I want to endorse these features, sometimes in tension, but in a way that avoids the abstraction and oversimplification plaguing standard theoretical accounts.[60]

At the same time, Jackson recognizes the potential limitations of the biblical foundations he has elaborated:

> Scriptural warrants can be adduced for [this kind of agapism,] . . . but in the end many evidences will tend to be autobiographical. The Bible is not self-interpreting, and there are no knock-down arguments (exegetical, empirical, or metaphysical) convincing to all. Strong agapists are those who feel themselves touched by an infinitely loving Presence that allows them to be present to others and themselves. . . . Gratitude for the serendipitous and forgiving love of God, the *ens realissimum*, is where strong *agape* begins rather than where it ends, both existentially and logically. The God who is love simply invites and empowers a response in kind.[61]

Jackson can sometimes sound like the early Ramsey in urging the subordination of the well-being and priorities of the self. "Freedom of conscience, freedom of speech, freedom of assembly, the right to vote, the right to keep and bear arms, and the like are crucial checks on tyranny and the human tendency

57. Jackson, *Priority* 5, 14.
58. Jackson, *Political* Agape x.
59. Jackson, *Love* 1–31; cp. Jackson, *Priority* 8–10.
60. Jackson, *Love* 15.
61. Jackson, *Priority* 14–5.

to abuse power, but a Christian exercises (or declines to exercise) these liberties for the sake of service to God and neighbor."[62] At the same time, as is clear from his general account of *agape*, he rightly emphasizes a basic equality between self and other.

Congruence between a Creational Love Ethic and Jackson's *Agape*

A creational love ethic will be able to acknowledge the value of a number of features of Jackson's conception of *agape* and to exhibit its own capacity to ground them. For this kind of ethic, every person (and, if I'm right, every non-human sentient above a certain threshold) is irreplaceably, nonfungibly valuable in a way that rules out purposeful injury and that entitles each to moral consideration. A creational love ethic thus seems to capture the unconditional character of *agape* Jackson emphasizes: neither actual reciprocity nor the potential to confer a benefit is required for a sentient to count as morally considerable, and behaving badly does not deprive any sentient of moral standing, which is unconditional.

The understanding of THE GOLDEN RULE embraced by a creational love ethic does not involve the kind of equal regard that is affirmed by, say, utilitarianism, in which each moral patient is treated as quantitatively equivalent. However, this kind of ethic definitely incorporates the idea of a basic moral equality with which making arbitrary distinctions among those affected by our actions is inconsistent. And everyone, not only those who reciprocate or otherwise behave well, is entitled to the fair treatment required by THE GOLDEN RULE.

Self-Sacrifice in a Creational Love Ethic

Talk of openness to self-sacrifice, an essential element of Jackson's understanding of *agape*, is *conceptually* in tension with the assumptions embodied in a creational love ethic. For such an ethic understands the opposition of self and other as questionable on a variety of grounds, as I have noted. When I do something that might count under some description not informed by the considerations I have adduced here as self-sacrificial, my action not only fosters another's well-being but also plays a part in my own flourishing. I can act deliberately in a way that *injures* my own well-being, and perhaps in some cases my injuring myself will be intended to benefit another and might even succeed in

---

62. Jackson, *Political* Agape x.

doing so. However, a purposeful attack on my own well-being is never consistent with love any more than an attack on someone else's is: either kind of attack violates THE PAULINE PRINCIPLE. Loving the other in accordance with the various specifications of love is, at the same time, loving the self.

Despite these qualifications, though, living out a creational love ethic can certainly involve making choices that result in significant damage to one or more aspects of one's own well-being, even when doing so at the same time contributes to and affirms one's own well-being. Sometimes, indeed, such choices may be obligatory in light of the understanding of love embodied in this kind of ethic.

(*i*) Someone might be required to act in a way in virtue of which she might undergo death or serious injury (physical or otherwise) because not doing so would violate THE PAULINE PRINCIPLE. So, for instance, I might be able to save my life only by torturing someone. Given that torture clashes with THE PAULINE PRINCIPLE, I would be required to act in a way that might be regarded as self-sacrificial. I might thus be thought to be sacrificing myself out of love for the person I might have been tempted to torture.

(*ii*) Someone might be required to act in a way in virtue of which she might undergo death or serious injury (physical or otherwise) or suffer a serious material loss because failing to do so would violate THE GOLDEN RULE. I might, for instance, take on a role—as, say, the lead clearer of mines on a battlefield—in which it would be unfair of me not to assume a serious risk of death or great injury. I might be perfectly free, per THE GOLDEN RULE, not to agree to accept the relevant role; however, once I've agreed to do so, I'm obligated to place myself in danger. Doing so could be seen as exhibiting self-sacrificial love for those relying on me—comrades and others who might later enter the field.

Similarly, I might (given that the obligation of promises is rooted in THE GOLDEN RULE) make a promise the fulfillment of which could involve profound self-sacrifice—if, say, I promise to care for a spouse who then becomes seriously unwell and requires sustained care. I might in this case be seen as engaging in self-sacrificial love for my spouse. Or I might find that THE GOLDEN RULE required that I disclose information about a certain financial transaction with the predictable result that I suffered a catastrophic financial loss. Doing so might be seen as involving self-sacrificial love for (say) the fellow investors to whom I tell the truth.

(*iii*) I might also act wrongly if I failed to do something potentially very costly in virtue of COMMITMENT. A resolution might obligate me to risk my life for fellow workers on a drilling rig, to give away a great deal of money to support a suddenly insolvent charitable institution, or to care for a vulnerable child. While my resolution wouldn't in such a case obligate me *to* my colleagues, the institution, or the child, it *would* obligate me *with respect to* the colleague, the institution, the child, channeling my love and structuring its expression.

(*iv*) I've focused on cases in which THE PAULINE PRINCIPLE, THE GOLDEN RULE, or COMMITMENT might require me to take on great risks or suffer substantial losses. In addition, a creational love ethic would often permit me to risk or undergo serious losses in cases like the ones I have considered here even when I wasn't obligated to do so.

Passionate Service

A creational love ethic may thus require or welcome the kind of behavior Jackson evidently has in mind when speaking of self-sacrifice, though there is good reason for a proponent of this kind of ethic to resist seeing such behavior as self-sacrificial. Exhibiting potentially costly generosity is, however, distinct from being engaged in "passionate service."

If, per both Saint Paul and the Jesus of the Gospels, THE GOLDEN RULE captures the meaning of, for instance, prohibitions of adultery and theft, it should be clear that *love*, highlighted in one depiction of this way of loving in the Gospels and in both of Saint Paul's explications of it, need not embody or find expression in any discriminable affective state or any kind of positive action.[63] I go through the day not stealing from innumerable people, most of whom I do not know, the existence of most of whom never crosses my mind. Fulfilling the commandment not to steal does not require or depend on a consciously empathetic awareness of any potential victim (though I might well seek to resist the serious temptation to steal by immersing myself in this kind of awareness), much less passion. This commandment is negative: obeying it requires no thought, feeling, or action apart from the choice not to steal. While the commandment is a specification of love, the kind of love ordinarily reflected in obedience to it is passive and unconscious. Love in the relevant sense is not directly related to how one feels.

Whether in a given case a creational love ethic would require "passionate service" will depend on COMMITMENT and THE GOLDEN RULE. Some people will opt for roles to which service in what I take to be Jackson's sense is integral. And, even for those who do not, to avoid engaging in service of one kind or another

---

63. See Matt 22:39; Mark 12:31, 33; Gal 5:14; Rom 13:8–10.

in a given case may be precluded by love in the form of THE GOLDEN RULE. When one does engage in service, welcoming passion will matter both because fulfilling one's responsibilities in many contexts is far easier if one is passionate than if one is grudgingly engaged and because, if one's service involves interpersonal interaction, passion may enable one to be more fully present to particular people one serves.

Jackson's account of *agape* is not identical with the account of love rooted in and responsive to creation I've tried to limn here. However, there are interesting and significant overlaps. The right way to resolve the differences between the two positions aside, it is clear that Jackson has articulated a vision of love that is moving and inspiring and that deserves continuing attention.

Making Space for *Agape*

Jack Provonsha engages in a distinctive appeal to *agape* in ethical decision-making, emphasizing that the prime focus of such decision-making should be securing the *possibility* of *agape*, which he understands as creative love.[64] The capacity to exhibit *agape* thus understood is the primary basis for moral standing, though not being able to exhibit *agape* doesn't automatically exclude one from moral consideration. Creation is the ground of ethics, but just what that means as regards *agape* and the treatment of the nonhuman world requires further exploration. Moral rules matter, on this view, but just to the extent that they foster the free and effective exercise of *agape*. There are difficulties with this position, including its narrow focus on moral judgment and action to the relative exclusion of flourishing, its limited regard for nonhuman sentients, and its potential overvaluation of nonsentient realities. But Provonsha has pointed toward an unexpected way of taking *agape* into account.

64. To the extent that readers are already familiar with Provonsha's work, they are perhaps most likely to be aware of the multiple interventions in bioethics facilitated by the experience as a practicing physician that began before his graduate work in theology and that continued after the completion of his PhD. But, while he certainly found biomedical questions of great interest, Provonsha devoted considerable attention not only to topics in applied ethics but also to ones in normative ethics as well as to ones in theology.

Understanding and Fostering *Agape*

Provonsha roots a love-centered account of Christian ethics in the conviction that "responsible human love . . . , *agape*, is an act of creative freedom."[65] Because "it is spontaneous and underived, [*agape*] cannot be directly the consequence of any so-called ethical action. Only its possibility, that is, the situation for its occurrence, can come directly under human control. This means in practice that the right action, the loving action, will be the one rendering *agape* possible."[66]

He proposes several simple formulations of the ethic he believes can be derived from a recognition of the centrality of *agape*:[67]

[1]　one ought so to act in every case that one's acts may render *agape* a possibility

[2]　so act as to guarantee the highest possible integrity of persons

[3]　so act in any situation that the highest level of "personhood" is produced

He emphasizes the importance of "maximiz[ing] the potential for *agape*," asserting that "the question in any situation will be[,] . . . which act or actions will produce the greatest amount of personhood, defined as creative agency, and thus potentially the greatest realization of *agape*?"[68] He maintains: "The right act will be that act which renders the greatest amount of *agape* possible. The wrong act will be the one that reduces the possibility of *agape*—taking the total situation into account—including the long-range consequences of the act."[69]

---

65. Jack W. Provonsha, *Making the Whole Person Whole: Papers and Presentations on Religion, Ethics, and Medicine*, ed. David R. Larson (Loma Linda, CA: Loma Linda University Center for Christian Bioethics 2018) 69.

66. Jack W. Provonsha, "Christian Ethics in a Situation of Change" (unpublished manuscript 1967) 5–6. This essay is an extract from Jack W. Provonsha, "An Appraisal of Hallucinogenic Drugs from the Standpoint of a Christian Person-Agapic Ethic" (PhD diss., Claremont Graduate School 1967).

67. For all three of these formulations, see Provonsha 58. They are italicized in the original; despite Provonsha's general pattern elsewhere, "*agape*" is italicized here rather than being set contrastively in roman.

68. Provonsha 60, 64.

69. Provonsha 64; cp. Provonsha, *Making* 69, 86.

The Value of Persons

Provonsha suggests that "'persons' . . . are valuable *because* of *agape*."[70] He seems
to have in mind the view that persons are valuable because they can exhibit *agape*,
because they can exercise creative freedom. Given this understanding, he proposes a scale of value, beginning with "fully integrated, rational, free" persons
and proceeding through a range of other kinds of creatures, from "higher level
person" to "low level person—e.g., child" to "more potential person—infant"
to "potential person—embryo, fetus" to "person symbol" (a category which
"may include [nonhuman] animal forms") to "animal" to "plant" to "thing."[71]
He also emphasizes "special social obligations" on the view that they ground
institutions "without which integrated personality (and thus freedom for *agape*)
would be impossible." They include "family," the "immediate social group," the
"state," and "humanity at large."[72] "Conflicts between the individual's social
groups . . . are resolved in terms of the importance of the group to the agapeic
context."[73]

The Value of Rules

On Provonsha's *agape-based* view, rules, including the provisions of the Decalogue, are valid just insofar as they foster or protect the capacity to love.[74] "The
rules can serve *agape* to the extent that they provide the occasion for *agape*. They
do not and can not in any sense take it prisoner!"[75] The same observable behavior can result from routine rule following or creative attention to particulars (and regard for the human capacity for free creativity), with only the latter
qualifying as *agape* in action. Rules can't obviate the importance of attending
to what love involves in particular circumstances; love may therefore require
alteration of or disregard for a rule or practice.

---

70. Provonsha, "Ethics" 57 (I've italicized "because").
71. Provonsha 61. Provonsha capitalizes these phrases in the text and uses the plural form of
"plant."
72. Provonsha 62. Provonsha (63) characterizes "government as the possibility of order and stability" but does not defend this claim.
73. Provonsha 63.
74. See, *e.g*, Provonsha, *Making* 179–84.
75. Provonsha, "Ethics" 55.

The Limits of an Ethic of *Agape* Facilitation

This is a creative and fruitful proposal, and Provonsha explores it sensitively in a variety of contexts, particularly ones related to bioethics. But there are reasons to question its sufficiency.

(*i*) By suggesting that we focus on what sustains or impedes creative love, Provonsha makes something like what I have called *practical wisdom* the master good. Practical wisdom involves choices among goods to be pursued and among means of pursuing them, which is another way of saying that it is concerned with love. Significant as it is, however, treating it as the master good seems problematic. There are multiple goods, and the exercise of practical wisdom ordinarily *depends on* the availability of these goods.

We exercise practical wisdom when we discern the consistency of our goals with love and identify appropriate ways of seeking those goals. However, once discerned, the goals (ultimately, the basic aspects of well-being) and the specifications of love take on independent significance in our deliberations. They are not dependent on practical wisdom; rather, practical wisdom (itself among these goods) discerns them and guides us in selecting among them. Even if we acknowledge the *importance* of creative love, we still need to know what loving involves.

If we take love to be, at minimum, appropriate regard for well-being, then we need a substantive account of well-being to make sense of love. Even if we need to acknowledge the importance of sustaining and protecting creative love, we still need to confront the prior question of what it makes sense for the creatively loving person to do. For such a person cannot simply be concerned with fostering and safeguarding and not impeding creative love, important as these activities might well be; she must also be concerned with actually loving creatively. To do this, she will need an account of what well-being, including appropriate regard for well-being, looks like.

Such an account will push us beyond *agape* facilitation because much of the time what we want is not to exercise or be the object of creative freedom but, rather, something else entirely. Creative freedom can—practical wisdom can—enable us to participate more effectively in various goods. But, when I'm sitting languidly with my partner as the sun comes up, creative freedom isn't the object of any choice I'm making. The same is true if I'm contemplating an architectural marvel. Creative freedom may have contributed to the development of my relationship with my partner (though dumb luck may also have been decisive), and it may have contributed to the construction of the building I'm observing. But just now, as I engage with my partner or reflect on the lineaments of the building, creative freedom isn't an essential aspect of what I'm doing. And the same seems likely to be true as we participate in a variety of goods.

Provonsha enthusiastically affirms the importance of rooting ethics in creation.[76] So it would hardly be inconsistent with the spirit of his proposal to seek to identify a rich account of flourishing as constituted by diverse, qualitatively distinct elements like the one I've sought to defend here. But such an account generates internal constraints on moral choice—certainly those encapsulated in RECOGNITION, THE PAULINE PRINCIPLE, and COMMITMENT. Recognizing what it means to participate in specific goods like friendship and play might add further definition to the moral life. And considerations related to love conceived of as appropriate regard for oneself and others prompt the acceptance of THE GOLDEN RULE and EFFICIENCY. The result is a theory that is unlike Provonsha's in important respects, even while sharing his concern for a creational basis for ethics.

(*ii*) Given that there are other goods worth pursuing, it's not clear why the fact that a given action affects practical wisdom in a particular way should be decisive as regards the moral status of that action. It is not consistent with love to *intend* to attack the exercise of or the capacity to engage in practical wisdom. However, various activities might be largely orthogonal to the exercise of practical wisdom without therefore being inconsistent with love, since they might involve the pursuit of genuine goods. Some actions might unintendedly but foreseeably impede the exercise without thereby proving inconsistent with love.

(*iii*) Even if practical wisdom were the only good, if individual instances of that good were nonfungible, as we might take them to be, it would not be possible to aggregate and therefore to maximize the potential for *agape* in a given situation as Provonsha's view appears to suppose we should.

(*iv*) It is at least open to question whether Provonsha's model can, without a stretch, capture all of the key precepts of common morality, which I presume he genuinely does want to affirm (he's a reformist, not a revolutionary), and provide them with a plausible rationale. Creative love—of others or of oneself—is doubtless relevant to these precepts. But it is not obvious that what's wrong, and especially that what's *centrally* wrong, with, say, ingratitude to parents or

---

76. See, *e.g.*, Provonsha, *Making* 190–1, 300–4; and Jack W. Provonsha, "Creation," *Remnant and Republic: Adventist Themes for Personal and Social Ethics*, ed. Charles W. Teel Jr. (Loma Linda, CA: Loma Linda University Center for Christian Bioethics 1995) 37–50.

disloyalty to a partner is that it lessens someone's capacity for creative freedom or that it embodies insufficient regard for or willingness to exercise one's own creative freedom. Both of these objections may be apposite in particular cases, but practical wisdom, whether or not manifested as creative freedom, doesn't seem central to what's problematic about ingratitude or disloyalty.

Good judgment need not always be creative—habit is just fine much of the time. But creativity can be a welcome expression of excellence in the exercise of practical wisdom. Still, there is good reason not to treat protecting the capacity to display creative freedom as the only or principal or foundational ethical concern: there is good reason to acknowledge and focus on a range of basic goods. Because Provonsha sees a single variable as uniquely significant, his various formulations of what he takes to be the central ethical norm understandably urge maximization of the potential for *agape*, the production of "the greatest amount of personhood." The nominal employment of a single principle operating on a unitary good as the basis of moral judgment helps to explain why Provonsha is inclined to think of moral rules as worth adhering to but as perfectly capable of being transcended in particular situations. If there is a single good, capable of maximization, it might seem foolish to avoid maximizing this good simply in order to follow a rule. (I ignore the obvious point that trying to maximize a good isn't the only way to take it seriously.) By contrast, if there are diverse goods with which love should be concerned and diverse ways in which love's concern with these goods will be manifest, maximizing approaches to moral decision-making will rarely be viable, and some judgments expressible as generic rules ("Don't purposefully kill noncombatants") will truly be unrevisable.

Creation and *Agape*

Provonsha's approach to ethics is explicitly creational. "If God is Creator of 'all that is,'" he observes, "the only facts of existence that do not share in the value that statement suggests are those that distort the Creation."[77] "The Creator of the world affirms the world. . . . God is in favor of the world and its creative institutions."[78] (As the reference to institutions suggests, Provonsha recognizes the social world as part of God's creation with genuine value.[79]) And, more comprehensively, "all valid patterns of moral behavior (ethics) will necessarily

77. Jack W. Provonsha, *God Is with Us* (Washington, DC: Review 1974) 93.
78. Provonsha 94.
79. Provonsha, "Creation" 45, 48.

reflect the divine creation and can be considered descriptions of it (in contrast with being arbitrary or merely prescriptive)."[80] And "to be unethical . . . [is] to oppose, to negate or destroy the creation."[81]

Provonsha's way of putting things sometimes suggests that some sort of voluntarism lies at the root of his creation-focused proposal, as when he emphasizes "the divine will" or "the divine creational intent."[82] However, he seems here to be focused not so much on the will as arbitrarily authoritative as on the will as the source of creation's deep character: his goal is to identify a basis for distinguishing between creation as essentially good and creation as distorted by sin.[83]

In general, we might think of Provonsha's twofold emphasis on creation and *agape* as operating on different levels. Belief that everything that *is* is the creation of a perfectly good God provides decisive evidence of the inherent goodness of finite existence, while an ethic focused on making space for *agape* guides our choices in light of that goodness—a goodness particularly evident in the resemblance of free and creative persons to their Creator. When he maintains that a choice "whose total effect is to diminish the Creation in any significant way is immoral," he may thus be suggesting (we might think, despite the reference to diminution rather than maximization) a more general criterion, one of which the call to maximize the potential for *agape* is perhaps best understood as a key instance.[84]

However, Provonsha's understanding of the ethics of creation can sometimes bring creation and *agape* into potential conflict as sources of moral requirements, as when he rejects what he takes to be overly ambitious biotechnological undertakings by insisting "it is an act of high blasphemy for human creatures to attempt to usurp the role of their Creator."[85] His focus on "unknown and possibly dangerous new life forms" and "some superman of the future" might suggest that his conclusion is a matter of risk mitigation.[86] But the underlying theological rationale seems to concern the *impiety* of ambitious undertakings that might in fact serve to enhance possibilities for the exercise of creative freedom and thus pass muster when gauged by his official moral criteria.

80. Provonsha 45.
81. Provonsha 48.
82. Provonsha 47, 48.
83. Cp. Provonsha, *Making* 190–1.
84. Provonsha 190.
85. Provonsha, "Creation" 39.
86. Provonsha 39.

His criticism also seems problematic insofar as humans are themselves parts of the good creation, and their transformative impact on the world around them displays their created potential. In addition, to describe even quite dramatic transhumanist projects as somehow usurping the role of the Creator seems to misstate the relationship between God and the created world. God is not a competitor with creation, and what creatures can do with their created powers is not and could not be the kind of thing God can do as Creator. In engaging in bold biotechnological ventures, humans are not trying to bring anything into existence out of nothing or otherwise deny their finitude; they are simply seeking to expand human capacities. This doesn't mean that there can't be credible objections to such ventures. But, to be credible, these objections should be framed with reference to love and thus to creaturely well-being rather than to blasphemy.

We might also think of a concern with diminishing creation as at odds with the concern to maximize the potential for *agape* in connection with our behavior in relation to nonsentient things. When Provonsha insists that "it is God's sky; these are God's streams and lakes; it is God's soil" and consequently urges the "respect and nurture" of nonsentient things, he seems to be registering a silent qualification on what he otherwise takes to be the imperative to produce the greatest amount of personhood.[87] One can't *simultaneously* maximize capacities and opportunities for the exercise of creative freedom and nurture nonsentient things for their own sakes or as a matter of piety (doing so for the sake of sentients is perfectly sensible), since the focus on nonsentient things will sometimes limit one's efforts to render the greatest amount of *agape* possible. I'll talk more about Provonsha's treatment of nonsentient things below.

Moral Patients

Provonsha offers an approach to identifying the moral patient that deserves further attention.

For Provonsha, what matters as regards whether an entity counts as a moral patient is primarily whether that entity is capable of *agape*. There are, he emphasizes, reasons to take entities with limited or nonexistent capacities for *agape* into account, but these are, in general, derivative reasons, rooted in regard for those

---

87. Provonsha, *Making* 301. Provonsha's focus here is on "the living environment," but I think sentience is a better criterion of moral considerability than bare life.

capable of *agape*. We might question this way of determining who counts morally because of its implications for nonhuman sentients.

Provonsha suggests that creatures that cannot offer *agape*, that are incapable of creative freedom, might be morally considerable, in effect, because of their resemblance to persons. But his view appears to be that they're not as important as persons so that their well-being can be ignored or attacked more readily than that of persons. If *agape* is conscious, deliberate, rational, reflective, determined, we may reasonably doubt that it is frequently, if ever, exhibited by the nonhuman sentients we regularly encounter on our planet. On the other hand, however, these sentients do seem perfectly capable of beneficence, exhibiting loyalty, friendship, compassion, fairness, and a willingness to engage in risky acts of rescue.[88] They are capable of being our friends and partners in what seem like more than merely analogical senses. Our relationships with them should make clear to us that they are not, as Descartes imagined, mechanical constructs: we can discern their capacities to act and appreciate. As a result, it seems as if they can flourish. And we might think that it was this capacity to flourish in virtue of which they qualified as moral patients, even if their capacities for action did not always amount to full-blown moral agency.[89]

Clearly, many vulnerable humans are limited in what they can give—perhaps more limited in some respects than nonhuman sentients. Still, their capacity to participate in some genuine goods and so to welcome gifts that help them to do so means, we tend to think, that they enjoy moral standing. Were we capable only of the agency of appreciation, of flourishing only because of others' gifts, we would still want to be treated as worthy of moral consideration. So it makes sense for us to treat not only vulnerable humans but also nonhuman sentients as members of the moral community.

Perhaps "the *imago Dei* is minimally a function of the need to receive . . . agapic love."[90] Suppose we can answer "Yes!" to the question, "Is this creature

88. Cp. Stephen R. L. Clark, *The Nature of the Beast: Are Animals Moral?* (Oxford: Clarendon-Oxford University Press 1981).

89. For an extensive, careful, thoughtful analysis of these issues, see Gary E. Varner, *Personhood, Ethics, and Animal Cognition: Situating Animals in Hare's Two Level Utilitarianism* (New York: Oxford University Press 2012) 105–221. As a nonconsequentialist, I am not, of course, inclined to make the kind of distinction between near persons and other sentients Varner finds appealing.

90. Jackson, *Political* Agape 107.

capable of receiving Christlike love?"[91] Why not think of this as all the evidence we need of moral standing?[92]

Moral Standing for Nonsentients?

Provonsha draws the net too tightly, it seems to me, when he suggests that non-human sentients might at best be morally considerable because of their capacity to *symbolize* persons. But he is unnecessarily inclusive, I think, with respect to nonsentient things. He quotes with approval Fletcher's succinct and (as long as nonhuman sentients aren't treated as things) entirely reasonable observation: "Things are to be used; people are to be loved. It is 'immoral' when people are used and things are loved."[93] Then, however, he seems to want to retract the implications of this sensible claim by suggesting that a nonsentient thing is "also of value as the divine creature."[94] He implies that we should respect a nonsentient *for its own sake* because it's part of God's good creation, that it should be treated as presenting moral agents with reasons for action independent of its capacity for welfare and significance for sentients' welfare. Indeed, he argues for a relatively conservative stance with regard to nonsentient realities on the basis of the doctrine of creation: "Humanity's role is that of caretaker, one of maintenance and preservation, and[,] after the Fall, one of restoration, rather than one of modification and innovation."[95]

To treat nonsentient things, objects, as having moral standing might lead us to worry that transforming such objects could be wrong. However, God is surely capable of creating some things in order for them to be used by sentients. The fact of something's having been created isn't sufficient, therefore, to show that it has some kind of moral standing. And we should be skeptical about the notion that we should accord something independent moral standing even if it's not valuable to itself.

91. Jackson, *Priority* 48. To be clear, Jackson himself is doubtful that nonhuman sentients can receive *agape*.

92. Provonsha does, indeed, urge compassion for nonhuman sentients. See, *e.g.*, "Creation" 39. But his focus seems to be primarily on the significance of concern for these creatures for the fate of human persons, and his theoretical approach wouldn't make it difficult to disregard them. Consider his own support for xenotransplantation requiring the death of a simian heart donor; see, *e.g.*, Jack W. Provonsha, "Ethics of Experimental Surgery: The Baby Fae Case—an Interview and Comment," *Pharos* 49.4 (Fall 1986): 23–6 (interview by Jack E. Bynum).

93. Fletcher, *Situation Ethics* 51. Quoting this passage, Provonsha ("Ethics" 59) has "are to be love."

94. Provonsha, "Ethics" 61.

95. Provonsha, "Creation" 39.

While not every object of love can actively return love, an object of love must be able to *value, welcome,* or *appreciate* love at least to some degree—it must be capable of being benefited or injured—if it is to enjoy independent moral standing, if it is to merit care and loyalty. Nonsentient things cannot be injured, and their welfare can't be enhanced. So they don't enjoy independent moral standing.

The frivolous or malicious destruction of a nonsentient object is inconsistent with RECOGNITION because it is not undertaken in pursuit of any genuine good. And such an object, even if incapable of appreciating love, can contribute to, support, and, in some instances, help to constitute the welfare of both human beings and nonhuman sentients, and moral agents should value it for that reason, choosing in relation to it in light of THE GOLDEN RULE and EFFICIENCY. Something may be valuable to me in virtue of COMMITMENT if I've chosen to incorporate it into my identity, but my commitment doesn't give anyone else reason to treat it as being inviolable, protected by THE PAULINE PRINCIPLE, in the way my body is. At best, others have reason to take my concern with it into account as a matter of fairness in accordance with THE GOLDEN RULE. Doing so will leave them free to make trade-offs in light of all of the goods involved in and affected by any decision. That a nonsentient object contributes to the welfare of human and nonhuman sentients doesn't make it valuable *apart* from their welfare.

Love is concerned with the well-being of its object. For an ethic of love, reasons for action are reasons to protect, respect, promote, or realize well-being—certainly the well-being of persons, probably, more broadly, as I've suggested, the well-being of sentients. To treat a given consideration as a potential reason for action when it is not intelligibly related to the well-being of one or more sentients is to opt out of an ethic of love. It is to choose in a manner inconsistent with RECOGNITION. And to treat such a consideration as a *decisive* reason for action, one that trumps countervailing considerations that *are* related to well-being, is to act *against* love and so to contravene THE GOLDEN RULE and perhaps EFFICIENCY and THE PAULINE PRINCIPLE.

To treat things as morally significant when doing so is not a matter of showing appropriate regard for the well-being of created sentients could be justifiable, then, only if doing so involved showing appropriate regard for the *divine* good, as Provonsha suggests. For classical theism, this isn't even possible: God is self-contained and complete in a way such that the divine life could not be affected by anything that happened to a finite thing, sentient or nonsentient. For neo-classical theism, there's a sense in which God is enriched when we are enriched, injured when we are injured, but that is because God's own life incorporates our lives and God identifies with and loves us. A nonsentient thing doesn't have a life to be incorporated into the divine life, a life with which God could in any sense identify. God's own welfare can't be enhanced as the welfare of a nonhuman sentient is advanced because nonsentient things don't *have* welfare.[96]

We should thus assume that an aspect of reality that doesn't have any such thing as its own welfare is of *instrumental* value to sentients and that this is how God—whether understood classically or neoclassically—treats it, so that it forms no part of the divine well-being. It might, to be sure, yield aesthetic experiences for God, but it won't be *needed* to generate these experiences. Any divine aesthetic experience can be had in virtue of the divine nature. There is no strictly aesthetic experience, just as such, that God could have only by contemplating the creation.

Even if all nonsentient things are constituents of the divine good—a notion that makes sense only if we reject classical theism and that doesn't seem especially obvious from the standpoint of neoclassical theism—it's not clear that this would place any limit on our treatment of any genuinely nonsentient object. Transforming such an object need not be thought to injure God.

Understood in neoclassical terms, God is enriched whenever creatures are enriched, so that any choice on the part of creatures that's consistent with love will benefit God, yielding a benefit incommensurable with the benefit resulting from any other choice. If this is the case, then, if whatever we do to a nonsentient thing is consistent with the specifications of love, it will enrich the divine life.

A moral agent might damage a nonsentient object as an expression of hostility to God, purposefully injuring harmony or friendship with God and so violating THE PAULINE PRINCIPLE. However, the transformation of such a thing needn't be undertaken for this reason. If the object isn't transformed out of hostility to God and if it's transformed in a manner that is otherwise consistent with the specifications of love, transforming it will enrich the divine life. There is no basis on which we could imagine that the enrichment of the divine life resulting from whatever we do to a nonsentient object in a manner consistent with the specifications of love will somehow *outweigh* whatever loss might be associated with our treatment of the object. The goods involved are qualitatively different and so incommensurable. But that means outweighing isn't even possible, which means, in turn, that it can't be and therefore isn't necessary.

96. It may have multiple insides, if some version of panpsychism turns out to be correct, as I suspect it might. But it won't have a single, unified, developed center of conscious experience and action.

Because God's relationship with creation is noncompetitive so that God's own good is not even potentially at odds with that of any creature, we need say no more than that: transforming a nonsentient object need not *attack* the divine good and can, if it enriches a sentient creature's life, contribute to the divine good. It won't be the case that creatures could or should ever think of their own welfare as something to be disregarded in favor of benefiting God. On a noncompetitive account of God's relationship with creatures, transforming a nonsentient object in a way that benefits creatures can never be counter to the divine good (presuming it doesn't injure and benefit creatures at the same time). And perhaps that's as much as we can say or need to say.

Provonsha's emphasis on the protection of *agape* as creative freedom rightly calls our attention to the importance of careful regard for people's autonomy and their exercise of practical wisdom. And Provonsha rightly stresses the goodness of creation as the basis of ethics. We might wonder about the merits of his advocacy of independent moral weight for nonsentient things. We might also wonder about integrating his broader concern for creation with his emphasis on maximizing the potential for *agape* as the focus of human morality. And we might suspect that exceptionless moral rules were more valuable than he seems to suppose. It would be possible to retain his appealing foci on love and creation while avoiding some of the difficulties his position confronts by embracing an account of love as focused on the well-being of sentients, a richer conception of well-being, and, as a result, a differentiated understanding of the character of enacted love.

A creational love ethic can incorporate a variety of the appealing features of alternative accounts of the moral life centered on love. To clarify the character and dynamics of this kind of ethic, I attempt in chapter 5 to explain what it looks like when used to address issues related to the use of force and to interpersonal eros.

5

Enacting Love

A creational love ethic can offer insight into a range of issues. In this chapter, I want to look at two clusters of issues in relation to love. I will begin by considering issues related to violence and war. Then, I will go on to reflect on eros—on erotic interactions and relationships. I will not be developing or articulating new bases for judgment; rather, I'll be showing what eros and war look like from a love-centered perspective. I hope that putting a creational love ethic to work will clarify the meaning of this kind of ethic while also helping provide some background for my subsequent examination of the Ten Commandments, New Testament injunctions from the Gospels and the Epistles, and the seven Christian virtues and the seven deadly sins.

Loving Forcefully

To accept a creational understanding of love is to embrace serious limitations on the use of force under any circumstances. Because of the terrible destructiveness of war, the deployment of force in war should be subjected to even more austere limits.[1]

Limiting Force

We ordinarily regard forcible interference with people's justly acquired possessions as unwarranted. But I want to put the issue of using force to interfere with possessions (some of what I say about the Eighth Commandment in chapter 6

---

1. What I say throughout this section reflects what I've learned from Finnis, Boyle, and Grisez, *Nuclear Deterrence*. See also Augustine Regan, *Thou Shalt Not Kill* (Butler, WI: Clergy 1979).

will be relevant here) to one side here and focus specifically on actual or threatened forcible harms to people's bodies.

Such harms target the good of life and bodily well-being and so contravene THE PAULINE PRINCIPLE. To love is to act with suitable regard for flourishing. And, since the good of life and bodily well-being is an aspect of flourishing, to seek to injure this good is to choose against flourishing and so essentially incompatible with loving those the actor attempts to harm.

At the same time, love for ourselves and our neighbors sometimes means opposing the unjust use of force. We can love our neighbors both when we oppose the unjust use of force against them and when we oppose their unjust use of force against others.

We may sometimes oppose the unjust (actual or threatened) use of force by attempts at persuasion, sometimes by simple avoidance or flight, and sometimes by interposing barriers between potential victims and aggressors. On occasion, these barriers may be our own bodies. Regarding these kinds of opposition to aggression as instances of love seems straightforward enough. We may also sometimes oppose the unjust use of force by using force. This, too, can be consistent with love.

Using force can be consistent with love provided, first of all, that our goal in the kind of case I'm envisioning is to protect those who are being subjected to the unjust use of force or threatened with this kind of force. Using force would not be consistent with love if the *purpose* of using force were to injure or kill the aggressor. But forcible resistance need not involve this purpose.

Consider a simple illustration of the kind of distinction I have in mind: a dentist drills into my tooth to treat a cavity and in which doing so causes pain. The pain, we may assume, is neither intentional nor brought about as a means to the dentist's goal (assuming the dentist isn't *Marathon Man*'s Christian Szell). Rather, it is a predictable but unintended outcome of the act of drilling.[2] Similarly, someone might use what proves to be and might be expected to be lethal force to defend herself or someone else against a violent assailant. The purpose of doing so need not be to kill or maim; the agent might simply intend to stop the assailant's violent action. At the same time, she might be aware that death or serious injury was a likely or even a virtually certain result of her defensive action. The assailant might in fact die, but death needn't be the defender's goal, which would be achieved as long as the attack ended even if it turned out that

---

2. The example is Grisez's; see, *e.g*, Germain Grisez, "Toward a Consistent Natural-Law Ethics of Killing," *American Journal of Jurisprudence* 15.1 (1970): 77.

the assailant had survived. Because the agent does not in any way intend injury to the attacker, the attacker's death is an unintended, even if anticipated, side effect of her use of force to stop the attack.

An act that involves injury to the aggressor can, as I have suggested, have the aggressor's own well-being in view insofar as one seeks to prevent the aggressor from injuring oneself or someone else. Unintentionally injuring the aggressor while preventing this injury is an act of love. It seeks to stop the aggressor's serious wrongdoing but does so because it is intended to keep the aggressor from engaging in forcible wrongdoing she would ultimately have good cause to regret. And people benefit when they are compelled by appropriate resistance to understand the wrongness of their treatment of others.

An act that, while causing injury, doesn't involve *purposefully* causing injury is consistent with THE PAULINE PRINCIPLE. But this requirement is not the only specification of love. Whether it is consistent with love to act in a way that will or might result in a given *unintended* injury is a function of the other specifications of love. Is one's action undertaken in direct or indirect pursuit of a genuine aspect of well-being (RECOGNITION)? Is it wasteful, involving pointless loss to one or more goods (EFFICIENCY)? Is it inconsistent with any serious plan one has made (COMMITMENT)? And—often most importantly—is it fair (THE GOLDEN RULE)? Would one be willing to accept a standard that allowed the unintentional infliction of injury in relevantly similar circumstances on oneself or one's loved ones?

Where the defensive use of force, in particular, is concerned, one might realize that, say, one would be using force to stop an injury *but* that one need not use probably lethal force to do so. It might be clear that a nonlethal action one could take without subjecting oneself to a risk of serious injury would suffice to stop the aggressor. Action likely to prove lethal would *also* stop the aggressor, but it wouldn't be necessary to do so, and one would hardly be willing to accept the use of lethal violence against one's child, say, under comparable conditions. As a result, to love in accordance with THE GOLDEN RULE is to avoid the use of lethal force in this case. Or consider a different set of circumstances in which one has made a commitment to avoid using lethal force (perhaps because of a particular relationship with the attacker or a general intent to model nonviolence). In this case, using lethal force would be ruled out by COMMITMENT.

Force in War

Participants in war are moral agents. The fact that their actions take place in the context of large-scale violence means that the facts they need to take into account when making moral judgments will be different from those of someone confronted by a lone attacker. However, love matters for their choices regarding the use of force just as it does for the choices of people in otherwise peaceful situations. And the fact that political authorities have encouraged or even commanded them to go to war doesn't absolve them of responsibility for making good choices. Rather, participants in war, like all other moral agents, must love in a way shaped by THE PAULINE PRINCIPLE. That means that they may not injure others as a way of achieving some goal. Instead, and for the same reasons that limit the choices of people not participating in war, their purpose in using force must be to *stop* the unjust use of force by others, not to kill or maim them.

Accepting that constraint is perfectly compatible with using force to stop combatants who are not currently deploying or bearing arms. Such combatants can be committed to effective participation in ongoing programs of unjust violence even though they are not currently engaged in violent acts. Among these combatants are not only frontline warriors who happen to be off duty but also people who are providing strategic and tactical direction to immediately violent actors.

However, while warriors may sometimes fairly use force to stop any actual combatant, they must always adhere to THE GOLDEN RULE's demand that we love others as ourselves, that we love fairly. Here as elsewhere, then, they must ensure that, even when they choose to use force without intending death or injury, their choices are consistent with standards they would be willing to see applied not only to their adversaries but also to themselves and their loved ones.

This means, in particular, refusing to engage in the purposeful injury of noncombatants,[3] including

accountants, actors, marketers, graphic designers, advertising account executives, clerical workers, architects, artists, authors, bakers, bankers, barbers, bookkeepers, brokers, canners, cashiers, cleaners and dyers, cobblers, salespeople, sex workers, cooks, decorators, delivery workers, dentists, personal assistants, editors, farmers, food processors, foresters, fruit and vegetable canners, furniture makers, mechanics, home

---

3. For classic treatments of particularly brutal violations of this constraint on the use of force, see G. E. M. Anscombe, "Mr. Truman's Degree," *Ethics, Religion, and Politics*, Collected Philosophical Papers of G. E. M. Anscombe 3 (Oxford: Blackwell 1981) 62–71 <https://www.law.upenn.edu/live/files/3032-anscombe-mr-trumans-degreepdf>; and John C. Ford, "The Morality of Obliteration Bombing," *Theological Studies* 5.3 (1944): 261–309 <http://theahi.org/wp-content/uploads/2013/10/Ford-Morality-of-Obliteration-Bombing.pdf>.

repair and maintenance workers, hat makers, members of hotel staffs, housekeepers, institutional inmates, insurance agents, janitors, judges, laboratory assistants, lawyers, librarians, lumberjacks, stay-at-home parents, musicians, nuns, nurses, retirees, painters, paper hangers, hospital patients, photographers, physicians and surgeons, piano tuners, plasterers, plumbers, priests, printers, prison inmates, professors, disaster relief workers, reporters, teachers, sculptors, social workers, statisticians, stenographers, sugar refiners, tailors, teamsters, computer programmers and other IT professionals, theatre owners and staff people, undertakers, wholesale dealers, upholsterers, and window washers.[4]

Using force against noncombatants can't be a way of stopping them from engaging in violence, since they're not doing so in the first place. The same is true of adversaries who have laid down their arms and surrendered. So the use of force against noncombatants and those who have surrendered must be purposeful. Because it is purposeful, it cannot be consistent with THE PAULINE PRINCIPLE.

It *could* be consistent with love to injure or kill noncombatants *unintentionally* in the course of stopping combatants from engaging in unjust violence. But it is not sufficient to announce piously that the noncombatants have not been *targeted*. There will be no justification for injuring them if adversarial combatants can be stopped from engaging in unjust violence without injuring noncombatants. And, even if they cannot be, causing injuries to noncombatants who are not purposefully harmed will be an apt way of loving only when injuring them is consistent with THE GOLDEN RULE. Stopping combatants is not an infinitely valuable goal that trumps all other considerations; love will sometimes require inaction.

A Bright-Line Limit on States' Decisions to Use Force

I have so far focused on constraints that are directly relevant to the choices of particular warriors. The crucial limit on their use of force is the same as the crucial limit on anyone's: it must be designed to stop others' unjust use of force rather than to cause death or serious injury, and it must involve no more harm than necessary, as gauged by THE GOLDEN RULE, to adversarial combatants and to noncombatants. But *war* is, as I've noted, especially destructive because it involves large-scale, coordinated violence. The additional risks posed

4. I draw most of these from Ford, "Morality" 283–4.

by war justify embracing constraints on the *large-scale* use of force that are more demanding than those applicable to all instances of the use of force.

The most straightforward and substantial limitation is that the overall project embodied in a given state's participation in a war should be designed to *stop the unjust use of force*. It should not be intended to acquire territory, punish evil, or preempt imagined bad behavior. Undertaking war with any of these purposes in view would mean asking warriors to use force unjustly. For them to use force justly, they would need to be doing so in order to stop others' unjust uses of force (presuming they understood and shared the decision makers' purposes). But those others *wouldn't* be acting unjustly if they sought to prevent or end territorial acquisition, self-righteous punishment, or premature preemption.[5] An attack for any of these purposes would likely be inconsistent with THE GOLDEN RULE; injuring people to punish them or facilitate stealing from them would be inconsistent with THE PAULINE PRINCIPLE. A state engaging in military action for any of these reasons, then, would be asking its warriors to engage in wrongdoing by using force against others not acting unjustly and would thus not be entitled to its warriors cooperation.

The inherently defensive character of individual acts involving the just use of force sets substantial limits on the kind of state military action that might count as just. But there are good reasons to limit state-made war even more than this. Consider a range of relevant considerations that count against the use of force by a state outside the context of defending its people and their land and other goods.

Appeals to humanitarian goals for warfare are often used to cover strategic mischief making. Blowback can be expected to result from foreign wars. Invaded societies are frequently economically vulnerable. Invading them is likely to make things worse both politically and economically by destroying institutions and infrastructure and upsetting stable political alliances. It is profoundly difficult to predict, and therefore to plan, where war is concerned. War making often involves the injustice of conscription. Because a state-made war will be tax funded and quite possibly fought by conscripts, the scale of any such war can be enormous and its destructiveness correspondingly great. The desire to promote a war can lead politicians to engage in manipulative propagandizing—inherently harmful to the people targeted and likely to lead

---

5. That is to say, preemption undertaken before there has been a clear commitment to and initiation of the behavior to be stopped (as, for instance, the Cold War notion that the Western powers should attack the USSR to keep it from attacking them).

to ill-informed and thus probably unwise decisions to begin or continue wars. The victor in a war, including a putatively humanitarian one, characteristically ends up with more wealth and power, no doubt not coincidentally, at the expense of the loser; support for war can thus contribute to the growth of empire. Unjust violence frequently accompanies war—affecting both combatants and noncombatants. When a state undertakes a war, some of its own people will be killed and maimed, and resources will be directed from projects its people prefer to the war making favored by politicians. Wars funnel resources to military contractors, who can use these resources in part to encourage further conflicts and further contracts. We can expect bad behavior from state decision makers who don't bear the costs of their own war making and who can shift those costs to others. When a country goes to war, paranoia, intergroup hostility, and domestic repression may result within the country, with vulnerable and marginal groups especially likely to be disadvantaged as a result.[6]

Love gives us good reason to want to minimize the occurrence of war and thus to favor a general policy that makes it likely that any state adopting it will avoid going to war. The policy should be clear and simple: states shouldn't send military personnel to engage in violent acts outside their own borders, and they should use military technology outside those borders only to repel immediate attacks. This policy would be easy to understand and defend in general terms. And it would be easy to apply in specific cases. Embracing it would thus make resisting the destructiveness of war easier than obvious alternatives. Protestors and political opponents of war could point easily to a generally accepted simple rule limiting state military action. And the consistent acceptance of this rule would mean that the resources and personnel needed to conduct aggressive, imperial wars would not be available in the first place. The state would be expected to limit itself to planning and budgeting for the defense of its territory. As a result, movements preparing for other kinds of war, including the acquisition of personnel and equipment, would be readily detectible; preparation couldn't be masked behind other kinds of activities with defensive objectives. Movement toward war could thus be opposed well in advance and so more likely stopped.

Using force in a way that involves only the unintentional infliction of injury to stop unjust violence can be consistent with love in the form of THE PAULINE

---

6. Versions of this cumulative case argument have appeared elsewhere in my work, including Chartier, *Flourishing Lives* 226–9.

PRINCIPLE. Using force in a way that involves only the fair infliction of un-intended, even if anticipated, injury on combatants and noncombatants can be consistent with love in the form of THE GOLDEN RULE. Provided COMMITMENT and the other ways of loving don't rule out using force in a given case, forcibly defensive action can thus express love. However, given the dangers associated with using force, state actors, NGOs, and others should accept a robust standard precluding the nondefensive use of force by states.

Loving Erotically

You turned here first, didn't you?

We're generally fascinated by erotic interactions. They captivate us because of their complexity and drama, because of their connections with a multiplicity of human goods. I seek here to explore the things that make eros worth-while, to consider its empirical concomitants, and to think about what we might say regarding the ethics of erotic relationships generally given its features and consequences. I go on to attempt to develop a satisfactory general understanding of marriage in particular in light of its significance for human goods and to consider when divorce might be consistent with love. Finally, I explain why I believe criticisms of LGBTQ+ relationships as inherently objectionable fall entirely flat.[7]

The Dynamics of Eros

Erotic activities offer us intense sensory pleasure. That's a real good. But it's hardly the only good associated with eros. Interpersonal erotic interactions provide opportunities for people to become acquainted, attached, and, in some cases, deeply bonded—opportunities for friendship. They can also lead to procreation and thus to occasions for another sort of friendship, friendship between children and parents. Such interactions can render people vulnerable and thoroughly open to one another—fostering knowledge. Erotic interactions are very much instances of play, not to mention occasions for aesthetic

---

7. For a more extended treatment of these issues, see Chartier, *Public Practice, Private Law* 101–26. Though that discussion is rather more leisurely than the one here, I think I've clarified the issues in this chapter somewhat for myself as well as readers.

experiences.[8] Freed from the constraints that often obtain in the course of other kinds of activities, people interacting erotically can put often hidden aspects of themselves on display and link them with others in a welcome exercise in self-integration. Learning to discover someone else erotically and to offer that person exquisite pleasure in and through an erotic interaction involves the development and display of one kind of skillful performance. And eros can be a way in which vulnerabilities are exposed and confronted and psychic wounds healed—and thus a way of fostering the psychic well-being that is a crucial aspect of the basic good of life.

Not all of these goods are realized in every erotic encounter, even when unqualifiedly well-intentioned and consensual. Sometimes, indeed, none is. But there are, at minimum, very few varieties of human activity in which so many different aspects of well-being are at least potentially implicated.

There is no set of moral requirements uniquely specific to eros. We don't need to appeal to unique standards to sort out the moral questions that arise in the context of erotic activities. We simply need (*i*) to recognize the multiple goods in which people can participate erotically, realizing these goods in their own lives and offering them to their partners. (Some, like play, will often be constitutively shared.) We need (*ii*) to be aware of the accompanying features of real-world erotic interactions. And we need (*iii*) to think about what it would mean to realize and promote the aspects of well-being involved in erotic interactions in light of the empirical characteristics and consequences of these interactions and the specifications of love.

Predictable Empirical Features of Eros

To think about eros helpfully is to take its empirical features seriously. The intensity of the sensory pleasure promised, and not infrequently delivered, by erotic activities is perhaps the most obvious of these features. This intensity is important on its own. But it's also important because of its potential to make such activities sufficiently appealing to many people so that they may not always think carefully about the consequences of their actions in the moment. The other goods involved can be expected to render a possible erotic encounter even more alluring and to increase the likelihood that people will be captivated by desire.

8. Finnis, *Law* 86.

That fact is worth taking into account because erotic activities have consequences. Among other things, they have the potential to connect people with one another, sometimes quite powerfully.

(*i*) Erotic interactions tend to generate and sustain romantic feelings. Romantic connection is not *dependent on* or *constituted by* these feelings, but they can prompt and support it, and people often find it easier to maintain intimate and delight-filled connections when they experience these feelings.

(*ii*) As a result, erotic interactions can lead to erotic love, either generating it directly or providing the occasion for it. Erotic love as I understand it is an orientation of the self that involves the reconception of one's identity so that the other (or one's relationship with the other) comes to play a constitutive role in that identity.[9] This kind of love, love as identity, whether or not reflected in or reinforced by intense romantic delight and desire, can occur without much, if any, intense physical contact. But erotic interactions certainly have the potential to help bring this kind of love about.

(*iii*) Even when they don't lead—initially or ever—to erotic love as I've characterized it, erotic interactions can result in neurochemical events (say, the release of oxytocin and phenylethylamine) in virtue of which people can come to be attached to one another, experiencing the instinctive desire to be near to and open with one another.[10] People can become attached over conversation or in the course of shared experience. But attachment can emerge very rapidly from eros in particular.

(*iv*) Because *eros* is very pleasurable, one person can come to associate another with intense pleasure and thus, viewing that person as a source of pleasure, seek repeated erotic encounters with that person. This may not include any intent to seek a more comprehensive relationship, but, even if it does lead to such a relationship, it can still involve bonding that, even if narrowly focused, may nonetheless prove quite intense.

(*v*) Even when erotic encounters don't render people immersed in erotic love, yearningly attached, or pleasure bonded, simple shared appreciation for eros can lead *indirectly* to powerful bonds. By prompting people to keep interacting, eros provides opportunities for mutual knowledge, vulnerability, and affection to develop because of persistent familiarity and conversational interaction.

---

9. See Robert Nozick, "Love's Bond," *The Examined Life* (New York: Simon 1989) 69–86.
10. See Helen Fisher, *Why We Love: The Nature and Chemistry of Romantic Love* (New York: Holt 2004) 77–98.

Familiarity and conversation can lead, in turn, to the development of stronger and more intense ties.

Eros and the Challenges of Bonding

Intense pleasure is ordinarily expected and experienced as a feature of eros. However, people may or may not anticipate a connection of any of the kinds I've mentioned. After all, none of these kinds of connection is anything like a *necessary* characteristic of erotic encounters. When a connection of one of these kinds does occur, it may occur for only one participant. And it may not occur at all, even when the experience is unequivocally positive: people may participate thoroughly in multiple goods in the course of a given erotic encounter without bonding. But the occurrence of potentially powerful attachment as an often unbidden aspect of erotic engagement is a persistent enough empirical feature to play a role in any thoughtful person's moral deliberation about eros.

That's not because bonding is undesirable. Quite the opposite. It can help people overcome insecurities and move toward greater intimacy. It can solidify a relationship and help the participants resist external pressures. It can lead to promises and commitments sustaining lifelong fidelity. However, it can also yield genuine challenges. Awareness of the possibility of these challenges might prompt someone to avoid an erotic interaction.

(*i*) Someone might opt against an erotic interaction aware that bonding might lead her or him to move toward a serious romantic relationship when she or he doesn't really want to do so. Someone contemplating an erotic encounter can realize that, because of the encounter, she or he will strongly desire a serious romantic relationship *but* that there is good reason not to want the relationship or that the person with whom she or he will want it won't reciprocate or both. In order to avoid this strong desire, someone might well opt not to participate in a given erotic interaction.

(*ii*) It is a truism that people's erotic interactions may end. A set of erotic interactions might end never having led to a romantic relationship. Or such a relationship might result only to break up. In either of these cases, someone who becomes attached to a partner in virtue of erotic interaction will be vulnerable to potentially debilitating distress. Recognizing that erotic interaction might lead to a connection of one kind or another and that rich connection might be a precursor to distress in the absence of greater security than a contemplated erotic interaction offers, someone might well choose not to engage in the interaction, whatever its potential appeal on other grounds.

Thinking about Conception

Another empirical feature of many erotic encounters is their potential to result in conception. There are, obviously, many sorts of encounters that do not have this feature. It will often, though not always, be possible for participants to assess the potential for conception readily and, where this potential exists, to take steps realistically likely to preclude it. But the possibility of conception can't simply be ignored.

Conception can lead to a range of consequences for parents and, if they arrive, children. And these consequences need to be recognized when there's a realistic chance of pregnancy. They include not only the social, relational, vocational, financial, and other complexities that accompany the birth and development of any child but also the particular capacities of potential parents to shoulder responsibilities for children and for each other, particularly if shared parenthood prompts them to form a more serious relationship than they had otherwise intended. And additional challenges are associated with procreation by people who share large numbers of genes or who belong to populations in which particular genetic disorders are likely to be passed on to children.

Love's Specifications and the Moral Limits on Eros

The potential contributions of erotic interactions to interpersonal bonding and the capacity of such interactions to lead to pregnancy don't determine just what people contemplating an erotic encounter should do. But the potential consequences of real-world erotic interactions matter for people's erotic choices.

Eros involves multiple goods, so RECOGNITION won't typically limit erotic choices, which can be made in view of one, some, or all of those goods. While EFFICIENCY might have some limited significance in a particular case, it is unlikely to play a meaningful role in most erotic contexts (unless it is incorporated in a certain sort of play). And an erotic interaction won't typically involve any purposeful attack on any good,[11] so THE PAULINE PRINCIPLE won't ordinarily be

---

11. The new classical natural law theorists will maintain that some varieties of contraception do, indeed, represent attacks on bodily integrity. Because many instances of nonprocreative *eros* don't involve contraception at all and because those that do need not involve the kind of contraception these natural law theorists regard as injuring bodily integrity, I won't address this set of complex concerns here. I will also bracket their other objections to nonprocreative *eros*, though my identification of sensory pleasure as a basic good responds implicitly to what I think is the most serious one.

germane.[12] Limits on erotic choices will ordinarily flow from love in the forms of COMMITMENT and THE GOLDEN RULE.

Both of these specifications of love are especially relevant in the context of eros to the management of risk.[13] We cannot predict the future with any certainty, and it's very clear that things might turn out in multiple ways. In an erotic context, we need to consider multiple possibilities: a participant might become deeply attached, for instance, or become pregnant. We need to recognize that we may have good reason to pursue an erotic interaction because intense pleasure may be a feature of the interaction, because we place a high priority on such pleasure, and because we look forward eagerly to the other goods. At the same time, we may also need to recognize that the prospect of participating in the various goods involved might make it easy to ignore the relevant risks.

We can't realistically determine just what might be the likelihood that any potential outcome will occur (and some outcomes may be quite unlikely), though we can make suitable assessments. In addition, even if we knew for certain what the likelihood might be, that would not determine how we should proceed. We need to *choose* priorities, which we may solidify in virtue of COMMITMENT.

Some people will be risk tolerant in virtue of their commitments (and priorities may play much the same role in the absence of settled commitments), while others will be risk averse. Some will give priority to realizing one or more of the goods made available in an erotic interaction, while others will give priority to avoiding the potential negative outcomes. While some people may lack clear commitments or priorities with respect to risk, their preferences may nonetheless dispose them to welcome or resist risk in the context of a given erotic interaction. And people's preferences may shift as an interaction continues, as resistance is replaced by desire or openness is transformed into firm refusal.

Whatever one's own priorities, which may be expressed in or constrained by commitments, THE GOLDEN RULE will be of particular relevance as regards the priorities and vulnerabilities of someone with whom one is or might be

12. Because of the intense feelings erotic encounters can bring to the surface, *eros* can serve as a way of expressing hostility. And when this is a matter not of exploration and resolution in the context of play but, instead, of attempted or actual injury, it will be precluded by THE PAULINE PRINCIPLE.

13. One kind of risk posed by erotic interactions may be the risk of disrupting preexisting relationships in which one or both of the participants are involved. For simplicity's sake, I assume the absence of relationships with others here. But I discuss some of the issues raised by this kind of risk in connection with the Seventh Commandment in chapter 6.

interacting erotically. It will be important to be alert to these priorities and vulnerabilities and, if context and standard behavioral expectations leave relevant features of the situation sufficiently unclear, to offer and request appropriate clarity.

It will also be important to recognize the degree to which someone is en route to making a decision she or he will clearly have good reason to regret and to resist the temptation to move forward when this is the case. Spontaneity is part of the charm of eros. And background conditions, immediate circumstances, and nonverbal behaviors may obviate discussion in many cases. But, in whatever way relevant information is conveyed, communication effected, and understanding fostered, it's important to proceed only when one's acceptance of the relevant level of preparatory engagement as well as of the risk inherent in the interaction itself is consistent with THE GOLDEN RULE.

It will be crucial to avoid telling lies (here THE PAULINE PRINCIPLE will be relevant, paired with THE GOLDEN RULE). (This is a minimum expectation of decent social interaction in any ordinary case, but it is especially important given the significance of trust not only for an individual erotic interaction but especially if there's the possibility that something more serious might develop.) Relatedly, it will be important (per THE GOLDEN RULE), even when not lying, to avoid recklessly fostering misunderstanding and to volunteer information when it's reasonably expected that one will do so even if one hasn't been asked and hasn't antecedently offered or when one would expect it to be volunteered were roles reversed.

Engaging in an erotic interaction in a given way will be consistent with love just in case one would be willing to accept a standard permitting someone else to interact erotically with one—or with someone one loves—in a relevantly similar way, under comparable circumstances.

Marriage

If an erotic interaction or a series of such interactions turns into something more serious, or if erotic love develops without such interactions, THE GOLDEN RULE and COMMITMENT become relevant in new ways. Here, concerns with vulnerability arise not just because of the potential for attachment to emerge from eros but also because shared experience and intimate exchange can create what will often be quite reasonable expectations. Intending to solidify a relationship—both because one values it and because one wants to offer greater security to another—one may seek formally to establish a relationship with mutual promises. And one may seek further to solidify it by making commitments. The terms of these promises and commitments will depend on the developing nature of the relationship.

Promises and commitments can ground intimate partnerships of many different sorts, with diverse expectations and requirements. These may be short term and open ended, with many explicit or implicit grounds for unilateral termination. They may, by contrast, be intended to be lifelong and comprehensive, with few mutually accepted justifications for unilateral termination—or perhaps none at all. I will refer to a partnership intended to be lifelong and comprehensive (making no assumptions about institutional recognition) as a *marriage*.

We initially desire people (and I think this applies to friends as well as to lovers) on the basis of particular characteristics; but, over time, our ties to them become detached from these characteristics and become focused on those we love *as such*. The histories we share with them are occasions for our becoming attached to, perhaps in a sense imprinted on, those we love.[14] Our lives are woven together, and our identities, then, are as well. Over time, one becomes bonded not with an array of qualities but, rather, with the person whose qualities they are.

A marriage need not be a physically erotic relationship. A decades-long celibate marriage that genuinely flourishes seems perfectly conceivable.[15] So too is a marriage in which the partners are erotically active but not with each other. Both can involve deep, comprehensive love. But a marriage as I conceive of it is erotic, whatever the partners' physical interactions, because it embodies the erotic nisus toward connection more richly and deeply than any other kind of relationship.

We can draw conclusions about the appropriate shape of marriage from the specifications of love together with an understanding of the factors that constitute and contribute to our flourishing. That account can readily be spelled out in relation to different varieties of commitments and promises.[16] But I am convinced that love is most powerful, most liberating and empowering, when it involves the simple declaration "I will never leave you."[17] My attitudes, my

---

14. See Nozick, "Love's Bond" 75–6.
15. See, *e.g.*, Charlotte Robinson, "Author and Gay Icon Gore Vidal Dies," *Outtake*, Aug. 1, 2012 <https://blog.outtakeonline.com/2012/08/author-gay-icon-gore-vidal-dies.html>.
16. As I have emphasized throughout, I take the two to be different.
17. See Hugh Prather and Gayle Prather, *I Will Never Leave You: How Couples Can Achieve the Power of Lasting Love* (New York: Bantam 1995).

circumstances, my instincts may all fluctuate. I may find it terrifyingly attractive to flee from you in panic or out of a desire for someone else. But I will never leave you. You can count on me.

Emotions fluctuate in a range of ways. They are frequently not under our control.[18] Because they fluctuate, it makes no sense to promise just as such that one will experience particular emotions. And, similarly, there is no reason to treat their occurrence or nonoccurrence as rightly warranting the end of a romantic relationship. Love as identity need not involve particular emotional responses; and there is good reason to treat marital love, in particular, as independent of such responses. Erotic love may and surely often does involve particular feelings, but those are not *essential* to it. And we should want a *kind* of erotic love that is best understood as ideally supported and signaled by feelings but not as essentially incorporating them. We should want to do so precisely so that, in virtue of the commitments and promises we make, we can, indeed, offer each other the confidence that we will never leave.

Cultural Particularity

It's almost certainly a mistake to assume that there's a single model of marriage that's equally conducive to flourishing in widely varying historical epochs and cultural environments. Love as identity constitutes a powerful and evocative alternative to understandings of such love as constituted by feeling or by the disposition to give rise to feeling, understandings that are, I think, difficult to square both with love's own internal dynamics and with the ethical features we have increasingly interwoven with erotic love.

A number of social circumstances make this kind of love possible. They include increasing appreciation for social equality without respect to sex or gender; legal safeguards for women's autonomy; the greater sense of the distinctiveness of the particular person, with a rich inner life and a range of identify-conferring characteristics that might not be widely shared; the ready availability of contraception; economic patterns and institutions in virtue of which women and men are both, in large numbers, independently employed outside their family homes; reliable ways of identifying children's parents; the availability of education without respect to sex or gender; and the influence of

---

18. This may or may not be true if emotions "can be *defined* in terms of . . . evaluative recognitions alone." Martha C. Nussbaum, *Upheavals of Thought: The Intelligence of Emotions* (Cambridge: Cambridge University Press 2001) 64 (my italics).

traditional Christian teaching regarding the indissolubility of valid sacramental marriage.[19] Given these historical contingencies, the effective prerequisites for the emergence of a particularly rich and powerful variety of marital love are in place. I have no illusions that everyone must embrace the particular relational package on which I'm focusing here. But I think it's possible to acknowledge the undoubted reality of historical and cultural specificity while recognizing that relational variety as well worth pursuing because of the intimacy, security, connectedness, and opportunities for growth it offers.

Staying Focused

The simple promise expressed in the declaration "I will never leave you" can be a tremendous source of security. It can offer people the space they need in order to be vulnerable, to grow, to thrive, to flourish. And people can support their promises with commitments to give their partners unqualified loyalty, commitments that may become especially relevant when partners don't keep their promises or when they become too incapacitated for consistent mutual engagement.[20] We want to know that we can count on love even when we are maimed, when our bodies change, when our interests shift. And, yes, we want to know that we can count on love when we act very foolishly or very wrongly. To love someone when she or he fails or disappoints profoundly is to exhibit the kind of care for a precious other that is, ultimately, what each of us needs. So each of us has reason to choose to offer this kind of love to a partner.

Marital promises and commitments don't obligate one to have, and don't presuppose that one will have, particular feelings or dispositions to feel. Rather, they obligate one to welcome and accept the other as sharing a *we*. Because erotic love is an orientation of the self that can be chosen, one *can* both promise to maintain it and commit to persisting in it. By making promises and commitments, we establish priorities in virtue of which we can evaluate our circumstances. We would be

19. For somewhat different perspectives on the relevant history, see Steven Horwitz, *Hayek's Modern Family* (New York: Palgrave 2015); and Ferdinand Mount, *The Subversive Family* (New York: Free 1992).

20. See Murphy, *Natural Law* 268n21: "I am, of course, not claiming that to be adequately cognizant of the other goods that one is forgoing in forming . . . [a commitment] need involve enumerating all such goods, or anything of the kind. I take it that one could reasonably form a commitment 'come what may.' One understanding of . . . marriage would involve just such a commitment; it would be made reasonable in part by the sort of goods that are available only through such a thoroughgoing commitment."

undermining our own flourishing by disregarding those priorities and the promises and commitments that underlie them. We can evaluate changes in circumstances and fluctuations in feeling in light of those already determined priorities.

We can and should respond to serious bad behavior, in particular, by offering forgiveness. Forgiveness is the renunciation of retribution or retaliation, of barriers to connection reflective of the sense that the other deserves to be *punished* or of the sheer desire to hurt the other. (More about this in chapter 7.) Forgiveness is healing to the forgiver and the forgiven alike. But it's quite compatible with maintaining distance because the other is in one way or another *dangerous*. What we ought to say about dangerous people is probably quite situation-specific; but I want it to be very clear that I do not suppose for a moment that there is any general, ordinary obligation to put oneself in harm's way. Forgiveness doesn't require giving opportunities to inflict injury to a lover who is potentially dangerous. While it can open the way to reconnection, forgiveness as such in no way entails exposure to the risk of physical harm. (It can make sense to reflect on situational particularities in light of THE GOLDEN RULE.)

The Possibility of Divorce

The promise "I will never leave you" doesn't rule out a genuinely mutual parting of the ways, but it does preclude unilateral abandonment. By contrast, many relationships are structured by quite different promises and commitments, ones that implicitly or explicitly render those relationships dissoluble.

A relationship is not somehow indissoluble because the participants label it "a marriage." After all, people may call their relationship a marriage while explicitly building grounds for divorce into the promises with which they create it. They may leave things wide open, promising to stay together only "as long as we both shall love" (while understanding love as a matter of feeling) or "till choice do us part." They may assume that adultery justifies divorce without saying so to each other privately or in the course of making marital promises, or they may, indeed, announce this quite explicitly. And they may use the language of a traditional wedding ceremony while understanding such language as evocative but nonbinding, as leaving them free to end their relationship unilaterally for what they regard as serious reasons. A great deal depends on context and mutually embraced background assumptions.

> When it is intended by the parties that . . . [a] promise shall afford a
> virtually indefeasible exclusionary reason, the promise will have to be

expressed with solemnity and precision as being one that binds them "for better for worse, for richer for poorer, in sickness and in health . . . till death . . ." (and even such a form of words may be given a reduced obligation-creating significance by the practice in which it is rooted).[21]

A relationship might evolve in such a way that, while begun with the expectation of easy divorce, it's ultimately regarded by the partners as permanent come what may. And THE GOLDEN RULE may preclude divorce not because of promises but, rather, because of the way mutual intimacy and reliance have developed. But, absent circumstances that render the partners' explicit promises less relevant than later developments, those promises as understood by the partners should be treated as decisive.

What matters, finally, for someone contemplating unilateral divorce is THE GOLDEN RULE; it will be reasonable for me to break up in a given case if doing so is consistent with a standard I would be willing to see applied to others' actions affecting me and my loved ones. It's important, however, not to apply one's analysis narrowly to one's immediate circumstances. Initial promises, which may set robust limits on divorce, matter a lot, and they should be taken at face value absent evidence to the contrary. Expectations and vulnerabilities that develop over time may play significant roles in determining what's consistent with love as well. And commitments may also be relevant. A commitment I've made doesn't establish a claim on the part of my partner, but it may nonetheless obligate me to avoid leaving at all or to do so under quite limited circumstances.

Jesus and Divorce

Christians have rightly stressed the importance of security in intimate relationships. Their stances have often been rooted in Jesus's undoubted proscription of divorce.[22]

Jesus seems clearly to have welcomed women into his circle and to have treated them with a level of respect surprising for the first century. His rejection of divorce may have reflected the awareness that women, already subordinated in his culture, were rendered especially vulnerable, both economically and socially, when divorced. Divorce could render a woman both socially outcast and destitute. In particular, a woman who had interacted erotically with one

21. Finnis, *Law* 308–9.
22. See Meier, *Marginal Jew* 4: 74–181.

man would have been, for that reason, viewed as undesirable by many other men. Under these circumstances, it would be thoroughly irresponsible for a man not to marry and to remain married to a woman with whom he had been erotically active.

We can see Jesus as overturning traditional assumptions about male power and equalizing the status of women and men in marriage by precluding divorce.[23] And his description of a husband's divorcing his wife as an act of "adultery" treats divorcing a wife in this way as an affront to her honor in the same way in which a wife's adultery could violate her husband's honor. The honor of wives and the honor of husbands, Jesus is saying, deserve equal regard.[24] As a result, his declaration "makes marriage a more equal institution in its first-century context." In "its own social context what was most radical about the teaching on divorce was the equal treatment of women and men."[25]

Perhaps, then, in the form that most likely goes back to Jesus himself (Luke's, which makes no reference to adultery as warranting divorce or to the divorcing of husbands by wives), the teachings on divorce recorded in the Gospels are intended to increase the status and protect the economic and social position of women.[26] We can see Jesus as offering "a prophetic utterance" condemning irresponsible male behavior in a patriarchal society, an utterance responsive to an immediate circumstantial problem that doesn't address the topic of divorce in a very different cultural environment.[27]

While there will have been exceptions, marriage in first-century Palestine will have served first and foremost as the enlargement of an extended family, with the formation of associated alliances, the development of a social unit more capable of household management than its individual members, and a means of propagating a family line. For wealthier families, it will have served to expand access to wealth. There will likely have been some genuinely intimate, loving marriages. But this will not have been part of many ordinary people's expectations of marriage. So the bar for the adequate contribution of a

23. See Richard A. Horsley, *Jesus and the Spiral of Violence: Popular Jewish Resistance in Roman Palestine* (San Francisco: Harper 1987) 235–6.

24. John S. Kloppenborg, "Alms, Debt and Divorce: Jesus' Ethics in Their Mediterranean Context," *Toronto Journal of Theology* 6.2 (1990): 195.

25. Joanna Dewey, "The Gospel of Mark," *Searching the Scriptures* 2: *A Feminist Commentary*, ed. Elisabeth Schüssler Fiorenza (New York: Crossroad 1994) 591.

26. Luke 16:18.

27. See Raymond F. Collins, *Divorce in the New Testament* (Collegeville, MN: Glazier-Liturgical 1992) 222, the source of the quote. I leave open the question of whether Collins would endorse this response to the text.

marriage to people's flourishing and their expectations will have been relatively low, something that will have rendered divorce harder to justify than it might be in a different cultural environment. Indeed, once we move from a high level of generality, the institution of marriage and the practice of divorce in our culture are in significant part simply not the same institution and practice as those with which most first-century inhabitants of Palestine were concerned. Drawing conclusions about contemporary marriage and divorce from norms in first-century Palestine may thus be inappropriate.

It might also be reasonable to read Jesus's remarks hyperbolically, or as articulating a general standard to be elaborated on and applied in different ways in particular cases by his followers. Just, on this view, as one should not literally pluck out one's eye if it offends, so one should not regard Jesus's intent as being truly to identify divorce with adultery or unequivocally to prohibit all divorce.[28]

Marriages Made in Heaven?

Some Christians have opposed divorce on the basis that each marriage has been brought into being by God. But God cannot be thought to be responsible for the occurrence of each individual marriage. That's because of the mediated and constrained character of particular divine action in the world. God's intentions are frequently not realized in the world, and it would be curious indeed if, despite the general impediments to the realization of God's will, it turned out that each marriage happened to reflect God's efficacious intentions. In addition, there are many choices of marriage partners consistent with love; there would be no reason for God to prefer or demand or impose one over another. (Divine providence would presumably seek to influence us away from choices that *wouldn't* be consistent with love.) And, given the untenability of voluntarism as an account of obligation, divine joining of individuals would not itself create any obligation on the part of those joined.

If we assume that God has the power to determine the joining together of two people in marriage and exercises this power, then it is presumably impossible or highly unlikely that their *divorce* would be against the divine intention. After all, as soon as we grant God the capacity to determine creaturely behavior

28. Cp. Robert Guelich, *The Sermon on the Mount: A Foundation for Understanding* (Waco, TX: Word 1982) 211; Craig S. Keener, *And Marries Another: Divorce and Remarriage in the Teaching of the New Testament* (Peabody, MA: Hendrickson 1991) 20; and A. E. Harvey, *Promise or Pretence? A Christian's Guide to Sexual Morals* (London: SCM 1994) 21–5.

in such a way that our choosing in marriage is also God's choosing, then the same must be true for our choosing in divorce as well (as in every other setting). One might suppose that God only acted to effect marriages but otherwise left people alone. However, this seems oddly ad hoc. The idea that God brings marriages about fits better with an understanding of divine providence as meticulous, and meticulous providence will be as responsible for divorce as for marriage.

We do not and cannot share the "first-century belief that God unites males and females before they are born."[29] But we can agree that God *has* joined people together in marriage in another way. God's activity lies behind human biology and the dynamics of human cultures and societies. This does not mean that these aspects of humanness perfectly embody God's intentions even at the macro level. But they do provide the background in virtue of which many people value—and have good reason to value—permanent, comprehensive connection with one another. People make multiple kinds of choices against this background, and it's their choices that determine the terms of their own particular relationships.

Sex, Gender, and Eros

The morality of an erotic interaction is not a function of the sexes or genders of the participants. This conclusion flows from two considerations: (*i*) The availability of the various goods potentially on offer in and through erotic acts does not depend on the sexes or genders of those participating in these acts. Participants in an erotic interaction will ordinarily be seeking to promote or realize one or more of these goods and so to be choosing in a manner consistent with RECOGNITION. (*ii*) The crucial window on the moral appropriateness of erotic acts is THE GOLDEN RULE. It is, at minimum, difficult to see how this specification of love could rule out a consensual erotic act because of the sexes or genders of the participants.[30]

One argument that a morally appropriate erotic act must be between two persons, a woman and a man, trades on the fact that only this kind of act is even potentially procreative. Because (on this view) only procreative erotic acts

29. Phillip Sigal, *The Halakah of Jesus of Nazareth according to the Gospel of Matthew* (Lanham, MD: University Press of America 1986) 91.

30. I'm bracketing COMMITMENT because it's very situation-specific and grounds no general requirement regarding the sexes or genders of the partners, and EFFICIENCY and THE PAULINE PRINCIPLE because I think, for reasons I noted earlier, that they're unlikely to be salient in most cases.

are justifiable, any act that doesn't involve (only) a woman and a man is always morally objectionable.

One can't take this kind of approach while embracing a creational love ethic. For such an ethic, love is about appropriate regard for well-being. Multiple varieties of well-being can be realized and fostered in and through eros; it is the specifications of love that identify morally appropriate ways of realizing and fostering these varieties of flourishing. Once one has determined that a given choice involves the (direct or indirect) effort to promote, protect, respect, or realize a genuine good in a manner consistent with the specifications of love, one can see that the choice qualifies as aptly loving. One can choose to pursue genuine goods by engaging in a given erotic interaction whether or not procreation is a live possibility.

The Good of Pleasure

Most people don't really believe that erotic acts need to be procreative in order to be morally appropriate. They typically recognize on a day-to-day basis that, for instance, experiencing sensory pleasure is itself a perfectly good reason to engage in erotic activity—except when criticizing the erotic behavior of others. The same people who might, for instance, assail a lesbian couple's erotic relationship as immoral will often be quite comfortable with an erotic relationship between the members of an infertile different-sex couple, nonprocreative erotic contact between the members of a fertile heterosexual couple, and adolescent masturbation.

Some Christian thinkers have maintained that nonprocreative eros is inherently alienating because it involves treating the body as a source of experiences for the conscious self, and this, they have suggested, involves dualistically separating the body and the conscious self.[31] But this doesn't seem like a plausible analysis. Bracket eros for the moment. Think about scratching one's back, chewing a stick of gum to enjoy the flavor, taking a painkiller, or contemplating a painting en route to an aesthetic experience.[32] All of these activities seem designed simply to alter the contents of consciousness. Seeking sensory pleasure

---

31. See, *e.g.*, Robert P. George and Gerard V. Bradley, "Marriage and the Liberal Imagination," George, *Defense of Natural Law* 150–1.

32. Thanks to the late Gareth Moore for the back-scratching and gum-chewing examples and for other helpful comments and suggestions related to my treatment of this issue, offered in connection with my first attempt to address this topic in print.

in and through eros is no more alienating than these activities, about which people normally have no moral qualms.

People don't ordinarily experience any of these activities as alienating, and they don't experience seeking or finding sensory pleasure in and through eros to be alienating, either. The notion that they *are*, nonetheless, alienated, divided, when they seek or find pleasure in this way seems intended as an objective claim cut off from experience. But it also, therefore, seems uninformative: in effect, seeking a subjective experience, or at least *this* subjective experience, is being *defined* as alienating.

It's not clear that seeking sensory pleasure for its own sake is very closely related to any sort of dualism. One could perfectly well embrace a fully materialist view of persons while understanding one part of the body as behaving in a way that led to an outcome for another part of the body—in this case, sensory pleasure. My point is not that materialism is correct; I think it encounters serious difficulties, especially from the standpoint of orthodox Christianity. I refer to it simply to suggest that one could seek to bring about particular conscious experiences while embracing a thoroughly reductive and, in this way, unified understanding of the self, an understanding in no way disrupted by attempts to bring about these experiences.

There would be something alienating about seeking pleasure for its own sake if pleasure could only be experienced rightly as a concomitant of participation in some underlying good. And this is surely right as regards emotional satisfaction: emotions *signal* value and meaning; they highlight the fact that things are going well or poorly. It would at least ordinarily be an exercise in confusion deliberately to seek a given sort of emotional satisfaction apart from circumstances that *warrant* that sort of emotional satisfaction; it would be, in effect, an attempt to deceive oneself. But sensory pleasure, as opposed to emotional satisfaction, *does* seem worth pursuing on its own. It need not be taken to be a signal of or pointer to anything else, though it may also be just that in some cases. To say that seeking it for its own sake is alienating because one has disconnected it from its role in signaling the value or meaning of some good or goods would make sense only if that role were its only possible or likely one. If, however, it is itself a basic good as well as a signal of value, then there's no reason to regard pursuing it in accordance with the specifications of love as alienating or unwise.

Complementarity?

Another kind of Christian defense of the view that only the members of different-sex couples may engage in eros, marriage, or both focuses on complementarity. Based, often, on its proponents' interpretations of Genesis 1, this defense insists that each of us is deficient without a complementary partner. God has, on this view, made women with certain personality characteristics and men with different personality characteristics. These characteristics match, fit, or counterbalance one another in such a way that a different-sex couple purportedly embodies a kind of complete humanness that would not be possible for any other kind of couple. The members of a same-sex couple, on this view, reinforce each other's existing ways of being and prompt each to curve inward, while the members of a different-sex couple give each other the gift of otherness and help each other open out toward the world.

This view is interestingly reminiscent of the notion, voiced by Aristophanes in Plato's *Symposium*, that we all—at least act, think, and feel as if we—are looking for specific life partners from whom we were previously separated by Zeus at a time when each now-distinct pair formed a single physical being (thus the notion of a partner as one's "other half").[33] That view captures something important about the sense of incompleteness we find it easy to feel and which a partner can help to assuage. The realities the Aristophanic picture is designed to capture don't have much to do with imagined sex or gender complementarity, however. In Aristophanes's story, someone can discover a same-sex as well as a different-sex partner, and, in either case, not just any partner will do; the complementarity of partners simply isn't guaranteed by sex or gender.[34]

The complementarist view runs into difficulties at several points.

(*i*) If it is intended as an argument against the moral permissibility of same-sex eros as well as same-sex marriage, it seems clearly unsuccessful. Erotic interactions as such needn't evoke the sort of interaction, mutual self-exposure, and personality development with which the complementarist perspective is concerned. Even if (as I unequivocally deny) a given long-term relationship were morally appropriate only because it caused or reinforced particular personality characteristics, an individual erotic encounter, whether or not different-sex,

---

33. See, *e.g*, Plato, "Symposium," *Dialogues of Plato*, trans. Benjamin Jowett, ed. J. D. Kaplan (New York: Washington Square 1950) 188–93.

34. On personality complementarity, see, *e.g*, Harville Hendrix and Helen LaKelly Hunt, *Getting the Love You Want: A Guide for Couples*, 3d ed. (New York: St. Martin's 2019).

could hardly be expected to do this, so its inability to do so doesn't seem like a good argument against its permissibility.

(*ii*) The argument might be read as presupposing that there is something like "the eternal feminine" that all women exhibit and "the eternal masculine" that all men exhibit. But the idea that women and men just as such consistently exhibit clusters of personality characteristics is difficult to square with the wide variations among actual women and among actual men. Even if, with respect to particular characteristics, there turned out to be statistically discernible differences, this wouldn't change the fact that many individuals didn't possess these traits or that differences *within* sexes and genders were likely to be greater than differences *between* sexes and genders.

As a result, it seems as if many different-sex or different-gender relationships will likely unite people who do not fully or without qualification embody, respectively, the personality characteristics of the eternal feminine and the eternal masculine. And, if this is the case, then either (*a*) these differences aren't morally decisive for different-sex or different-gender relationships or (*b*) an indeterminate number of different-sex and different-gender relationships are likely to be morally deficient for the same kind of reason complementarists evidently believe same-sex or same-gender relationships are morally deficient. If complementarists opt for (*b*), this seems rather like a reductio ad absurdum of their position, given that they do not characteristically object to same-sex or same-gender relationships that don't meet the complementarity standard and that there seems to be nothing inherently problematic about these relationships. If, however, complementarists opt for (*a*), it's unclear why same-sex or same-gender relationships wouldn't be morally acceptable on their preferred terms.

(*iii*) Given the actual configurations of real people's personalities, if complementarity is morally important, it seems as if people should be actively seeking *not* partners who are standardly feminine or standardly masculine *but*, rather, partners who differ from them in ways that match their own distinctive characteristics. This kind of complementarity, complementarity between people's actual traits and attitudes, has no obvious connection to sex or gender. It can't, therefore, serve as the basis for any sort of criticism of LGBTQ+ relationships.

(*iv*) It's difficult to see how "Seek a partner with complementary (gender-stereotypical) personality characteristics" could qualify as morally obligatory. One could welcome an erotic or romantic partner who didn't exhibit the relevant sorts of characteristics without choosing unfairly and so violating THE GOLDEN RULE. It's not clear that choosing such a partner would injure any basic aspect of one's own or the partner's well-being. Perhaps a complementarist might argue that doing so would adversely affect *practical wisdom* by somehow making it harder for one to make good choices or *knowledge* by making it easier for one to avoid self-understanding. But, even if choosing a partner did injure these basic goods, the injury wouldn't be the *purpose* of one's choice or a means to the *fulfillment* of that purpose, so choosing a (putatively) noncomplementary partner wouldn't violate THE PAULINE PRINCIPLE. Provided one chose one's partner with *some* good, most obviously friendship, in view, one's choice would comport with RECOGNITION. And it would also be consistent with EFFICIENCY, since it wouldn't be wasteful. One might commit to limiting oneself to (supposedly) complementary partners. However, (a) this won't be true in the vast majority of cases. In addition, (b) even if one were among the tiny number of people making commitments to complementarity, if one's resolution were premised on false beliefs about the significance of complementarity, it wouldn't be binding.

Eros is only one of multiple topics addressed crisply in the text we often call the Ten Commandments, at the heart of the Jewish and Christian moral traditions. We can and should think about this profoundly influential text through the lens provided by a creational love ethic. I seek to spell out this model of love more fully while also clarifying some central elements of the moral life in the course of focusing on the Decalogue in chapter 6.

6

Creational Love
and the Decalogue

The Jesus of the Gospels and Saint Paul both maintain that the negative commandments of the Decalogue can be encapsulated in the requirement of love; sometimes, they suggest that this is true of the entire law.[1] That's what we would expect if ethics is fundamentally a matter of love so that any moral requirement must flow from love. In this chapter, I want to explore how we might think about each of the Ten Commandments in relation to the specifications of love; THE GOLDEN RULE will play a central role, but I will also call attention to the significance of the other specifications of love.

The provisions of the Decalogue can be read as highlighting various ways of loving not only others but also God and ourselves. Others benefit substantially from our willingness to adopt an appropriate stance before God. Our infinite Creator is not insecure and in need of attention, but (as I noted in chapter 1) we can see orienting ourselves aright in relation to God as a way of loving God; and, at least on a neoclassical view, God's life incorporates ours so that when we and other creatures benefit, we contribute to that life. And we, too, are better off when we choose in accordance with the specifications of love.

Shun Other Gods

You shall have no other gods before me.[2]

---

1. Matt 7:12; Matt 22:40; Rom 13:8–10; Gal 5:14.
2. Exod 20:3; Deut 5:7.

Judgment and choice consistent with love presuppose understanding and so concern for truth. We should worship no other deities in preference to God because the truth is that there are no such deities. Whatever powerful creatures there might be in the universe apart from human beings, these creatures, no matter how powerful, are *creatures*. No creature, whatever its capacities, is "a Universe-class contender" with God.[3] "The infinitely great is not a very large number: even a Mind that exceeds ours (whatever that would mean) by a factor of a googolplex to one (that is to say, 10^{googol}, where a googol is 10^{100}) is no closer to the infinite" mind of God than we are.[4]

To ascribe divinity to a creature is to oppress and disappoint. It is to oppress because God, the infinite Creator, is not a competitor with creatures for love or loyalty. We can acknowledge God as God without in any way undermining the integrity or value of any creature. But creatures *are* competitors with one another for love and loyalty. To treat a creature as divine is thus to ascribe absolute status to a reality that can be loved and worshipped only at the expense of other creatures. To do this is, then, to lay the groundwork for oppressing those other creatures, for treating them as less valuable and important than the false divinity.

To treat a creature as divine is to disappoint because it simply cannot bear the burden of divinity. It can't ground the meaning of my life, offer me comprehensive or unqualified love, or secure me against finitude and death. Any finite source of ultimate consolation is a fake.[5]

This means, in turn, that there is a second sense in which divinizing any creature is linked with oppression. A divinized creature will tend to oppress other creatures with which it competes for attention and loyalty. But the devotees of such a creature will also be inclined to treat *it* controllingly because they want to make sure that it actually delivers on its promises, actually performs as advertised. Controlling the worshipped other won't succeed in making it perform divinely, but its worshippers will often *seek* to make it perform in this way. (This doesn't matter particularly if the worshipped creature is a human artifact, but it does if the worshipped other is a human person, community, or institution or perhaps another sort of creature.)

---

3. Jack W. Provonsha, qtd. Gary Chartier, "'More Needs to Be Said': Jack Provonsha on Fundamentalist Geology," La Sierra *Criterion* 57.6 (Nov. 8, 1985): 4; cp. Provonsha, *Making* 259, 266.
4. Clark, *Biology and Christian Ethics* 107.
5. I echo Iris Murdoch here; see *The Sovereignty of Good*, 2d ed. (London: Routledge 2001) 18. Murdoch thinks God-talk itself an example of fakery.

To divinize a creature is to injure the good of harmony with reality, mis-aligning ourselves with what is. This is an attack not on God but on our own well-being and that of others. By contrast, to decline to divinize any creature is thus a way of loving every creature by refusing to absolutize anything finite to the detriment of other valuable but also finite realities. It is also a way of loving ourselves, in particular, by refusing to set ourselves up for disappointment by relying on any creature for impossibly unqualified solace. And it is, in addition, a way of loving each creature by refusing to subject it to the burden of divinity, a burden it cannot shoulder, or to place it in a position in which would-be wor-shippers seek to control it in order to force it to deliver the divine grace it in fact cannot provide.

To keep the First Commandment is thus both a consequence of and a rein-forcement for adherence to THE GOLDEN RULE, THE PAULINE PRINCIPLE, and the other ways of loving insofar as they protect against behavior that involves deny-ing the reality and value of each sentient creature and each aspect of each creature's well-being. To keep this commandment is also to avoid taking up a stance—spiritual, psychic, moral—likely to dispose one to choose in ways inconsistent with love and so to disregard what it means to love others and ourselves. Resisting idolatry is a prophylactic against injustice and a safeguard for love.

Shun Idols

> You shall not make for yourself an idol, whether in the form of anything that is in heaven above, or that is on the earth beneath, or that is in the water under the earth. You shall not bow down to them or worship them.[6]

There's no sharp distinction between avoiding the worship of unreal gods and avoiding the worship of *idols*. But concern with idolatry is, in particular, concern with the tendency to treat as divine or quasi-divine something *tangible, percep-tible*. In the critical sense implicit in the Second Commandment, an idol is a concrete, tangible reality that serves as an object of religious devotion. An artis-tic representation of ultimate reality isn't necessarily an idol: no one worships Michelangelo's Sistine Chapel portraits of God. What matters is the *function* an object performs in the life of a person or group. A finite object counts as an

---

6. Exod 20:4–5a; Deut 5:8–9a.

idol when it not only *evokes* devotional attitudes, as literary or visual art can do, but also serves as the *focus* of those attitudes, when it is *itself* treated as powerful and sacred. A statue, say, is an idol if people act as if it can work magic on their behalf or are inclined to respond violently when it is, as they suppose, mistreated.

Reading the Second Commandment prompts us to acknowledge the risks associated with our active attempts to represent God and to treat our representations as accurate. To pay religious attention to something one knows to be other than God the Creator seems simply irrational and foolish. No doubt we *can* respond with devotion to some finite reality, but no such reality merits or can reward our devotion. The only kind of idolatry that isn't clearly wrongheaded involves the direction of religious devotion toward something taken to *represent* the Creator. But this kind of idolatry poses risks, too.

In the nature of the case, God, as infinite, isn't tangible, accessible. But we want to *touch* God, *see* God, *hear* God. So we look for creaturely realities that mediate God's presence to us. That's the point of *sacraments*. While, as Creator, God is present in, with, and under all of created reality, we can discern and respond to some mediations of God's presence more effectively than we can discern and respond to others.

The problem is not with mediation but with losing sight of the created character of mediating realities. We can begin interacting with a reality fully aware that it mediates, that it is altogether creaturely; but we can begin to lose sight of its mediatorial character, treating it as if it partook of the perfection, the infinity, the otherness of God. In so doing, we attack the good of harmony by misconstruing our relationship with ultimate reality and also lay the groundwork for choices inconsistent with the specifications of love.

It's clear enough that idolatry happens in connection with explicitly religious objects—not only artistic representations of divinity but also human persons, like religious leaders, human institutions, like churches and states and military forces. When we treat these tangible realities as divinely sanctioned, holy, and authoritative, we give them a status that renders them oppressive. Activities ranging from the punishment of a child for after-hours rambunctiousness in a sanctuary (a word that nods toward an idolatrous conception of what a church building is) to the punishment of an adult for treating a church leader as fallible or for daring to question the claims of a text like a conciliar declaration highlight the harmfulness of idolatry.

Idolatry is most insidiously dangerous when it's least obvious—when it doesn't concern religious figures, texts, traditions, or objets d'art at all. It is all too easy to treat other finite realities as mediating the transcendent and thus, ultimately, as if they themselves were transcendently important. The most obvious examples are states. People aren't very likely to speak of or act in relation to these political entities in explicitly religious terms. A nationalist won't tell you, ordinarily, that her favorite state is divine (though Thomas Hobbes famously described the state as a "mortal god"). But they can in fact respond to the state or another political institution as a focus of absolute loyalty, a loyalty that they may instinctively regard as justified because the state *feels* worthy of worship: it transcends, they may think, the various individuals who make it up; identification with it confers a sense of higher purpose. People may respond in the same way to a system of beliefs or practices, whether religious, political, moral, aesthetic, or scientific.

Idolatry undermines, attacks, competes with entirely appropriate loves for finite realities. We love the Creator as we love the creation. But we cannot combine idolatry with love for creation, since the idol is itself a part of creation and will thus seek to supplant other parts from their places as objectives of love.

Predictably, when we do love an idol, we will treat creatures unjustly, ignoring THE GOLDEN RULE in particular but also likely THE PAULINE PRINCIPLE and perhaps also other specifications of love. Saying "No!" to idolatry is a centrally important way of refusing unjustly to subordinate some sentient creatures to others and to disregard their inherent dignity and beauty. Idolatry is wrong not because it involves mistreating God—who does not depend on our recognition or adulation—but, rather, because it either is or lays the groundwork for the failure to love our fellow creatures well or at all.

Shun Wrongful Reference to God

You shall not make wrongful use of the name of the Lord your God.[7]

We find it easy to invoke God in support of our projects. In ancient Israel, turning God into a guarantor would likely have meant swearing with God as one's witness—perhaps in court, perhaps in some social setting, perhaps looking to God to endorse the truth of what one claimed, perhaps asking God to punish one if one failed to fulfill one's undertaking. The Third Commandment demands that people be responsible. It insists that they avoid calling on God

---

7. Exod 20:7a; Deut 5:11a.

as a way of supporting their lies or of leading others to expect that they won't behave irresponsibly.

Formal oath taking is not an especially common feature of life in contemporary Western societies. But it is still easy for people to treat God as standing behind their assertions or demands. A parent can seek to strengthen her authority over an unruly child by declaring, "Jesus doesn't like it when you do that." An ecclesial bureaucrat who is seeking a committee's approval of a controversial decision can begin with a self-serving prayer insisting that the Holy Spirit has providentially ensured the correctness of the decision. A politician can seek to prompt support for a war by referring to it as a "crusade" and speaking of the nation's cause as God's.

Part of the good of harmony is recognizing ourselves as creatures while acknowledging God as God. We damage this basic good when we treat ourselves as elevated beyond creaturely moral and epistemic limitations. In addition, to regard God as the guarantor of our projects can sometimes encourage us to sit lightly to the specifications of love. We can lie, torture, or treat people unfairly because we believe that we are acting on God's behalf in the world. Spiritual arrogance can lead us to relativize the demands of love, to treat them as only holding for the most part and as inapplicable to us when we function as God's agents.

God is on our side in the sense that God is our loving Creator, but God has given us no mission to dominate our children, the people with whom we work, the church, or the world. God does not insulate us against the possibility of error, even when we're attempting to discern the implications of love. And God has not authorized us to ignore the specifications of love. To make the claim that God is our guarantor is thus *false* and so counter to love. It represents an attack on the goods of knowledge and practical wisdom insofar as we (even if unknowingly) deceive others and ourselves when we invoke God as the guarantor of the importance of our cause or the correctness of our beliefs. Violating the Third Commandment may also lead us to attack the good of friendship if we separate ourselves from friends by uncritically, self-righteously invoking God's support for our convictions.

If we knowingly embrace and encourage a false understanding of God's relationship to our projects, we may purposefully attack the goods of harmony, knowledge, and self-integration; in so doing we will contravene THE PAULINE PRINCIPLE. But we do not ordinarily violate the Third Commandment knowingly. All too frequently, we declare that or act as if God is on our side because we really believe that this is the case. And we might really have been led to believe this in good faith.

When we do this, we are likely to act in a way that is inconsistent with love in the form of THE GOLDEN RULE. After all, if our projects are divinely endorsed, we may pursue them in ways that may involve riding roughshod over others, whom we treat, with unjustifiable arbitrariness, as less significant than ourselves. By acting as if God were our Divine Endorser, we urge those with whom we communicate to join us in treating others unfairly. We may even, sadly, urge them to treat themselves unfairly, to accept our dominance, to give priority to our projects, by announcing God's affirmation. Avoiding the vain—insubstantial, unsupported—invocation of God in support of our projects is thus a way of protecting against the unfair elevation of ourselves and the unfair denigration of others.

Remember the Sabbath Day

Remember the sabbath day, and keep it holy. Six days you shall labor and do all your work. But the seventh day is a sabbath to the Lord your God; you shall not do any work—you, your son or your daughter, your male or female slave, your livestock, or the alien resident in your towns. For in six days the Lord made heaven and earth, the sea, and all that is in them, but rested the seventh day; therefore the Lord blessed the sabbath day and consecrated it.[8]

Observe the sabbath day and keep it holy, as the Lord your God commanded you. Six days you shall labor and do all your work. But the seventh day is a sabbath to the Lord your God; you shall not do any work—you, or your son or your daughter, or your male or female slave, or your ox or your donkey, or any of your livestock, or the resident alien in your towns, so that your male and female slave may rest as well as you. Remember that you were a slave in the land of Egypt, and the Lord your God brought you out from there with a mighty hand and an outstretched arm; therefore the Lord your God commanded you to keep the sabbath day.[9]

8. Exod 20:8–11.
9. Deut 5:12–5.

Jesus famously insisted, "The sabbath was made for humankind, and not humankind for the sabbath."[10] The value of Sabbath rest lies in its support for and expression of love for those God has made. This kind of rest, which is what Sabbath holiness *is*, can be a way or source of support for loving ourselves and others. It can help us embrace the goodness of creation and liberation from the tyranny of work. While embracing Sabbath time bears a different kind of relationship to love than adhering to the other commandments, like each of them, it can be a valuable way of loving.

Rest and the Goodness of Creation

Sabbath rest carries multiple meanings.[11] Historically, it's linked with the goodness of creation and with liberation from slavery. In Genesis 1 and Exodus 20, celebrating the Sabbath is seen as an affirmation of creation: creation is good and needs no further work, so God can rest. We are to rest in imitation of God; and our rest makes sense only because, imaging God in the world, we don't need to work either, in recognition of the goodness of creation. Our work can contribute to the ongoing development of the creation, the unfolding of its potential. But whatever we might need to do isn't, as a general matter, some sort of emergency that demands our constant engagement. And our own value as

10. Mark 2:27.
11. See, *e.g.*, Lynne M. Baab, *Sabbath Keeping: Finding Freedom in the Rhythms of Rest* (Downers Grove, IL: IVP 2005); Donna Schaper, *Sabbath Keeping* (Cambridge, MA: Cowley 1999); Wayne Muller, *Sabbath: Restoring the Sacred Rhythm of Rest* (New York: Bantam 1999); Marva J. Dawn, *Keeping the Sabbath Wholly: Ceasing, Resting, Embracing, Feasting* (Grand Rapids: Eerdmans 1988); Tilden Edwards, *Sabbath Time: Understanding and Practice for Contemporary Christians* (New York: Seabury 1982); Charles Scriven, *Jubilee of the World: The Sabbath as a Day of Gladness* (Nashville: Southern 1978); Kenneth L. Strand, ed., *The Sabbath in Scripture and History* (Washington, DC: Review 1982); Sakae Kubo, *God Meets Man: A Theology of the Sabbath and Second Advent* (Nashville: Southern 1978); Roy Branson, ed., *Festival of the Sabbath* (Washington, DC: Association of Adventist Forums 1985); Karl Barth, *Church Dogmatics*, ed. Geoffrey W. Bromiley and Thomas F. Torrance, trans. A. T. Mackay (Edinburgh: Clark 1938–67) 3.1 (1945/58): 98–9, 313–38; 3.4 (1951/61): 47–72; Niels-Erik A. Andreasen, *The Christian Use of Time* (Nashville: Abingdon 1978); Niels-Erik A. Andreasen, *The Old Testament Sabbath: A Tradition-Historical Investigation* (Missoula, MT: Scholars 1972); Niels-Erik A. Andreasen, *Rest and Redemption* (Berrien Springs, MI: Andrews University Press 1978); John Brunt, *A Day for Healing: The Meaning of Jesus' Sabbath Miracles* (Washington, DC: Review 1981); Herbert W. Richardson, *Toward an American Theology* (New York: Harper 1967) 108–60; Samuele Bacchiocchi, *Divine Rest for Human Restlessness: A Theological Study of the Good News of the Sabbath for Today* (Berrien Springs, MI: Bacchiocchi 1980); and Abraham J. Heschel, *The Sabbath: Its Meaning for Modern Man* (New York: Farrar 1951). Thanks to Roy Branson, Fritz Guy, Sakae Kubo, and Charles Sandefur for bibliographic work identifying most of these sources.

persons doesn't depend on our performance: not only is the creation in which we work good, but we ourselves, as elements of creation, are good.

We are not *essentially* producers or workers. Production is for the sake of consumption, and all of us flourish by enjoying the goods and services we or others produce. Even though most of us produce during our adult lives, production is not essential to flourishing humanness. Some kinds of work may be opportunities to engage in skillful performance. They may prove to be stimulating creative outlets, but this is hardly true of all work; in many cases, we work simply for compensation, fully aware that other aspects of our lives provide more welcome opportunities for flourishing.

Rest and Liberation from Work

In Deuteronomy 5, celebrating the Sabbath is first of all a matter of representing emancipation: the Sabbath allows the Israelites, who are liberated slaves, and their descendants, along with others in their society, to experience something like liberation from slavery and so from the demand that they work. In a society adhering to the Sabbath commandment as recorded here, slaves would have been freed on the Sabbath from demands to work that might well have been backed up with physical force. But for everyone else, whose work was not mandated by means of physical force, the prohibition of work on the Sabbath would still have ruled out social pressure to work.

Whether or not this is true of those who inhabited biblical Israel, later observers of the Sabbath have also found in it a source of liberation from their own internalized demands. It's easy to see one's work as essential to one's value as a person. By insisting that one let go of the compulsion to work, the practice of Sabbath helps to free one from the illusion that the significance of one's life depends on how much or how intensely one works or on the value to others of what one produces through one's work.

By relativizing the importance of work, the Sabbath also helps to relativize the status distinctions that derive from work. The practice of Sabbath prompts one to step outside one's identity as a worker and producer. In addition, to the extent that, as in worship, others similarly move beyond *their* identities as workers and producers, the experience of Sabbath allows one to meet them as equals.[12]

---

12. Cp. Andreasen, *Use* 60–1.

The practice of Sabbath thus enables us to flourish in multiple ways. Sabbath rest can foster physical and emotional health. It can provide an occasion for the stress-free acquisition of knowledge and the rehearsal of narratives and engagement with ideas that can enhance practical wisdom. And freedom from work can mean freedom for friendship, for play, for sensory pleasure, for aesthetic experience, and for the pursuit of the good of harmony in and through study and worship.

Rest as Holiness

Sabbath rest *is* Sabbath holiness. To make holy is first of all to set apart, to render distinctive, to make or treat as *other*. To regard the Sabbath as holy is not a matter of adhering to the sorts of puritan constraints that can lead a child to sing, "Sabbath is a no-no day." It is, rather, precisely *to rest* and so to behave differently than one does on days in which one submits to the demands of work, productivity, and status.[13] Setting the Sabbath apart means welcoming its difference from the days on which one is pressured to perform.

Sabbath Rest and a Creational Love Ethic

One does not choose to injure oneself or another—and so violate THE PAULINE PRINCIPLE—if one does not rest from work and from the demand that one be productive. One does not act unfairly—violating THE GOLDEN RULE—if one fails to rest from work and productivity (unless not resting impedes one's fulfillment of responsibilities to others—as by, say, causing one to suffer a heart attack). Even if one is not resting (sometimes precisely because one is not resting), one can seek directly or indirectly to realize genuine goods and so act in a matter consistent with RECOGNITION. Declining to rest from work and productivity is compatible with taking proper account of the (material and other) costs of reaching one's objectives and so with EFFICIENCY. Since the other ways of loving, taken separately or together, don't mandate rest, one is under no obligation as a general matter to resolve that one will rest on a consistent basis. If one hasn't

13. This seems to be just what Exod 20 and Deut 5 are saying. The injunction to keep the Sabbath holy in these passages is not to be understood as an addition to the direction to rest or even as a call to engage in a given kind of rest, as if the original hearers and readers of these passages had brought to their interpretation of the language of rest a prior understanding of holiness that would inform their view of what rest involved. Rather, rest from work is presented as the way in which the Israelites are to keep the Sabbath holy.

thus resolved, not resting will be compatible with COMMITMENT (unless rest happens to be an essential prerequisite to fulfilling some other commitment). However, one might resolve to engage in Sabbath rest as a way of loving oneself and others. And, in this case, ignoring one's resolution will be inconsistent with COMMITMENT.

Because failing to rest can sometimes be consistent with the specifications of love in action, doing so is importantly different from, say, not murdering. However, choosing to rest from work and to welcome the opportunities to flourish in worship, friendship, play, and so forth made available by Sabbath rest can be a way of taking a tested path to flourishing. And a Christian community that acknowledges the value of Sabbath rest might well seek as much as possible to institutionalize this kind of rest.

A Christian hospital can hardly turn patients away or prohibit emergency surgeries. It can, however, seek to reduce the demands on staff members' Sabbath time by limiting nonemergency activities and encouraging work rotations that keep any one person from being expected to perform even essential work constantly during Sabbath time. A Christian university will need to provide cafeteria services at least sufficient to meet the needs of resident students and campus visitors, but it can avoid scheduling classes, laboratories, field trips, and committee meetings in ways that interfere with Sabbath rest. A Christian congregation can seek to avoid turning its worship services into theatrical productions that require excessive and thoroughly nonrestful activities during Sabbath time. And it can recognize that a pastor's time will need to be guarded jealously. She will need to be free to avoid demands for work on the Sabbath outside worship services. Rotations of pastoral responsibility will be important to help keep a day of rest from becoming a day of travail for any pastor. And a pastor may need to rest on a day different from the one on which the members of her congregation celebrate the Sabbath so that she can experience the gift of the Sabbath herself.[14] While recognizing the difference between Sabbath rest and the avoidance of theft or adultery, a Christian community can take the practice of Sabbath seriously by removing barriers to shared rest. (In addition to taking Sabbath seriously in their own planning, Christian communities might actively encourage members who are employers or who are otherwise

---

14. See Eugene H. Peterson, *Working the Angles: The Shape of Pastoral Integrity* (Grand Rapids: Eerdmans 1987) 66–83; and Eugene H. Peterson, "Confessions of a Former Sabbath Breaker," *Christianity Today*, Sep. 2, 1988, 25–8.

able to make decisions about others' work conditions to safeguard opportunities for Sabbath rest, too.)

Actively embracing Sabbath rest from work can help us to flourish and to help others flourish and thus to enact the kind of love that is grounded in and responsive to God's good creation.

Honor Parents

Honor your father and your mother.[15]

Our positive responsibilities to care for particular others and to invest ourselves in relationships with them flow from THE GOLDEN RULE and COMMITMENT. Honoring our parents is one way of loving particular people, a way in which love is channeled, focused, by these specifications of love.

Every one of us has a father and a mother. Some people's parents are simply sources of genetic material, while others offer nurture, stimulation, inspiration, and empowerment. Unavoidably, people's relationships with their parents will vary with what they have received from their parents and how they interact with their parents. Some will honor their parents by being grateful for the simple fact of existing, while others will do so as they celebrate and continue to deepen the ties that bond them with their parents.

In the broadest sense, THE GOLDEN RULE grounds and incorporates the norm expressed in the phrase "One good turn deserves another."[16] Each of us would want to be acknowledged appropriately by others for what she or he has offered them, for who she or he has been in relation to them, so each of us should acknowledge others in the same way in turn. The specifics matter: the gratitude we owe a person depends on what we have received from that person, on the kind of relationship we've had with that person. But, aware of the many different kinds of relationships people have with their parents, THE GOLDEN RULE grounds our obligations to them in the most general sense.

In some cases, in addition to the general obligation to treat parents in light of their gifts to us, there will be further requirements that flow from the close relationships we have developed with them. Parents can be good to their children without being friends, but, when they *are* friends, further responsibilities

---

15. Exod 20:12a; Deut 5:16a.
16. Finnis, *Aquinas* 140.

emerge for parents and children alike. These will flow in part, thanks to THE GOLDEN RULE, from the specific vulnerabilities and interdependencies that emerge as parents and children nurture warm, intimate ties and in part from COMMITMENT, as they make various self-investing decisions, plans, and resolutions intended to acknowledge the value of friendship and to solidify the friendships they have created. Thus, THE GOLDEN RULE and COMMITMENT both focus and channel the love between children and parents and specify the *kind* of love that's appropriate in a particular parent-child relationship.

To the extent that we value what we have been given by our parents, honoring them can also be a way of underscoring the value of who we are as persons constituted in part by their gifts. And this can be a useful prerequisite for actively loving ourselves and, by increasing our confidence and self-belief, loving others as well.

Shun Murder

You shall not murder.[17]

The prohibition of murder expresses and safeguards love. It embodies regard for the good of life and bodily well-being and also for the other goods in which someone protected by the prohibition on murder might participate or which such a person might promote, including the love embodied in various relationships that will be disrupted if someone is murdered.

The Sixth Commandment precludes not *killing* but *murder*. As I suggested in chapter 5, love similarly precludes purposeful killing but not some instances of unintended killing in defense of oneself or others. To kill another purposefully—as a means of eliminating a romantic rival, securing an inheritance, asserting oneself . . .—is inconsistent with THE PAULINE PRINCIPLE: it's an attack on the basic good of life and bodily well-being. To kill another recklessly is inconsistent with THE GOLDEN RULE. There may also be cases in which COMMITMENT rules out the use of lethal force. The refusal to kill as a means to an end, unfairly, or in violation of one's commitments is a crucial expression of love, providing a vital baseline for social interaction.

17. Exod 20:13; Deut 5:17.

Shun Adultery

You shall not commit adultery.[18]

Avoiding interactions that disrupt others' marriages or our own is a powerful manifestation of love.

Rejecting adultery need not be rooted in the false belief that we own our spouses. Rather, for contemporary persons, it can be a matter of adhering to one's promises and commitments and refusing to encourage others to ignore theirs. These promises and commitments can be rooted in an understanding of how erotic exclusivity can help to protect our too-often fragile intimate relationships; they establish priorities that offer us vantage points from which to view the relational possibilities we confront. Our partnerships can be unsettled by various kinds of interactions with those other than our partners and by concerns that erotic or otherwise disruptive interactions have taken place. Partners can agree on a variety of standards for each other's behavior, but these should be shaped in full awareness of the vulnerability of our intimate connections to disturbance. Making and keeping promises and commitments that safeguard those partnerships is a vital expression of love.[19]

Owning Spouses

People in ancient Israel seem generally to have believed that males owned their female spouses. The conviction that they did apparently grounded Israelite objections to adultery.[20] Thus, some contemporary people resist seeing adultery as morally troubling because they regard prohibitions of adultery as dependent on this mistaken conviction. On this view, once we affirm sex and gender equality and reject the idea that a married woman is absorbed into her

---

18. Exod 20:14; cp. Deut 5:18.

19. I've examined a number of the issues on which I focus here in Chartier, *Public Practice, Private Law* 81–100.

20. See, *e.g.*, L. William Countryman, *Dirt, Greed, and Sex: Sexual Ethics in the New Testament and Their Implications for Today*, rev. ed. (Minneapolis: Fortress 2007) 145–6, 152–5. Anthony Phillips, *Ancient Israel's Criminal Law: A New Approach to the Decalogue* (Oxford: Blackwell 1970) 117, argues that concerns with the husband's control over the paternity of the children he supports and the continuance of his family line ground the Seventh Commandment as originally understood. For a cross-cultural analysis, see, *e.g.*, Suzanne G. Frayser, *Varieties of Sexual Experience: An Anthropological Perspective on Human Sexuality* (New Haven, CT: HRAF 1985) 259.

husband's identity, the basis for any critique of adultery will have disappeared. But a creational love ethic gives us reason to think otherwise.

Adultery and Unfairness

When people think about adultery today, they will characteristically understand it as an instance of promise breaking. Often among the mutual promises that people make in order to constitute their marriages are promises to avoid extramarital erotic contact. And promise breaking is, as a general matter, inconsistent with THE GOLDEN RULE.

Relatedly, there's the sense that spouses who want to be erotically engaged with third parties while insisting that their marriage partners be erotically exclusive are being unfair by breaking rules they have accepted themselves and expect their partners to keep: they're *cheating*. This kind of unfairness is, similarly, a violation of THE GOLDEN RULE.

Why Promise Exclusivity?

On one level, it's sufficient to note that a choice is inconsistent with THE GOLDEN RULE to show that it's wrong. But we still need to understand why it would make sense to make promises to choose erotic exclusivity, to avoid adultery, in the first place, just as we need to ask how we should regard violations of those promises.

Some promissory violations, after all, are trivial. I act wrongly, for instance, if I promise you that I will turn up for dinner with a mutual friend and then fail to do so for no good reason. But no one would expect to find "You shall not skip a dinner you have promised to attend" accompanying "You shall not steal" and "You shall not murder" on a church or synagogue wall.

Promises to be erotically exclusive, by contrast, are important because adultery can and often does pose a serious threat to marriage partners' attachments to each other. Even if people continue to live together while an adulterous relationship persists or its aftereffects are felt, one partner may have partly or completely detached from the other in order to bond with a lover, while the other may have disengaged out of resentment. And an adulterous relationship may propel one partner to abandon the other entirely—in order to form a new relationship or as a means of punishment or retaliation for the other's adultery.

Sometimes, people experience erotic interaction as pleasurable but not as freighted with meaning. This kind of contact, casual and relatively detached, likely won't lead someone to seek distance from or abandon a spouse. Sometimes, however, the impact of sex on people's attitudes can be much more intense. It can lead to deep attachment or ecstatic passion for the various reasons I noted in chapter 5.

It is often not realistically possible to be at all confident that an erotic encounter *won't* lead to passionate ties that will undermine one's connection with one's spouse and even rupture it. A seemingly casual fling can turn unexpectedly into a grand passion. We can't know in advance what will happen in any given case. So it is certainly not unreasonable at all for people to worry about the consequences of erotic encounters by their spouses with others and thus for spouses to make mutual promises of erotic exclusivity.

Such promises help substantially to reduce the risk that a marriage will be undermined by the partners' interactions with others. Given the great importance of marriage in the lives of most of those who marry—a level of importance established by their comprehensive promises (and, sometimes, commitments) to share their lives and experiences and loyalties—safeguarding this central relationship by means of serious promises, even if keeping those promises may sometimes be onerous, makes perfect sense. Promises to avoid adultery are worth making and worth keeping; failing to keep them matters because of the risks adultery can pose to a marriage.

Promises, Commitments, and Attraction

Promises and commitments establish priorities one can use to gauge one's options. Suppose one finds oneself intensely, passionately, drawn to someone other than one's spouse: one desires not simply to enjoy a fling with this person but actually to form a new *we*, to start a new life, with him.[21] Perhaps, loyal and generous as it presents itself as being, one's passion seems as if it might be described as love. This kind of love, not only intense but also evidently well intentioned, is often taken in our culture as self-justifying. "I love him, so I should leave you to be with him." But the point is that one's promises and commitments have *already* established the focus of one's love, and that focus is one's partner.

To be loyal to one's partner in this case is not a matter of choosing duty over love. It is, rather, a matter of choosing one love over another and of choosing the love one has already promised, the love to which one is already committed. One has established priorities for oneself not as an alternative to loving but as

21. Thanks to David Gordon for discussion on this point.

a way of loving, to determine the direction and intensity and character of one's love. Declining to risk experiencing disconnection from or the temptation to abandon one's partner by keeping not only one's promises to love her or him but also one's promises to avoid unnecessary hazards is a profoundly important expression of love.

Varieties of Disruption

The kind of threatening attachment I've envisioned need not in principle be rooted in physical erotic contact. Physical erotic contact isn't the only kind of engagement that can disrupt a marriage. An intimate nonphysical connection can similarly lead to disconnection and potentially even abandonment. The *frisson* associated with an overtly innocent flirtation can be enough to detach one from a spouse who seems all too familiar or with whom one is in conflict. Sex can bond us intensely, but so can conversation. People can fall in love without ever touching. If a promise to avoid adultery is intelligible, if we can see how such a promise fits within and helps to sustain marriage as we conceive it, then it will similarly be clear why it makes sense to avoid any other kind of interaction likely to lead to serious disruption in one's marriage, whether it's physical or not.

Worry, Fear, Anger, and Deception

If it makes sense to be concerned with erotic exclusivity in order to reduce the risk that one's marriage will be disrupted, then it's clear why someone might be gripped by the fear that a valuable relationship will be undermined, even destroyed. This kind of concern can embody one's entirely reasonable appreciation of the high priority one has assigned to a relationship.

By contrast, other kinds of reactions to—real or imagined—adultery are unwarranted and unhelpful. Some people are notoriously insecure, confident that betrayal lurks around every corner and consequently seeking to dominate their partners to prevent them from beginning or continuing down paths leading to abandonment. This kind of overly fearful behavior is itself a source of disconnection, since a dominated, bullied partner can hardly feel safe and free and is thus likely to grow increasingly detached, whether or not involved with anyone else. It is also likely to contribute to the misery of the person engaging in it, both because it's inherently unpleasant and because of the disconnection it will breed.

Fear and anger rooted in the mistaken view that a partner is one's possession have no place in a flourishing life. On this sort of view, a partner's erotic contact with someone else is a violation of one's imagined possessory rights. One's partner's adultery flouts one's authority. It interferes with one's dominance. The spouse who thinks of adultery as violating her possessory rights can experience fear and anger as a result of resentment at her partner's imagined rebellion. A thoughtful spouse who cares about her marriage, by contrast, will regret and challenge an adulterous partner's heedless risk-taking. But she will worry, if she does, because of the likely impact of her partner's behavior on the partner's bond with her. Potential loss of connection will be what concerns her, not her partner's violation of her supposed entitlement to control her partner's body.

A partner is not a slave. And, while ignoring a promise of erotic exclusivity can be risky and dangerous and can evince a cavalier attitude toward the security of one's marriage, a simple act of adultery, a boundary crossing, will not necessarily result in destructive detachment or abandonment. However, while not every act or relationship that's inconsistent with someone's promise of exclusivity will necessarily have this effect, someone who breaks a promise of exclusivity to a partner will ordinarily assume that the partner might *respond* with worry, fear, or anger to the discovery of the act or relationship. (If such responses weren't to be expected, the partners likely wouldn't have asked each other to promise exclusivity in the first place.) Seeking to avoid conflict, the promise breaker will therefore likely attempt to conceal the act or relationship, often by lying. And the concealment itself will drive a further wedge between the partners, disrupting their relationship further by impeding their mutual knowing.

Erotically Open Relationships

Because erotic interaction with someone who isn't one's spouse can pose a serious risk to one's marriage, there's good reason ex ante to promise to avoid engaging in this kind of interaction and good reason ex post to keep promises of erotic exclusivity. However, opting for erotically open relationships, some partners may choose not to promise erotic exclusivity or may opt to release each other from promises of exclusivity previously made. There are many different reasons partners choose erotically open relationships. They may see such relationships as means of spiritual discipline—because they challenge people to move beyond jealousy and possessiveness. They may regard such relationships as sources of enriched erotic experiences the partners can share directly or indirectly. They may understand them as occasions for growth and discovery for individual partners (with or without the further thought that the partners' experiences may enhance their primary relationships). They may be sources of drama and pleasure for participants in primary relationships from which erotic interaction is absent. And there are doubtless various other reasons. The important thing is that, because erotic openness is allowed and shaped by the promises the partners make, they are able (whether or not they do this in any particular case) to treat erotic relationships with others as contributing to and limited by the needs of their primary relationship.

It is easy to understand the appeal of these sorts of arrangements for many people. And there's nothing in virtue of which they're inherently inconsistent with love. However, they *can* pose risks. And it is important to be genuinely alert to the challenges erotic openness can create for a marriage.[22] The negative consequences that can flow from the violation of promises of exclusivity can also flow from nonexclusivity even when it is consistent with people's marital promises. The surreptitious, unfair character of adultery can augment disconnection and detachment and make betrayal and abandonment more likely. But even when no lying, concealment, or promise breaking is involved, one's erotic interactions with people other than one's spouse can lead inadvertently to intense, disruptive attachments with the potential to end one's marriage.

There's nothing just as such that renders a particular level of risk intolerable in principle. As long as people are open about the risks and how to manage them, they may be able to choose in a manner consistent with THE GOLDEN RULE to assume these risks in and through the promises that constitute their relationship. At the same time, however, partners' individual commitments with respect to their marriage and their promises to each other will characteristically treat it as of great importance. For those for whom their marriage is a comprehensive relationship that trumps relationships with other creatures, it will be essential, at minimum, to place substantial safeguards in place to limit risks to the persistence and flourishing of their marriage posed by erotic interactions with others. And, for many, this will quite reasonably mean opting for erotic exclusivity.

---

22. In the high-profile Christian marriage of Hannah and Paul Tillich, wrestling with the demands of erotic exclusivity was an important theme. It surfaced initially in connection with Hannah's affair with Paul, at the time a former lover, during her marriage to her first husband. And it continued to be significant during a marriage marked sometimes by erotic openness and sometimes by cruelty. See, *e.g.*, Alexander C. Irwin, *Eros toward the World: Paul Tillich and the Theology of the Erotic* (Eugene, OR: Wipf 2004); and Hannah Tillich, *From Time to Time* (New York: Stein 1973).

Loving by Promising and Committing

When spouses say "No!" to adultery, they do so as a way of keeping promises and commitments. They do so, therefore, as a way of loving. Embracing exclusivity is a crucial way—hardly the only way—of loving by reducing risks to the well-being of the spouses and of their relationship. As partners, they share in a particularly intense—comprehensive, intimate—variety of friendship. Adultery threatens to attack this good, to disrupt their relationship and, potentially, end it. Through their promises and commitments, they have established this good in a position of great importance in their lives and in their identities.

Avoiding adultery is thus both a way of loving one's partner and a way of loving oneself, since, by avoiding the disruption adultery risks causing, one protects the especially important friendship in which one participates with one's spouse. One acts for one's own well-being and for that of one's spouse, and in this way, one loves. One's commitments and one's promises serve to *channel* one's love, to *focus* that love. Keeping a promise is a way of loving, as is adhering to a commitment—a way of determining who and how one will love. By making the promises that constitute and commitments that help to sustain and deepen a marriage, one determines that one will love oneself and one's spouse in particular ways, notably by building an intimate, comprehensive friendship and a corresponding and supporting shared life.

There are innumerable people other than one's spouse to whom one might have given oneself in love. But one *chooses* to unite in love with one's spouse. One need not love oneself by seeking for oneself the good of intimate union and shared life with this person or in just this way. As a free, creative person, one chooses the good of *this* kind of marriage with *this* person, shaping the instance of the good of friendship one intends to create with promises and, if one chooses to do so, establishing its priority with commitments that obtain independently of one's spouse's actions.

These considerations offer some insight into the once famous case of Mrs. Bergmeier, offered by Joseph Fletcher as evidence of the intuitive attractiveness of his Christian consequentialism.[23] Mrs. Bergmeier has been unjustly detained in a Ukrainian concentration camp at the end of World War II by the invading Soviet army. Her impoverished family languishes in a devastated Germany. Learning that her family needs her badly and recognizing that she will be sent home if she's pregnant, she prevails on "a friendly Volga German

23. See Fletcher, *Situation Ethics* 164–5.

camp guard to impregnate her."[24] When she reaches home, her family members are delighted—and not judgmental. And they agree that "little Dietrich" has "done more for them than anybody."[25] For Fletcher, it seems clear, this case highlights the appropriateness of ignoring what he takes to be a rule of thumb when breaking the rule will bring about better consequences than keeping it.

We don't need to think about this case as Fletcher does. To see why, we need to focus on the value of promises of exclusivity as safeguarding our intimate connections. We don't promise exclusivity because nonexclusivity is *inherently* destructive of an intimate partnership. We promise exclusivity, rather, as a risk-management tool. Exclusivity reduces the likelihood that (*a*) one will bond with someone other than one's spouse in a way that might lead to disruption, distance, and abandonment and (*b*) one's erotic interactions with someone else might bring about disconnection from one's spouse by encouraging concealment and lying. Mrs. Bergmeier's action involved no intent to conceal or lie. (Though she could have misrepresented the quality of her relationship with the guard, she could hardly conceal the reality of her pregnancy.) And the odds would have been low that her erotic encounter with her helpful friend would lead to disconnection from her husband. Further, her continued separation from her husband will have contributed unavoidably to some measure of disconnection between them so that the capacity of her action to lead to their more rapid reconnection will have given her particular reason to become pregnant as she did—directly in support of her marriage. (We can be confident that, given the opportunity, her husband, yearning to see her, would have released her from her obligation of exclusivity to the extent necessary to effect her plan.) The opportunity her choice will have afforded for her to aid and connect with the rest of her family will also have been salient.[26]

Ordinarily, when we promise exclusivity, we do so with the intent of taking these sorts of risk calculations off the table. (*i*) We want to keep the relevant risks at an absolute minimum. If we've already decided to do this, calculation is unnecessary: we judge that no amount of potential erotic pleasure will be worth the risk that seeking such pleasure with someone outside our relationship could pose to that relationship, even if that risk might turn out, in a given case, to have been low. (*ii*) In particular, we know that risk calculations made in moments

24. Fletcher 165.
25. Fletcher 165.
26. I bracket any issues related to the guard's choice to assist Mrs. Bergmeier, assuming, in particular, that he wasn't married.

of desire are likely to be inaccurate. If I have to make a situational judgment about the likely consequences of an erotic encounter, I will probably, with all the goodwill in the world, underestimate the risk. And my partner and I might well judge that, in such a case, the results could be devastating for my marriage and that it would be better not to find out.

We don't, that is, ordinarily leave open the possibility of situational risk calculation when we promise exclusivity; that's the point of making a promise. But the obligation to keep promises flows from THE GOLDEN RULE. Whether it's reasonable to break a promise will depend on whether breaking it is (*i*) undertaken in pursuit of a genuine good and (*ii*) consistent with a standard one could reasonably accept as applicable to anyone in a situation with the same or closely comparable morally relevant features. Mrs. Bergmeier's promise of exclusivity to her husband has to be *assumed* here; that is, we're not asking about how someone might behave if that person hadn't made a promise. Rather, the promise must be taken into account. If Mrs. Bergmeier were willing to accept a standard that permitted people in general to violate promises of exclusivity in situations relevantly comparable to hers, her choice to violate her promise (absent the release her husband surely would have given her had he been able to do so) would be consistent with THE GOLDEN RULE.

Shun Theft

You shall not steal.[27]

Concern with physical possessions can often seem immeasurably far from love. In the abstract, talking about possessions in relation to love can call up images of Scrooge McDuck in his gold-filled vault. But possessions are integral to love's enactment. While physical possessions are not themselves basic goods, how we choose with respect to those possessions is an important way of fostering well-being and so of loving.

Just possessory claims are rooted in THE GOLDEN RULE, from which reasonable constraints on choices about legal rules related to possession can be seen to flow. They reflect our embodiment and a broad range of desiderata reflective of our created characteristics and the goods material possessions can foster. Variations in possessory norms are certainly consistent with THE GOLDEN RULE. But

27. Exod 20:15; cp. Deut 5:19.

there is good reason, at any rate, to adopt something like what I call the *baseline possessory rules*. These norms are appropriate for a flourishing legal system, and one has good reason to uphold such a system; but one might be warranted in acting counter to the baseline rules in a variety of circumstances, though one should be prepared to accept responsibility for doing so.[28]

The Practice of Possession

Possession is a practice. Social structures and institutions shape our engagement in this practice. They do so in recognition of the reality that physical objects matter to us in multiple ways. But they're also premised on the acknowledgment of the reality that a physical object that's not part of your body isn't, as a general matter, part of *you*, a constituent of your identity. (I leave wedding rings and family farms to one side for simplicity's sake.) It's something with which you have, as it were, an arm's-length relationship. Moral questions about your just claim to a given possession are not questions per se about your relationship to the possession; they're questions about your relationship with *me*, about how *I* should choose in relation to the thing in question.

Interference with my possessions isn't like interference with my body. Purposefully attacking someone's body is always wrong because it's always inconsistent with love in the form of THE PAULINE PRINCIPLE. By contrast, what's right and wrong as regards my choices with respect to your possessions is mainly a function of THE GOLDEN RULE, a matter of fairness. And that means that various sorts of interference with others' possessions could be more defensible than interference with their bodies. Nonetheless, THE GOLDEN RULE grounds robust safeguards for just claims to possessions.

Constraints on Interference

To begin with, consider the simple case in which you currently possess something physical—a pencil, a bicycle, an apartment, or whatever. If our roles were reversed, if *I* possessed it, I wouldn't ordinarily be willing for you to appropriate it temporarily or permanently at will. So it would typically be inconsistent

28. I have explored these issues in other places, including *Anarchy and Legal Order: Law and Politics for a Stateless Society* (Cambridge: Cambridge University Press 2012) 44–156; *An Ecological Theory of Free Expression* (New York: Palgrave 2018) 13–22; and *Good Life in the Market* 47–60. In those texts, I cite a range of sources on which I've drawn appreciatively in developing my approach to the ethics of possession.

with THE GOLDEN RULE for me to do the same to you. There's thus a presumption in favor of avoiding forcible or fraudulent interference with other people's possessions.

To be sure, things are more complicated than this simple two-person case might suggest. Suppose, for instance, that you now possess a bicycle because you sneaked it out of my garage last night. To do so seems inconsistent with THE GOLDEN RULE, since you almost certainly wouldn't be OK with a standard that permitted me to sneak things out of *your* garage at will. My taking the bicycle from you might, then, be a matter of self-help, of my reappropriating from you something to which I *am* entitled and to which you were never entitled in the first place. This example points toward the need for a more complex account of the rules we need to order our relationships with respect to physical possessions.

From Persons to Systems

We need, therefore, to think not just about how to behave one-on-one, in relation to each other as particular persons in a given moment, but also about what kinds of social norms we should support and how social institutions like courts and legal systems should address disputes about people's claims to possess things justly.

To sort that out, we need to consider the significance of general rules about possessions, the functions such rules might play, and the values to which they should be responsive. By beginning with THE GOLDEN RULE, we recognize that whatever we say about possession shouldn't and can't be a matter of protecting some people's interests at the expense of everyone else's, of endorsing special privileges for some while ignoring others. A system of rules about possession needs to foster widespread well-being, to benefit people in general. This is the best way to understand what Christians have sometimes talked about as "the universal destination of goods": the overall scheme of possessory rules should conduce to general—in principle, universal—benefit.

Desiderata for Possessory Rules

Real-world standards regarding possession are social conventions. They reflect the habits and judgments of particular people in particular social contexts. And a range of different conventions could be consistent with love. But THE GOLDEN RULE—together with a range of considerations, arguably desiderata, that reflect the dynamics of the human and natural worlds and the character of human flourishing—places limits on what will count as good rules about possession.

To summarize these desiderata far too briskly: we are embodied creatures who undertake projects in the physical world, so we need to have clear rules about who makes what decisions with respect to the various elements of that world. Such rules should be *simple*: they should be easy to understand and follow. They should be *general*, applicable across multiple situations, so that it's hard to fudge them for the benefit of decision makers' cronies or the privileged on the basis of supposed situational particularities. They should be *impersonal*, applicable to people whatever their differences. They should be *impartial* in the sense that they don't privilege one person's peaceful objectives over another's. They should render possession *reliable* by precluding arbitrary intrusion or deprivation. And they should be *stable*, supported by the attitudes and circumstantial constraints that make them the kinds of rules that would predictably develop over time during the course of people's engagement with each other.

Along with these formal characteristics, good rules should foster *stewardship* by assigning accountability for particular physical objects to particular people and encouraging them to take good care of such objects. They should offer people the *space* they need to exercise practical wisdom about the ways in which they want to flourish. Good rules should also equip people to undertake their projects *freely*, without meddling by others. They should be premised on the recognition that a limited subset of physical objects may qualify as *parts of us*, even if lots of other things aren't. They should be free of barriers to our construction of personal relationships and mutually supportive connections with *people who differ from us* as regards how they look, behave, and think and where they are—they should, indeed, encourage the creation and maintenance of such connections. They should help us uphold societal *norms* of good behavior. They should foster *peaceful interaction* and minimize quarrels and controversies by making boundaries apparent. They should offer people encouragement and opportunity to *focus* on engaging in particular activities, nourishing particular skills and capacities, and flourishing in particular ways. They should facilitate the investigation and provision of what's *new and innovative*. They should lay the necessary groundwork for the *coordination* of the cooperation of the activities of people—friends and acquaintances as well as distant strangers—in making and delivering the things others want. They should make the things people want as easy to obtain as possible by facilitating and encouraging *creativity and efficiency*.

In addition, good possessory rules should make it easy for those who seek to do so to form, maintain, and express *mutual, reciprocal relationships*, and they should render it straightforward to *compensate* others for the ways in which they've aided us in the context of such relationships. They should empower people to *dissent* from the status quo in order to *experiment* with different ways of flourishing and to *display* the ongoing progress and current results of their experiments in living for others to see. They should foster interactions that encourage *the growth of character traits* like reliability and truthfulness. They should enable people to *become generous and to express generosity*. And they should *acknowledge* the reality that physical things don't exist in infinite quantities and aren't readily available in all contexts.

Baseline Possessory Rules

They should do all these things because good standards governing our choices about possessions should serve the ends of love. Upholding such standards should be a way of showing authentic regard for our own well-being and the well-being of others.

To decide what standards for possession it makes sense to affirm, we can consider our circumstances and the various desiderata I've elaborated in light of THE GOLDEN RULE. The desiderata constrain the form and substance of good standards for possession significantly. A first pass at identifying good standards, yielding what I call *baseline possessory rules* for a good legal system, might look something like this:

- EFFECTIVE POSSESSION. If something has been abandoned by someone else who acquired it justly, or if it's never been justly acquired by anyone, or if there's no way of characterizing someone as already having acquired it justly, you can come to possess it justly if you take effective possession of it—picking it up if it's a dropped pencil, say.
- VOLUNTARY TRANSFER. If you've justly acquired something, you can transfer it to someone else as a gift or in exchange for something else.
- REMEDIAL CONVEYANCE. If you've acquired something through theft or fraud, you can be deprived of it, along with the reasonable costs associated with getting it back. If you've injured someone's body or justly acquired possessions, some of your possessions can be taken to repair the injury and to cover, again, the reasonable costs associated with getting you to take responsibility for your actions.
- PERSONAL RESPONSIBILITY. While you possess something you've justly acquired, you're responsible for making decisions regarding how it's to be used and cared for.

"You shall not steal" can be understood, then, as an injunction to avoid interfering with someone's freedom to control a possession and to transfer it to someone else when she has acquired it voluntarily from another person or by taking effective possession of something unclaimed.

Variations

Nothing about the baseline rules requires that the acquisition or title of a just claim to a physical possession take on a particularly formal character. As long as they're relatively clear and unambiguous, informal conventions can do what's needed perfectly well. Similarly, there's nothing about the rules which implies that only particular people, and not groups, can acquire just possessory claims in accordance with EFFECTIVE POSSESSION or VOLUNTARY TRANSFER.

There are lots of other rules regarding possession that people might conceivably endorse. But there's a good chance, at any rate, that the baseline rules satisfy the desiderata I've noted above more effectively than most alternatives and that any alternatives that fulfill those desiderata to something like the same degree will probably be quite similar.

Systemic Rules, Personal Choices

The baseline rules make sense as guides for the general practices of legal systems. Actors in a legal system have good reason to uphold them without deviation or exception to ensure reliability and predictability. At the systemic level, in courts and similar venues, adhering to THE GOLDEN RULE means applying these norms on a consistent basis.

However, someone who finds herself, say, fleeing an avalanche doesn't violate THE GOLDEN RULE if she breaks into a mountain cabin in search of shelter, even though PERSONAL RESPONSIBILITY is one of the baseline rules and she's not responsible for the cabin. While she should compensate the owner for any damage she has caused, she is under no obligation to let herself die in order to avoid interfering with the owner's possessory rights. Because a good legal system operates dependably, systemic actors cannot have ongoing recourse to THE GOLDEN RULE in individual cases; but an individual person who isn't behaving as a systemic actor is perfectly free to remember that a just approach to possessory claims is rooted in and derivative from THE GOLDEN RULE, to which she, unlike a judge or other systemic actor, can appeal directly when deciding what to do in a case like the one I've envisioned.

The prohibition on stealing doesn't rule out emergency choices like the one contemplated in this section. But upholding it, as a general matter, enables legal systems and individual choices to embody and foster love.

Shun False Testimony

You shall not bear false witness against your neighbor.[29]

Declining to bear false witness expresses love to a range of others, including the neighbors against whom we might be tempted to witness falsely and those involved in making decisions about the matter under consideration. Bearing false witness against someone is not the same as lying, and it is an interestingly open question whether one might ever reasonably give false testimony *for* someone. Context means that some verbal performances that seem like lies aren't. But actual lying is harmful in multiple ways and will ordinarily be ruled out by THE GOLDEN RULE and THE PAULINE PRINCIPLE. It is possible that some lies are consistent with these specifications of love, but, even if this is the case, there is very good reason to shun lying in general.

Lying Testimony

The Ninth Commandment is not a general prohibition of lying. This commandment is concerned specifically with giving false testimony in court. Lying in court is inconsistent with love. It prevents an accurate, and thus a fair, adjudication of a dispute from taking place. And so it ensures that people's rights will go unvindicated. It may even, as in a capital case (which might be especially in view here), serve as a means of indirect murder.

Testifying falsely to bring about someone's death, whether for its own sake or in order to obtain something desired (an inheritance, say), is unloving because, as a purposeful or instrumental attack on the good of life and bodily well-being, it is always inconsistent with THE PAULINE PRINCIPLE. The same is true of false testimony designed to effect an injury to any basic aspect of someone's welfare other than life and bodily well-being.

Giving false testimony in order to bring about a decision inconsistent with THE GOLDEN RULE is itself likely to be inconsistent with THE GOLDEN RULE; if I

29. Exod 20:16; cp. Exod 23:1–3; Deut 5:20.

wouldn't be willing to accept a standard that permitted an unfair outcome for myself or a loved one in particular circumstances, it's not fair of me to attempt to bring about such an outcome in such circumstances. Similarly, if I wouldn't be willing to accept a standard that allowed someone to manipulate me or a loved one using falsehood in a relevantly similar case, then it's not fair of me to manipulate using falsehood in this case.

Testifying falsely to give myself or someone else an advantage at the expense of the neighbor against whom one gives false testimony is also likely to be inconsistent with THE PAULINE PRINCIPLE as a purposeful or instrumental attack on the good of *practical wisdom*. The person giving false testimony seeks to hamstring the exercise of practical wisdom by the judge or other decision maker. Giving false testimony will also often be inconsistent with THE PAULINE PRINCIPLE as an attack on the good of *knowledge*.

Helpful, Harmless Lies?

We may reasonably ask, then, whether it is ever consistent with love to give false testimony—or to lie—inside or outside the courtroom, even in a good cause.

I recall hearing a conversation in my church when I was a child in which someone suggested (roughly) this casuistical norm: a lie is permissible if (*i*) it won't hurt anyone and (*ii*) it will help someone. This approach seems rather too capacious. A lie injures whenever basic aspects of the target's well-being, including knowledge and the exercise of practical wisdom, are damaged. And these aspects of the target's well-being *will* be damaged if the target is prompted to adopt a false belief or is rendered less capable of reasoning properly with respect to a given situation in virtue of having such a belief. Not reasoning properly because of a lie may lead one to make various decisions that themselves lead unnecessarily to injuries to basic goods (as when a relationship is damaged because someone believes a lie) or instrumental ones (as when someone is defrauded of the instrumental good of money). When a lie disrupts mutual knowing, it may undermine friendship as well.[30] It may also injure those who overhear it in various ways. Lying is frequently contrary to love.

30. The best discussion of lying from a creational perspective is Christopher O. Tollefsen, *Lying and Christian Ethics* (Cambridge: Cambridge University Press 2014), though I disagree at various points. I engage with Tollefsen, offering my own perspective, in Chartier, "Lies," *Flourishing Lives* 68–85.

Seeming Lies That Aren't

Some verbal performances may not be lies because they occur in contexts in which it is clear, despite surface appearances, that they do not convey false-hoods, perhaps because they are not genuinely fact-stating at all. (Think of the things an actor or comedian might say or of Uncle Charlie telling a joke framed nominally as a true story at the Thanksgiving dinner table.)

In other cases, communication is already understood by both parties to be sufficiently *ambiguous* that a verbal performance is not taken to be a clearly truth-ful assertion. This will be especially true when both parties understand that trust has largely or completely broken down between them, though it may also occur in the context of a formally or informally structured game. (Think of military commanders engaged in a war game or a murderer and a captured likely victim playing verbal cat and mouse with each other.) In these cases, the participants will not take each other to be communicating unequivocally and will thus not accept each other's verbal performances as assertions intended to be taken as unquestionably correct.

Unintended Injuries

The kinds of verbal performances I've just discussed aren't lies, though they resemble lies. So judging that they're consistent with the specifications of love doesn't tell us whether any actual lies are (we know most aren't). It is at least possible that the damage done by a lie may sometimes be incidental, antici-pated even though not sought as either a means or an end. For instance, one might lie in response to someone's question *not* to manipulate her by inducing her to accept a false belief (and so deliberately attacking her well-being) but, instead, in order to avoid conveying something she isn't entitled to know but will learn on the basis of any sort of answer other than a lie. Perhaps—I think the issue deserves more reflection—one can tell a lie in a case like this without choosing injury for its own sake or as a means to one's end. If one can, the lie is consistent with THE PAULINE PRINCIPLE, though it might still be wrong on other grounds.

Whether a lie that doesn't involve choosing injury as a means to one's end is permissible depends on whether it is consistent with THE GOLDEN RULE. If you're willing to accept a standard that would permit someone to lie to you or one of your loved ones in particular circumstances, then you choose fairly if you lie in relevantly similar circumstances. If telling the lie is also consistent with

THE PAULINE PRINCIPLE and the other specifications of love, then telling it isn't contrary to love.

In a given case, telling a lie may perhaps comport with THE PAULINE PRINCIPLE and THE GOLDEN RULE (and any other applicable specifications of love). Even if this is the case, though, most lies are inconsistent with love. Attacking others with falsehood, in court proceedings or elsewhere, is thoroughly wrong. And acting in view of the worth of friendship, trust, and the autonomous exercise of judgment will mean avoiding the use of lies in a variety of other settings, including those in which lying might be expected to make our lives easier.

Shun Coveting

> You shall not covet your neighbor's house; you shall not covet your neighbor's wife, or male or female slave, or ox, or donkey, or anything that belongs to your neighbor.[31]

One doesn't choose in a way inconsistent with love if one simply *wants* something, including something currently possessed by someone else. What matters is whether one wants whatever one wants in a way that can't be squared with the specifications of love.

The specifications of love are relevant to wanting in various ways: RECOGNITION requires that, if I choose to open myself to desiring something, what I choose must actually *be* good or be reasonably viewed as a prerequisite to what is actually good; COMMITMENT might ground adherence to resolutions not to entertain various sorts of desires or to undermine them if they arise; and THE GOLDEN RULE might preclude behaving in ways that nourish particular desires.

There are many varieties of desire, most of them perfectly compatible with love. Appreciating someone else's home or fantasizing idly about what a relationship with someone else's partner might be like need not be inconsistent with love. Desiring a physical reality or a state of affairs (like an interpersonal relationship) is not itself choosing to do anything at odds with love as a way of bringing one's desire into being. However, a desire warrants concern when it becomes embedded deeply enough in one's motivational structure that there's a serious risk that it will prompt one to act against love.

---

31. Exod 20:17; cp. Deut 5:21.

When the choice to nourish a desire leads to an unfair risk that one will engage in an action inconsistent with love, the initial choice to nourish the desire is itself contrary to love. The test here is THE GOLDEN RULE. Imagine that nourishing the desire posed a certain risk of leading to an action that might wrongly injure another. Now, suppose the desire were someone else's. Suppose that that person's nourishing the desire posed a comparable risk of leading her to act in a manner that was inconsistent with love and that injured you or a loved one. If you wouldn't be willing to accept a standard permitting her to nourish a comparable desire with the relevant risk of injury to you or a loved one, it wouldn't be consistent with love for you to nourish the desire.

A GI who consoled and diverted himself in 1944 with endless fantasies involving Betty Grable might, indeed, have desired Grable (as he perceived her) very intensely. But he will almost certainly have posed no actual threat to her marital relationship with Harry James. By contrast, consider the triangle of Juliet, Peter, and Mark in Richard Curtis's *Love Actually*. Mark, Peter's loyal best friend, is obsessively smitten with Juliet, Peter's fiancée and then wife. Only after making a comical declaration of love is he able to let go of his desire for her. Mark has every reason to see that continuing to nurture his desire for Juliet will lead either to pointless frustration or else to disruptively bad behavior that could damage Juliet's relationship with Peter. He thus has every reason to stop nurturing his desire for Juliet and probably to try to quench it.

Declining to nourish a desire or actively seeking to extinguish it when to do so could lead one to injure another or oneself is an expression of love. THE GOLDEN RULE prompts us to refuse to nourish our desires when to do so would be to exhibit inadequate regard for the well-being of those our desires might lead us to injure (and so for our own well-being, too, since choosing in a manner inconsistent with love always harms the actor). It channels our love for genuine goods in ways that don't involve needlessly risking injury to others' flourishing or our own.

While it's easy to see adhering to the moral requirements I have examined in this chapter as a way of loving, love is not the *explicit* focus of the Decalogue. By contrast, it plays a much more overt role in the moral teaching of the New Testament, in which we read that love is the greatest commandment and that THE GOLDEN RULE's expression of love as fairness captures the central meaning of the Ten Commandments. Continuing to highlight the implications of a creational approach to love and to offer proposals regarding our own appropriation of the Christian moral tradition, I examine that teaching in chapter 7.

7

Creational Love and New Testament Teaching

The New Testament places great emphasis on love as a central aspect of Christian life. In this chapter, I want to reflect on some key New Testament moral injunctions with a focus on love understood in relation to creation.

The vision to which Jesus gave expression and the underlying principles he voiced, along with the moral understanding supported by his actions and ultimately his resurrection, will have been seen as authoritative among early Christians. But it is striking how infrequently specific sayings recorded in the Gospels are invoked in the context of moral instruction in the Epistles.

This may have been because "the specific ethical teachings of Jesus . . . concerned the specific religio-political crisis of Israel."[1] However, even when moral teachings in the Gospels or the Epistles might initially have been intended to apply to quite specific local circumstances, when they are framed in general terms and enunciated with little or no context, they have often been understood as applicable more generally. Sometimes, understanding teachings with historically particular meanings as generally applicable has exerted powerfully revolutionary effects on the moral attitudes of later generations. That's true, I think, of many of the teachings with which I engage here.

I begin with what may be Jesus's most powerful and memorable injunction, to love enemies, seeking to show how this directive does not need to be justified with reference to a special ethic but flows naturally from love understood in the light of creation. I turn to his blessing on those who make peace before going

---

1. Marcus J. Borg, *Conflict, Holiness, and Politics in the Teaching of Jesus* (Harrisburg, PA: Trinity 1998) 246n22.

on to examine his proscriptions of insulting and judging others. Then, I turn to a range of sometimes provocative directives offered in the Epistles.

I consider the encouragements to resist petty human regulations, to treat with respect and care those Saint Paul calls "the weak" (roughly, those with scrupulous consciences), to refuse to accept the assertions of prophets without critical scrutiny, to bear in mind the victims of torture, to address and heal rifts within the church, and to rejoice. I conclude with an analysis of the wrongness of enslavement, seemingly taken for granted at multiple points in the New Testament.

Love Your Enemies

But I say to you, *Love your enemies and pray for those who persecute you*, so that you may be children of your Father in heaven; for he makes his sun rise on the evil and on the good, and sends rain on the righteous and on the unrighteous.[2]

We may reasonably suppose that the precepts now included in the Sermon on the Mount were "intended . . . [to guide] a collective posture at a particular time in history toward a particular state," so that Jesus's call to love enemies will in its initial context have served to urge his listeners to avoid violent resistance against Rome.[3] We should hesitate to detach many of Jesus's sayings from their very specific contexts. But it is difficult not to see the universal significance of this one.

I begin by considering the varieties of enemies before explaining the grounding a creational love ethic offers for love of enemies, given not only the significance of THE GOLDEN RULE but also the inherent moral problems with the ideas of retaliation, retribution, deterrence, and reprobation. These are especially important as theories of criminal punishment, of course, but my concern is hardly limited to our relationships with those enemies who violate the criminal law; rather, these rationales for criminal punishment are, at the same time, justifications for everything from interpersonal antagonism to violence in war, and I intend what I say to apply, with appropriate qualifications, to all of the arenas in which resentment and enmity might rear their heads. After discussing

2. Matt 5:44–5; my italics.
3. Borg, *Conflict* 245n15.

these defenses of hostility, I point out the importance of recognizing the special ties that may exist with enemies in particular before explaining why I think we should see forgiveness as nonoptional and how we might think about the idea of nonresistance to evil.

Varieties of Enemies

There are multiple kinds of enemies we need to love. There are (*a*) *deliberate* enemies, those who act out of hostility toward us (as particular persons or as members of one or more groups). There are (*b*) what we might call *dismissive* enemies, who have nothing in particular against us but who are willing to disregard our personhood—using violence, fraud, theft . . .—in pursuit of their goals. And there are (*c*) *competitors*, who don't hate us and who don't regard us as nonpersons (they may not even dislike us or know we exist) but by whom we may feel threatened because they are seeking the same jobs, customers, lovers, or prizes we are. Sometimes enemies are people we know and with whom we have other kinds of relationships, while sometimes they are strangers. But, in virtue of their attempted or actual impact on our lives, they are, even if strangers, not *merely* strangers. Our lives and theirs are connected in particular ways.

Why Love Enemies?

Love for enemies is, in part, simply an expression of love more generally. The temptation to dehumanize those who oppose us—to treat them as irredeemably evil, as contemptible, as occasions for the expression of wrath—can be hard to resist. But our enemies aren't any of these things. We love them, then, because being our enemies doesn't keep them from *also* being God's unique, irreplaceable creatures and so members of the moral community.

Because they are created persons, THE GOLDEN RULE applies to our interactions with them. If I would be unwilling to accept a standard allowing someone to disregard, subordinate, exclude, or demean me just because I was in conflict with that person, then it would be inconsistent with love for me to disregard, subordinate, exclude, or demean someone just because that person was in conflict with me. Similarly, whether or not I am in conflict with someone, I cannot rightly choose, disregarding love in the form of THE PAULINE PRINCIPLE, to injure that person as a way of discouraging her future bad behavior, balancing the imagined scales of justice, or prompting others not to emulate her choices. Despite our conflict, I can acknowledge and remind myself of her value by blessing her in my mind and in my words and choosing not to view her as a nonperson ripe for destruction.[4]

Rejecting Retaliation

One rationale for not loving our enemies holds that it's practically important that we retaliate against them: we should return evil for evil as a way of playing tit for tat, because doing so will reduce the likelihood of future evils. We play tit for tat when we exhibit a consistent willingness to respond in kind not only to benefits but also to injuries. Thus, one matches what the enemy does as a way of signaling that one will escalate one's attacks on the enemy's assets as the enemy escalates her attacks on one's own assets—and so, ideally, discouraging further escalation and potentially encouraging de-escalation and even peace.

It's pretty clear why we often feel satisfied when we retaliate. In some contexts, playing tit for tat will likely have conferred a survival advantage on our ancestors by discouraging human predators and noncooperators, who could count on costly responses when they behaved badly. Those with instinctive *dispositions* to play tit for tat probably behaved more reliably, more predictably, than those deciding what to do on a case-by-case basis. We're probably descended from people with those dispositions. Exhibiting the impulses we inherited from them, we often favor retaliatory responses immediately and unthinkingly.

However, choosing to cause injury to a basic aspect of well-being, directly or indirectly, as a means of achieving some good, including influence over the behavior of the person one is injuring (or someone else), violates THE PAULINE PRINCIPLE. That's true whether one attempts to harm someone's body, her friendships, her aesthetic experiences, or her participation in play. Causing injuries in many cases will also be inconsistent with love in the form of THE GOLDEN RULE just because we would often decline to endorse standards permitting injuries to ourselves or our loved ones in comparable cases. In addition, retaliation can prompt a spiral of counterattacks and vendettas, and the likelihood that it will do so can easily render it at odds with THE GOLDEN RULE.

Rejecting Retribution

Sometimes, we rationalize playing tit for tat by suggesting that, when seeking to injure enemies, we're effecting retribution, purportedly a way of doing justice.

4. Rom 12:14.

To engage in retribution is to impose an injury of some kind on someone who has chosen wrongly. We tell ourselves that, just as "one good turn deserves another,"[5] so one *bad* turn deserves another. We appeal to the supposed righteousness of retribution to justify petty personal paybacks, but retribution is also a profoundly influential basis for law and policy. Immanuel Kant demonstrated with unsettling clarity where a firm belief in retribution can lead when he argued that, "if a Civil Society resolved to dissolve itself with the consent of all its members . . . [,] the last Murderer lying in the prison ought to be executed before the resolution was carried out."[6]

Despite the instinctive appeal of retribution, however, an appeal likely rooted in the same soil as the desire to retaliate by playing tit for tat, it's pointless. An injury to you may yield some indirect benefit to me, but it doesn't *constitute* a benefit to me. An injury to you does not in and of itself amount in any way to an enhancement of any basic aspect of my well-being. But retribution involves, uncontroversially, imposing an injury on someone.

Sometimes, it may be consistent with love for me to perform an action that amounts simultaneously both to injuring a basic good and to protecting, respecting, realizing, or promoting such a good. However, if I injure someone while simultaneously seeking to realize, promote, respect, or protect a genuine good, I'm not engaging in retribution. Retribution necessarily involves deliberate action. When I engage in retribution, I take myself mistakenly to be realizing an authentic good: the same act that injures you is also supposed to *constitute* doing what justice demands. Retribution doesn't enact a genuine good, however.

Consider the basic aspects of well-being—aesthetic experience, avoidance of physical pain, friendship, harmony with reality, imaginative immersion, knowledge, life, play, practical wisdom, self-integration, sensory pleasure, and skillful performance—in turn, if you like. It will be apparent that there is no basic good, no basic aspect of well-being, that retribution in fact realizes—not for victims, not for perpetrators, not for those who punish. However, an action is consistent with love only if, *per* RECOGNITION, it is undertaken to realize, respect, promote, or protect some basic good. Because retribution is undertaken to realize a putative good and because there is no good that retribution in fact realizes, imposing retribution is inconsistent with RECOGNITION.

Perhaps we find retribution attractive in part not only because it taps into the instinct to play tit for tat but also because of its superficial resemblance

---

5. Finnis, *Aquinas* 140.
6. Immanuel Kant, *The Philosophy of Law*, trans. William Hastie (Edinburgh: Clark 1887) 198.

to restitution. Suppose I injure you and then, voluntarily or as a result of the operation of the legal system, provide you with restitution. Perhaps I offer you enough to, say, repair the injury, cover your reasonable costs of recovering the debt I've come to owe by injuring you, and compensate you for not having had the resources or opportunities my injury took from you. As measured from the baseline after the injury's occurrence, you benefit, while I am, at least financially, worse off (though I also benefit by acting in a morally appropriate way as I take responsibility for my injurious behavior). You're better off because, having transferred resources to you to make you whole after wrongfully injuring you, I'm financially worse off.

Retribution superficially mimics restitution. If I injure you and am subjected to retributive punishment as a result, I am in some respect worse off. So it can seem as if I have paid a debt. But, unlike restitution, retribution makes victims no better off. My being (say) imprisoned, fined, executed, maimed, publicly humiliated, or the like because I've injured you constitutes no benefit to you and confers no benefit on you.

You may be pleased, satisfied, gratified as a result. But feelings of satisfaction are of no inherent value *on their own*. They matter, if they do, because they signal the awareness that something worthwhile has occurred—if your emotions are functioning well, something that's valuable because it's beneficial to you or to another sentient. If I feel satisfied when there's nothing worth being satisfied *by*, that's just reason to think that my psyche isn't in altogether good working order. If there's good independent reason to think that the occurrence of retribution is worthwhile, your being satisfied when it happens makes perfect sense. But whether it *is* worthwhile depends on whether it does, in fact, confer or constitute a benefit. Your feeling satisfied when it takes place doesn't necessarily mean that it has conferred or constituted a benefit.

Someone might suggest that a person imposing retributive punishment benefits because she is doing justice or that the person undergoing retributive punishment benefits because she submits to and accepts the demands of justice. But this would be the case only if retribution *were* demanded by justice. An action is an instance of fairness (or of loving action more generally) only if it confers or constitutes a benefit. Otherwise, it's pointless. Whether the action is in fact fair depends on whether it confers or constitutes a benefit in a manner consistent with THE GOLDEN RULE. There is no way to assess the consistency of the action with THE GOLDEN RULE without specifying the benefit or benefits conferred or constituted by the action. So, if imposing retribution doesn't confer or constitute a benefit, it doesn't qualify as fair. It makes no sense to say that the performance of the action *itself* constitutes or confers a benefit just because performing the action is nonarbitrary. I might impose retributive punishment consistently on others and be willing myself to be retributively punished. But my behavior and attitude don't tell us whether what I'm doing is actually beneficial to anyone and therefore consistent with love.

My choice to treat someone in a given way in particular circumstances is consistent with THE GOLDEN RULE only if I would be willing to accept a generic standard that allowed me or my loved ones to be treated in the same way in comparable circumstances. Many people, aware of the pointlessness of retribution, might not be willing to accept a standard permitting them or their loved ones to be subjected to retributive punishment. They, therefore, would act contrary to love by subjecting anyone else to this kind of punishment.

Saint Paul may well be reflecting on and seeking to elaborate Jesus's call to love enemies when he writes:

> Do not repay anyone evil for evil, but take thought for what is noble in the sight of all. If it is possible, so far as it depends on you, live peaceably with all. Beloved, never avenge yourselves, but leave room for the wrath of God; for it is written, "Vengeance is mine, I will repay, says the Lord." No, "if your enemies are hungry, feed them; if they are thirsty, give them something to drink; for by doing this you will heap burning coals on their heads." Do not be overcome by evil, but overcome evil with good.[7]

Saint Paul's attribution of vengefulness to God is, among other things, hard to square with Jesus's injunction to love enemies and with a plausible understanding of the merits of retribution. Retribution is irrational in all cases, without exception. So it never makes sense to repay evil for evil, to avenge oneself (or anyone else). And this would be true of retribution effected by divine action just as of retribution effected by creaturely action. But the central point of the passage, to encourage forgiveness and discourage retribution, seems thoroughly consonant with what Jesus is remembered as saying.[8] Abjuring retribution is part of the minimum content of love.

---

7. Rom 12:17–21; cp. 1 Thess 5:15; 1 Pet 3:9.
8. Saint Paul might be read as having retaliation rather than retribution in mind, but presumably, he takes God to be engaged in retribution, not retaliation, and if the divine action he envisions is supposed to be a substitute for human action, this might suggest that he envisions the human action as retributive.

Rejecting Deterrence

People also sometimes justify attacking enemies as an exercise in general deterrence: injuring one person (or more) who's behaved in a given way to discourage others (and sometimes also the injured person) from behaving in the same way. This might be true for an individual who chooses to "make an example" of someone to discourage others from challenging her authority. But perhaps the most obvious example of a direct attack on a basic aspect of well-being for deterrent purposes is capital punishment, the practice of killing people—attacking the good of life and bodily well-being—in the hope that doing so will prompt others to avoid behavior likely to lead to their own deaths. But, like retribution, deterrence can involve attacks on other basic goods.

If a court enacts an order precluding contact between two friends, for instance, in order to deter others from engaging in bad behavior of the sort to which it believes the example afforded by the relationship encourages, the court's purpose seems (we might conclude otherwise in a particular instance) to attack the relationship itself. Because friendship is a basic aspect of well-being, an attack for this purpose, an action with this structure, would violate THE PAULINE PRINCIPLE and would thus be wrong in all cases.

Attacking or being willing to attack people's bodies is also an aspect of another sort of deterrent punishment: incarceration. It's not possible to incarcerate people or to keep them incarcerated without engaging or threatening to engage in physical violence; the willingness to engage in the varieties of physical violence needed to keep prisoners submissive and to prevent them from escaping is integral to the practice of deterrent incarceration. But using force against someone's body to incarcerate or to continue incarcerating that person is not a matter of protecting anyone from that person's unjust use of force. Rather, force is used in the context of deterrent incarceration to keep people from evading the losses associated with confinement as a way, in turn, of discouraging others from behaving in ways that might result in *their* being confined.[9] Force is being used—a basic aspect of welfare is being attacked, in other words—to make it possible for confined people to continue serving as examples to others. Using force to maintain deterrent incarceration thus seems inconsistent with love in the form of THE PAULINE PRINCIPLE. And people would often not be willing to accept standards in virtue of which they or their loved ones could be

---

9. The hope is presumably also that confined people themselves will choose to avoid behaving in ways that might lead to further confinement.

incarcerated to serve as examples to others—potentially at all and certainly not given the conditions of many contemporary prisons. Their support for or implementation of policies of deterrent incarceration would thus often fly in the face of love in the form of THE GOLDEN RULE.

Deterrence can also involve interference with people's possessions. Possessions are not basic aspects of well-being, nor is the possessory relationship, so interfering with someone's possessions would not normally be a violation of THE PAULINE PRINCIPLE. In some cases, however, it might be. These would be cases in which someone interferes with another's possessions *for the purpose* of impeding her participation in one or more basic aspects of well-being. Someone might do this to assert herself, establish dominance, and so forth. But, more to the immediate point, she might also do this in order to influence the victim's behavior or the choices of others aware of what has happened to the victim.

Suppose, for instance, that I want to discourage you from publishing editorials critical of my business practices, so I steal from you money that I know you need in order to make an immediate purchase of a vital medicine, thus causing you to be hospitalized. I let you know that you can count on me to keep impeding your access to this medicine if you continue to publish critical editorials. My action interferes with your possessions and thus violates THE GOLDEN RULE. At the same time, I act in order to bring about injury to your physical well-being, and in so doing, I violate THE PAULINE PRINCIPLE.

Deterrent interference with someone's possessions that doesn't involve the choice to injure a basic aspect of her well-being isn't precluded by love in the form of THE PAULINE PRINCIPLE. However, it would seem to be in tension with love in the form of THE GOLDEN RULE in at least two ways.

Most importantly, punishing someone by taking her possessions for deterrent purposes involves using someone as a means, injuring that person in order to influence the behavior of others, for which she isn't in any straightforward sense responsible. They're free persons, not under her control, so she's not responsible for their actions. In addition, even her indirect influence—which may be morally problematic but shouldn't render her legally responsible—is likely to be limited insofar as others are unaware of whatever she's done to trigger the deprivation of her possessions or of the deprivation itself. If I wouldn't be willing to accept a standard that allowed me to be punished as an example to others, that allowed the punishment of my loved ones for exemplary purposes—and I suspect most of us wouldn't—then I'm ignoring THE GOLDEN RULE by subjecting someone else to deterrent punishment.

Depriving someone of her possessions for deterrent purposes also appears to be inconsistent with the baseline possessory rules, rooted in THE GOLDEN RULE. It's not consensual, so it isn't warranted by VOLUNTARY TRANSFER. But it's also not warranted by REMEDIAL TRANSFER, since it involves the nonconsensual deprivation of possessions that's not intended to provide a remedy for someone's imposition of an injury on someone else.

It's perfectly consistent with love to be glad when bad behavior is deterred; gladness in this case is, indeed, likely to be expressive of love. But causing, facilitating, or threatening injury to a basic aspect of well-being *for the purpose* of deterring behavior one doesn't like is inconsistent with love, just like retribution and retaliation. And interfering with someone's possessions for deterrent purposes seems at least often to be inconsistent with THE GOLDEN RULE. In addition, one might think that what are nominally exercises in deterrent punishment might in fact be engaged in or encouraged because they satisfy the pointless desire for retribution or retaliation. Participating in or otherwise furthering deterrent punishment for this reason is inconsistent with love even if there's no way for anyone else to be sure about one's underlying motive.[10]

Rejecting Reprobation

Loving enemies, as I've observed, is important in a wide range of contexts. I don't mean by devoting so much attention to grounds for criminal punishment to suggest that Jesus's call to love enemies is salient only in connection with the criminal law. However, criminals are often among those actual or potential enemies subjected to the most brutal treatment, and formal defenses of criminal punishment often track the moral rationales people offer for their treatment of enemies in other contexts.

A final defense I want to consider is what is sometimes called "reprobative" punishment.[11] For the advocates of reprobation, punishment is justified because of its symbolic meaning, because it serves to communicate unequivocal rejection, on moral grounds, of someone's bad behavior.[12] Punishment imposed

10. My own view is that all varieties of deterrent interference with people's possessions should be avoided. It is possible, however, that the arguments I've given will turn out not to be decisive in all cases and that some varieties of this kind of interference will in some instances be compatible with love, and so with loving one's enemies.

11. Wolterstorff, *Justice in Love* 193–8, drawing on Joel Feinberg, *Doing and Deserving* (Princeton, NJ: Princeton University Press 1970) 95–118.

12. Wolterstorff, *Justice in Love* 195, citing Feinberg, *Doing and Deserving* 98.

in accordance with the criminal law can serve a reprobative function because "hard treatment has gotten connected with a judgment of moral disapproval of deed and doer."[13] "Certain forms of hard treatment have become the conventional symbols of public reprobation."[14] We should see reprobation thus understood as "an intrinsic good in the life of punisher and wrongdoer and an important instrumental good for society in general, perhaps also for the wrongdoer."[15]

It's not obvious why we should regard reprobation in this sense as important in its own right, as a suitable justification for anything like the contemporary practice of criminal punishment. Communicating the truth fosters the good of knowledge, but we don't work hard to communicate all truths. Sending a message of condemnation certainly matters if it delegitimizes bad behavior and encourages changed attitudes. If it doesn't have these effects, it might well enjoy a lower priority, especially given that most people probably understand already that unquestioned cases of serious wrongdoing are not condoned by either individual people or the legal system.

I am doubtful, too, whether the social function of punitive acts really is primarily reprobative at present. I suspect that various criminal penalties, in particular, communicate moral rejection, if they do, only because they are *also* and primarily taken to effect retribution, and perhaps also deterrence and restraint. Even if "punishment conveys to those who have ears to hear that society does not condone what was done," we might reasonably wonder why various sorts of public announcements highlighting deep moral disapproval of someone's behavior might not convey noncondonation with more-than-adequate clarity and specificity.[16] The response that the disapproval would not seem or be serious enough without attacking or threatening the bodies and inhibiting the autonomy of those whose behavior is the occasion of disapproval seems, again, to presuppose the value of something like retribution. In this case, reprobation doesn't provide an independent justification for harming enemies; and, when reprobative acts are performed for retributive purposes, they are inconsistent with love for the reasons retributive acts generally are inconsistent with love.

---

13. Wolterstorff, *Justice in Love* 196; he adds "and with feelings of indignation, resentment, and anger," but considering the role of these feelings would unnecessarily complicate the discussion of reprobative punishment here, I think.

14. Feinberg, *Doing and Deserving* 100, qtd. Wolterstorff, *Justice in Love* 196.

15. Wolterstorff, *Justice in Love* 197.

16. Wolterstorff 197.

What about the possibility that reprobative punishment could be intrinsically worthwhile for the punisher and the wrongdoer?[17] If, even as it injured, an act of punishment were at the same time an inherently beneficial act, performing it would jibe with THE PAULINE PRINCIPLE, though, of course, doing so might still clash with THE GOLDEN RULE. Someone might well recognize that the putative goal of reprobation, conveying noncondonation, could be achieved clearly in some way less injurious than any of the standard criminal punishments. And this might mean, given THE GOLDEN RULE, that her imposition of any of those punishments was inconsistent with love.

It's not clear, in any case, that reprobative punishment *could* be an intrinsic good. Reprobative punishment is most naturally understood as communicative: it's not simply about venting but about conveying a *message* to an audience. An act performed without anyone's knowledge couldn't be an instance of reprobative punishment because this kind of punishment essentially involves communication, and communication occurs only when a message is received. Reprobation's goal is that the wrongdoer, at minimum, receives the message, that she comes to know what the act of reprobative punishment seeks to communicate. Unless she does come to know this, the putative value of reprobative punishment for the wrongdoer and the punisher alike isn't realized (the punisher's message hasn't been *heard*). But this means that reprobative punishment involves performing some act (or set of acts) *in order* to communicate a message. Performing this act just is *sending* the message, but sending the message isn't the purpose of the act. The purpose of the act, the goal of sending the message, is to bring about the *reception* of the message, to effect deepened understanding and awareness of the message on the part of the wrongdoer and perhaps others. Reprobative punishment involves injuring the wrongdoer in order to achieve a goal distinct from the act of sending the communication. And this means that, if the imposition of reprobative punishment involves injuring any basic good, it's inconsistent with THE PAULINE PRINCIPLE.

Certainly, when imposing a penalty reprobatively involves injuring an aspect of someone's well-being as a way of communicating a message to people other than the wrongdoer, as in the case of doing so in order to bring about "an important instrumental good for society," imposing that penalty is inconsistent with love in the form of THE PAULINE PRINCIPLE. Using force against someone's body for the purpose of corralling her *so that* a reprobative penalty can be imposed on her is, again, inconsistent with THE PAULINE PRINCIPLE, even if the penalty to

17. Wolterstorff 197.

be imposed is itself an intrinsic good. And depriving someone of justly acquired possessions to express condemnation of her behavior will often be inconsistent with THE GOLDEN RULE and will always be inconsistent with REMEDIAL CONVEYANCE, derived from THE GOLDEN RULE.

Reprobation is most obviously a rationale for harming enemies in the course of criminal punishment. But it might also seem to provide a warrant for the infliction of injuries by private persons. One might publicly dissociate oneself from a friend, for instance, on the basis that doing so was a way of communicating one's moral disapproval of her conduct. However, to attack the basic good of friendship in order to communicate a message would be to flout love in the form of THE PAULINE PRINCIPLE. (It may be perfectly consistent with love to distance oneself from a friend as a matter of self-protection, but to do so would not be a way of engaging in reprobation.) Purposeful injuries to basic aspects of others' well-being for reprobative purposes will clash with THE PAULINE PRINCIPLE even when they're nonviolent. And private reprobation will also not infrequently fly in the face of THE GOLDEN RULE: announcing one's moral condemnation may help one to feel smugly self-righteous, but it is unlikely to be an effective way of improving someone's behavior or character. Humbly and quietly confronting someone with the way in which her behavior has been harmful may be constructive, but public condemnation seems more likely to provoke resistance.

Special Ties with Enemies

Love for enemies matters not only because of the fact that they are irreplaceably valuable, and so entitled just as persons to a kind of moral respect we may be disinclined to show them, but also because in some cases, we participate in special relationships with them. They may *be* enemies precisely *because* of ruptures in what once were close relationships. Even if that's not the case, we may have special needs for reconciliation with them if we have treated them wrongly. We may also have special needs for reconciliation because we have, ironically, *established* special relationships with them just in the course of our ongoing enmity with them. And, even if we have not, we may have special needs and opportunities for healing where they are concerned just as they may have where we're concerned. Love for enemies, in particular, matters because of our special ties with them.

Forgiveness

Jesus pronounces God's blessing on the merciful.[18] And a crucial aspect of mercy is forgiveness. Forgiveness should be appealing because of its healing impact on the forgiver and forgiven alike: it releases the forgiving person's tight grip on the toxicity of resentment while helping to free the forgiven person from self-recrimination and, perhaps, social ostracism and at least potentially to free both from alienation from each other. But its healing potential is not the only or, indeed, the fundamental reason to embrace it. Forgiveness is not optional. It is not supererogatory. It is morally required in the precise sense that it involves giving up the will to retaliate or to engage in retributive or deterrent punishment.[19] Since retaliation, retribution, and deterrence are never consistent with love, the will to engage in these activities can never be appropriate. Forgiveness is an antidote to punitive impulses that we shouldn't embrace.

It's important to see that this *doesn't* mean any of several other things. While it is inconsistent with love not to forgive, we can still make prudential judgments about whether it is reasonable to seek *reconciliation* with someone one's relationship with whom has undergone a rupture. We should not resist reconciliation just because we have been injured. And we should recognize, with Saint Paul in Romans 12, that spirals of hostility and retaliation can be interrupted when someone stops playing tit for tat and reaches out to connect with an adversary in a new way. After all, our putative foes are irreplaceable and valuable just as we are. It also makes sense because we and they will benefit from the end of hostilities and the establishment of cooperative or, at least, nonconflictual relationships.

At the same time, an unqualified requirement of reconciliation does not flow from THE GOLDEN RULE. Sometimes it will be consistent with this requirement of fairness simply to embrace priorities other than reconciliation. Sometimes it will be fair not to attempt to heal a relationship with an enemy because of the low probability of success, though someone might nonetheless

---

18. Matt 5:9; cp. Col 3:13.

19. For Wolterstorff (*Justice in Love* 53–5; and he is hardly unique in this respect), we can only forgive by giving up "corrective rights," so there can be no entitlement to forgiveness. My own view is that there is a right not to be subjected to retributive or reprobative punishment or to retaliation, and at least in many cases (perhaps all) not to be subjected to deterrent punishment. It will often, however, be the case that one has no right to be trusted, to be welcomed into fellowship, to not be restrained if one is dangerous, or to avoid compensating someone one has injured.

quite reasonably seek to heal it.[20] And sometimes it will be fair not to attempt to heal a relationship with an enemy because engaging with the enemy is thoroughly dangerous to oneself or others (as, say, when people are on opposite sides of an armed conflict).

Forgiveness is distinct not only from reconciliation but also from *trust*. I can forgive you for embezzlement without taking my act of forgiveness to commit me to hiring you as my company's treasurer. Trust is a distinct issue that requires fact-sensitive judgments about what to expect from another. Taking a risk, giving someone a chance, when doing so might foster renewed self-respect and thus healing and spiritual growth can be a choice entirely consistent with love; perhaps in some cases, *not* doing this might even be incongruent with THE GOLDEN RULE. But whether reposing confidence in someone who has previously behaved in an untrustworthy manner is permissible or required can be determined only in light of what one actually knows about the person's character and circumstances.

We can never be certain how someone will behave, both because people are free and might thus make quite different choices than they've made in the past and because the factors that incline people to behave in particular ways and the impacts of these factors will often be unclear. There will always be some degree of risk involved, then, in trusting someone who has already demonstrated the capacity to choose disappointingly. But we can still make good judgments as we look at the facts and discuss them with others. To do so, we must be willing to trust in the face of punitive impulses and instinctive and fearful reactions. And we need to recognize that we ourselves would want to be given the benefit of the doubt so that, when there is substantial and genuine uncertainty (which there won't always be), we have good reason (when doing so doesn't pose risks to others that are inconsistent with love in the form of THE GOLDEN RULE) to take the risk of trust.

Just how much risk it might be appropriate to shoulder vis-à-vis a given person will depend in significant part on one's promises and comparable undertakings to that person and others who might be affected and one's commitments with respect to one's relationship with her and with respect to other relevant relationships. But THE GOLDEN RULE will be salient even in the absence of special obligations to or with respect to a given person. That's because risk-laden reconciliation and trust may have the potential to play valuable roles in healing

20. For a remarkable example, see Kathryn Watterson, *Not by the Sword: How a Cantor and His Family Transformed a Klansman* (Lincoln, NE: Bison 2012).

broken people and equipping them to move forward as responsible, reliable moral agents. So it will be important to consider one's potential to offer healing by engaging in reconciliation and trust. It will also be important to query oneself about any resistance one might feel in a given case, asking in particular whether it might have more to do with a desire to punish or with unnecessarily replayed memories of past harm than with actual ongoing threats.

Forgiving someone is also distinct from *abjuring restitution*. To forgive you for embezzlement doesn't mean ignoring the fact that you should return the money you've stolen, along with the reasonably incurred costs of recovering it. The point of asking for restitution isn't to punish the embezzler but to make her victim or victims whole. In addition, proffering restitution can be a morally and spiritually healing act for someone who's injured another.

Resistance to Evil

Not resisting evil—that is, declining to respond with force when someone unjustly interferes or threatens to interfere with one's own body or possessions or the bodies or possessions of others—has formed a central element of highly visible strands of Christian practice, notably those associated with the Radical Reformation. It has served as a powerful witness to the moral standing and precious irreplaceability of even those we think of as enemies and of the value of imagining alternatives to the use of force.

I would not be willing for one of my loved ones, even if acting unjustly, to be injured in the course of a just defense if her wrongful attack *could* have been repelled in a way that didn't injure her. So it would not be consistent with love for me to resist aggression forcibly when I could have done so nonviolently. More than that, if I expect to encounter such violence, it would be inconsistent with THE GOLDEN RULE not to reflect in advance, if I'm able to do so, on the ways in which I might be able to resist effectively without the use of force. Creative nonviolence can be a crucial expression of love.

Love for enemies is an essential element of a creational love ethic, as is thinking creatively about ways to avoid injuring others' well-being. But that doesn't mean that forcible resistance is inconsistent with love. Force that aims not at destroying the aggressor but only at stopping the aggressor's unjust violence and that does not injure the aggressor or anyone else unfairly can be perfectly compatible with the love embodied in THE GOLDEN RULE and THE PAULINE PRINCIPLE. And, indeed, when it *is* compatible, love for some of those whom I am responsible for protecting—because of promises or commitments or because failing to protect them would be inconsistent with THE GOLDEN RULE—may *require* the use of force. It may, that is, in a given case be inconsistent with THE GOLDEN RULE for me to *decline* to respond forcibly to violence in a manner consistent with THE PAULINE PRINCIPLE.

Jesus's injunction "Do not resist an evildoer" has provided the basis for much Christian nonresistance.[21] Presuming it has been accurately recorded, it may be seen as calling his hearers to avoid participating in the self-righteous, destructive, and ultimately futile project of violent rebellion against Rome, and so against the naïve or idolatrous identification of the human project of reestablishing the political independence of Israel as God's project,[22] rather than as abstractly precluding the use of defensive force.[23] At least as collected in Matthew 5, this injunction immediately follows Jesus's rejection of "an eye for an eye and a tooth for a tooth."[24] In this context, it is plausibly seen as a rejection of the ethics of retaliation, retribution, and deterrence, which I have already suggested should be understood as deeply problematic. Jesus can be understood here as "contrast[ing] his ethic of love with the reciprocity code" calling, in effect, for one form or another of tit for tat.[25] In Matthew's Sermon on the Mount, Jesus is articulating "vivid metaphorical and hyperbolic repudiations of the negative side of the reciprocity code and injunctions to put in its place the ethic of love."[26]

One reason to think that Jesus did have a more focused meaning in mind is provided by Luke 22:

21. Matt 5:39.

22. Cp. Oscar Cullmann, *The State in the New Testament* (New York: Scribner 1956) 20, 24. Cullmann proposes that Jesus's suggestion that the two swords possessed by the disciples are sufficient to be taken as a comment on the option of violent rebellion against Rome (33–4); while defensive weapons might be appropriate, the disciples should not aspire to be, should not become, and should not be mistaken for a fighting force.

23. N. T. Wright, *Jesus and the Victory of God* (Minneapolis: Fortress 1996), sees the rejection of resistance in Matt 5:39 as a rejection of "revolutionary resistance," "violent resistance." But he also assumes that the same injunction "would apply to local village disputes" (291); it is not clear that we know enough to affirm this point with any confidence. Wright notes Richard A. Horsley's opposition to this interpretation on the view that accepting it would undermine support for contemporary revolts against unjust regimes (290). But this conclusion would follow only if the injunction not to resist were taken to be a universal law rather than a tactical response to the actual circumstances of first-century Palestine.

24. Matt 5:38. The original function of this rule seems likely to have been to place an upper limit on the destructive practice of retaliation, not to legitimate it.

25. Wolterstorff, *Justice in Love* 121.

26. Wolterstorff 124.

He said to them, "When I sent you out without a purse, bag, or sandals, did you lack anything?" They said, "No, not a thing." He said to them, "But now, the one who has a purse must take it, and likewise a bag. And the one who has no sword must sell his cloak and buy one. For I tell you, this scripture must be fulfilled in me, 'And he was counted among the lawless'; and indeed what is written about me is being fulfilled." They said, "Lord, look, here are two swords." He replied, "It is enough."[27]

We cannot be certain of Jesus's intention here, but the preservation of this saying with no apparent qualification suggests that the first-century church did not read Jesus as mandating nonviolence in all circumstances.

Particularly if the book comes from the first century, perhaps before the destruction of Jerusalem,[28] it is noteworthy that the *Didache*—sharing as it does a thought-world and, perhaps, provenance with Matthew—repeats the injunction to turn the other cheek (which it identifies as a path to perfection)[29] but makes no reference to nonresistance. One might take this as evidence that first-century Christians didn't consistently understand Jesus as having issued a general mandate opposing resistance to evil.

Acknowledging the incompatibility of nonresistance (which he takes to be binding on all Christians) with responsibility for civic order, John Howard Yoder regards it as essential to "distinguish between the ethics of discipleship which are laid on every Christian believer by virtue of his very confession of faith, and an ethic of justice within the limits of relative prudence and self-preservation, which is all one can ask of the larger society."[30] But to adhere to THE GOLDEN RULE is precisely to take love seriously. It is not to abandon faithful love in favor of "prudence and self-preservation" (though these are themselves aspects of love). And THE GOLDEN RULE may sometimes not only permit but, indeed, require the use of force.

---

27. Luke 22:35–8; cp. Cullmann, *State in the New Testament* 31–4 (Cullmann believes Jesus rejects participation in revolution unequivocally).

28. See Thomas O'Loughlin, *The* Didache*: A Window on the Earliest Christians* (London: SPCK 2010) 25–7.

29. *Didache* 1:10, *Ante-Nicene Fathers* 7. The *Didache*'s first chapter contains multiple references to or echoes of the Sermon on the Mount but not to the injunction to avoid resistance.

30. John Howard Yoder, *The Christian Witness to the State*, 2d ed. (Scottdale, PA: Herald 2002) locs. 503–6 of 2008 (ch. 3, part B), Kindle.

Because God is Creator, because the *Logos* is the light that enlightens everyone, it will not do to maintain "that Christian ethics is for Christians."[31] If nonviolence were (as I believe it is not) morally required of all people, it would be required in virtue of the kinds of creatures we are, the kind of world God has made, the kind of order the *Logos* shapes and structures, the kinds of insights the *Logos* reveals. Embracing it would need to be consistent with THE GOLDEN RULE.

Advocating nonviolence as a duty, Yoder argues that "the axiom *I am Everyman* . . . must be denied *when* it operates to determine the way in which the sons and daughters of the Kingdom participate in the world of nations."[32] Presumably, Yoder wouldn't want to suggest that THE GOLDEN RULE isn't significant for Christian ethics. But if it is this specification of love in virtue of which we are permitted or required to use force to defend others, we're not, in using force in this way, importing some alien element into Christian ethics. Instead, we're drawing on a central constituent of Christian ethics—a way of making moral judgments actively encouraged by Jesus.[33]

Blessed Are the Peacemakers

Blessed are the peacemakers, for they will be called children of God.[34]

Peace is a crucial enabler of love, peacemaking a vital expression of love. Both are thus important concerns of a creational love ethic.

A general moral requirement to practice peace can be seen as rooted in the specifications of love. Love places substantial limits on the use of force, as I've already noted, with THE PAULINE PRINCIPLE ruling out the instrumental use of force against sentients' bodies and THE GOLDEN RULE further limiting foreseen but unintended forcible injuries. In addition, THE GOLDEN RULE provides a further reason to affirm the practice of peace. Force constrains people's choices; and, since most of us would prefer ordinarily that our exercise of our own autonomy not be limited, we would likely not accept standards that would allow widespread forcible interference with our choices. It would thus

31. Yoder loc. 661 of 2008 (ch. 4, part A).
32. John Howard Yoder, *The Priestly Kingdom: Social Ethics as Gospel* (Notre Dame, IN: University of Notre Dame Press 1985) 162.
33. In emphasizing love's role here, I happily acknowledge my dependence on Paul Ramsey's work.
34. Matt 5:9.

be inconsistent with love for us to accept standards permitting widespread forcible interference with others' autonomy, and therefore standards permitting the widespread disruption of peace through such interference.

More broadly still, peace makes possible voluntary cooperation, including the extended, voluntary social cooperation among strangers that enables the production and distribution of goods and services that enhance people's lives in innumerable ways. Peace also allows people to engage in social experiments of diverse kinds. These experiments often benefit those who engage in them, enabling them to make discoveries about fruitful and not-so-fruitful approaches to human existence. At the same time, however, they also benefit others, people who do not engage in them but who observe those who do, learning at a distance about the merits of ways of being human.

In short, peacemakers are blessed, not least because peace helps others to flourish by fostering the conditions that make for personal safety, social cooperation, experimentation, and personal choice.

Do Not Insult

If you insult a brother or sister, you will be liable to the council; and if you say, "You fool," you will be liable to the hell of fire.[35]

An insult can be troubling for more than one reason. (*i*) It can amount to a threat, making clear that the person who has uttered it regards one with contempt and can be expected to act accordingly. (*ii*) If it's uttered by a person one otherwise thought was a friend or ally, or even simply neutral, it can signal a rupture—a person one expected to be able to count on is now an adversary—or make clear, disturbingly, that one was mistaken in the first place in believing that one could trust the person pronouncing it.

The first two troubling aspects of an insult's significance have to do with the information it conveys. There are also ways in which the *consequences* of an insult can be problematic.

(*iii*) When delivered publicly, it can encourage others to look at one in a new and contemptuous way. Suppose I'm aware that someone has pronounced an insult directed at me. In this case, it might make sense for me to worry that, influenced by that person's evident attitude, others will come to view me more

---

35. Matt 5:22; cp. Col 3:8.

disdainfully than they otherwise would have. And I might fear that, as a result, they might prove more inclined to subordinate or exclude me than they otherwise would have been.

(*iv*) Perhaps most insidiously, an insult can threaten one's own self-understanding. Hearing or reading the insult, knowing that someone else regards one as meriting the insult, imagining others hearing the insult and reflecting their own embrace of the attitude it embodies in their behavior, can lead one to reassess oneself. Taking an insult to heart or even simply *fearing* that it might embody an apt understanding of who one truly is can result in a loss of self-confidence and prompt one to view and treat oneself as detestable.

Given these negative consequences, one would not ordinarily be willing to be insulted or willing that one's loved ones be insulted. Uttering an insult is thus typically a violation of THE GOLDEN RULE. To voice an insult *for the purpose* of undermining another's psychic health, capacity for judgment, or relationships, or other aspects of her well-being—to establish dominance, to make oneself appealing to others, to reinforce bigoted attitudes toward a group to which the victim belongs . . .—is, further, at odds with love in the form of THE PAULINE PRINCIPLE.

Expressing the insult will also be wrong if it conveys false information—empirical or normative—as true. If, for instance, I tell you explicitly that you are contemptible or if I say something to you that makes sense only on the presupposition that you are contemptible, I am lying: you are not contemptible—you are an irreplaceably valuable creature of God. As I've already noted, making a knowingly false assertion is, as an ordinary matter and certainly in this case, inconsistent with THE PAULINE PRINCIPLE and THE GOLDEN RULE alike.

One sometimes says things others don't want to hear, things that may in fact undermine their confidence and change their perceptions of themselves. If I make clear to a hockey player that I can no longer employ her as a member of my team because of her performance on the rink, I am trying to contribute to her own self-understanding and to treat her with respect by refusing to manipulate her with sweet falsehoods. I can tell an actor that his portrayal of Langston Hughes has entirely failed to capture the poet's charisma without trying to attack his self-confidence; my goal can be, rather, to give him information he can use to make better decisions. In instances like these, my purpose can be to foster various basic goods; the potential harms resulting from what I say are unintentional, even if I anticipate them, so my saying what I do is consistent with THE PAULINE PRINCIPLE. And, presuming I would be willing for someone to tell me or a loved one these truths in relevantly similar circumstances, it's consistent with love for me to do so here. (It may even be unavoidable, either because to say anything else in these circumstances would violate THE PAULINE PRINCIPLE or because it would be unfair, inconsistent with THE GOLDEN RULE, to avoid communicating clearly about them.)

But cases like these require careful analysis precisely because what we say *can* be insulting. It's important to recognize this and to avoid speaking in a manner that's inconsistent with love.

Do Not Judge

Do not judge, so that you may not be judged. For with the judgment you make you will be judged, and the measure you give will be the measure you get. Why do you see the speck in your neighbor's eye, but do not notice the log in your own eye? Or how can you say to your neighbor, "Let me take the speck out of your eye," while the log is in your own eye? You hypocrite, first take the log out of your own eye, and then you will see clearly to take the speck out of your neighbor's eye.[36]

We can love by saying "No!" to judgment. To judge in the context of the Sermon on the Mount is, I take it, to confront someone with a negative evaluation—in effect, to criticize. "Experience has shown that the only predictable result of criticism is the weakening of trust in human relationships."[37] A criticism may be considerably less dismissive than an insult. But the reasons to avoid confronting people with criticisms are similar to the reasons it's important to avoid insulting them. Judgment can threaten, signal, and (when done within the hearing of others) encourage dismissiveness; undermine confidence; and prompt inaccurate self-understanding. But criticism can be more insidious because it's often cast as positive, as helpful.[38]

Criticism is often inconsistent with THE GOLDEN RULE. If you want to know whether the kind of assessment you have in mind counts as the sort of judgment challenged in Matthew 7, consider the messages it might convey and the consequences it might yield in light of this specification of love. And, with THE PAULINE

---

36. Matt 7:1–5; cp. Rom 14:10–3.
37. Thomas W. McKnight and Robert H. Phillips, *Love Tactics: How to Win the One You Want* (Garden City Park, NY: Square One 2002) 89.
38. Cp. McKnight and Phillips 89–91.

PRINCIPLE as well as THE GOLDEN RULE in view, ask yourself about the truth of the assessment and your actual purpose for voicing it.

Jesus's words imply that the person offering criticism will characteristically assume that she is superior to the person she is criticizing. These words prompt us to ask ourselves about our own limitations, to ask ourselves whether we're as good or as competent as we might suppose. Reflecting on these things is a way of increasing our knowledge. It's also a way of enhancing our practical wisdom, since it enables us to make better decisions. I never have to seek every possible good. Indeed, I shouldn't do so, since I won't be able to participate deeply in any if I seek all. But, if I avoid the kind of self-scrutiny Jesus encourages for the purpose of keeping my illusions in place, I'm acting against my own flourishing (at least against the good of knowledge) and thus violating THE PAULINE PRINCIPLE.

What Jesus says also suggests an additional kind of reason to avoid criticism: it often serves to support inaccurate self-perception on the part of the one offering it. If I'm able to criticize your performance, that means I'm an expert who knows or can do more than you know or can do. I can reassure myself of this, I can try to persuade observers of my superiority, and I can hope you will submit to me as a result of my superior knowledge or skill. If I'm able to criticize not your technical skill or intellectual ability but, instead, your moral performance, even better: I may feel morally inadequate, but I can assure myself that at least I'm more virtuous than you are, and I can signal my virtue to others, too, by acting as a member of the morals police.

Propping up my sense of competence or moral superiority can be a satisfying aspect of criticizing you. Sometimes, I'll be mistaken in my criticism—as regards your performance or the norm I invoke to assail it. And I'll characteristically be fostering a false sense of moral superiority when I criticize in order to shore up my moral smugness. But, even when I'm not, the very fact of criticizing for the purpose of reinforcing my self-righteousness is a moral deficiency, likely inconsistent with THE GOLDEN RULE and possibly inconsistent with THE PAULINE PRINCIPLE (depending on how I intend that you and others think and feel and act in light of what I say).

It's sometimes helpful—perhaps even, given THE GOLDEN RULE or COMMITMENT, necessary—to tell others hard truths about themselves. But we need to be very much aware of our motives and of the way we characteristically communicate. Bringing our inclinations to light, assessing our purposes with THE PAULINE PRINCIPLE in mind, and examining our communicative strategies and their likely outcomes in light of THE GOLDEN RULE can prepare us to choose wisely.

Test Everything

Do not quench the Spirit. Do not despise the words of prophets, but test everything; hold fast to what is good; abstain from every form of evil.[39]

The willingness to test everything is an expression of love for ourselves and others. We are not God. We are not omniscient; rather, we are finite, fallible, and ignorant. There is a great deal we don't know. And our own desires and commitments can dispose us to believe some things rather than others. As a result, we often don't welcome surprises. However, to value the basic good of knowledge is to be open to being surprised. Absent situational constraints made relevant to our choices by THE GOLDEN RULE and self-investing resolutions rendered significant for those choices by COMMITMENT, we have no positive duty to seek knowledge actively. However, if we deliberately *avoid* knowledge—because, say, we don't want to be unsettled by what we learn—we are acting against our own well-being and so violating THE PAULINE PRINCIPLE.

The *Logos*, according to John 1, is "the true light, which enlightens everyone."[40] And this means not only that God seeks to inspire us individually to understand the world and its Creator more fully but also that God works through our encounters with others to increase our knowledge. That hardly means, however, that we should heed every voice that clamors for our attention by claiming to offer us truth—on the purported basis of everything from direct divine revelation to logical dexterity to scientific expertise.

Rather, like those who encountered claimants to prophetic authority in the first-century churches of Saint Paul, we can and should test the assertions of those who seek to use their purported grasp of truth to tell us what to do. To do so is a reflection of our regard for the good of knowledge. (It also reflects our regard for every other good, since how we participate in any aspect of well-being depends on what we believe. We undermine our ability to exercise practical wisdom, in particular, when we are inadequately informed.) While it is surely often sensible to accept things on say-so, on embracing what we're taught, there's still value in looking critically at what parents and teachers tell

39. 1 Thess 5:19–22.
40. John 1:9.

us.[41] This is even more the case with many of today's would-be prophets, speaking to us from pulpits, newsrooms, or social media platforms; simply accepting what they say doesn't often seem to be a reliable guide to truth. If we value actual knowledge, then, we won't give up our critical faculties in response to their pronouncements.

We may not be seeking knowledge in any given case, and we don't violate THE PAULINE PRINCIPLE just by employing sloppy methods of acquiring beliefs. But we don't treat others fairly, in a manner consistent with THE GOLDEN RULE, if we act in relation to them on the basis of beliefs acquired with undue carelessness. Fairness doesn't mean obsessively trying to obtain perfect knowledge with respect to every matter, but THE GOLDEN RULE undoubtedly precludes using information acquired without scrutiny to make or encourage serious decisions affecting others' lives. Indeed, simply accepting what a would-be prophet maintains isn't even fair to that person: we love her or him, offering the gift of otherness, by presenting a challenge: *Are you sure you're right? Have you considered* this *objection?* While THE GOLDEN RULE ordinarily wouldn't *require* us to disagree, when we do, we also help the would-be prophet recognize her or his own creatureliness and come closer to the truth.

Do Not Submit to Human Regulations

> Why do you submit to regulations, "Do not handle, Do not taste, Do not touch"? All these regulations refer to things that perish with use; they are simply human commands and teachings.[42]

Resisting petty, unwarranted demands is a way of loving ourselves and others. A creational love ethic is not antinomian. It affirms the objectivity not only of morality but also, indeed, of many general (*e.g.*, "Keep promises") and a few truly exceptionless (*e.g.*, "Don't purposefully injure noncombatants") requirements. But to acknowledge that love is essential and that it exhibits specific features

---

41. See Nicholas Wolterstorff, "Can Belief in God Be Rational If It Has No Foundations?," *Faith and Rationality: Reason and Belief in God*, ed. Alvin Plantinga and Nicholas Wolterstorff (Notre Dame, IN: University of Notre Dame Press 1985) 135–86; Nicholas Wolterstorff, *Reason within the Bounds of Religion*, 2d ed. (Grand Rapids: Eerdmans 1984); and Stephen R. L. Clark, *Civil Peace and Sacred Order* (Oxford: Clarendon-Oxford University Press 1989) 1–26.
42. Col 2:20b–2.

and a determinate structure is not to accept any and all requirements upheld by social consensus or announced by those who claim authority.

Communities and individual authority figures uphold petty regulations for all sorts of reasons. Such regulations may foster community cohesion. They may link community members with admired predecessors. They may serve to preserve the power and influence of those charged with interpreting and enforcing them. Perhaps most insidiously, they may have embodied love in what are now long-passed circumstances, even though now, with background conditions different, they don't.

It's worth being alert to these possibilities, then, and thus asking of any assumed or announced demand whether it really does embody love. If it doesn't embody love, there may still be good sensible pragmatic reasons not to flout it, presumably to avoid conflict. But, if ignoring it isn't inconsistent with love, one is perfectly free in principle to ignore it. "Human commands and teachings" may be useful, but they are not entitled to the claim on our loyalty that only love enjoys.

To submit to regulations that disregard one's own well-being or the well-being of someone else or that even undermine flourishing is precisely to act counter to love. To resist dubious rules, by contrast, is to love oneself, if they restrict one's participation in genuine goods. It is also to love others who might be subject to petty demands that restrict their flourishing, since one's resistance may offer an inspiring example. In addition, to resist can also be to love anyone who formulates (if they're deliberately crafted) or enforces these regulations, since resistance can prompt reflection (*If they weren't problematic, would they be flouted like this?*) as well as awareness of personal limitations (*How did I fail to see why someone might object to this?*) and thus offer the gift of otherness.[43]

Welcome Those Who Are Weak

Welcome those who are weak in faith, but not for the purpose of quarreling over opinions.[44]

---

43. I owe this evocative phrase to Luke Timothy Johnson, *Faith's Freedom: A Classic Spirituality for Contemporary Christians* (Philadelphia: Fortress 1989), *e.g*, 68–70.
44. Rom 14:1.

Since some have become so accustomed to idols until now, they still think of the food they eat as food offered to an idol; and their conscience, being weak, is defiled. "Food will not bring us close to God." We are no worse off if we do not eat, and no better off if we do. But take care that this liberty of yours does not somehow become a stumbling block to the weak. For if others see you, who possess knowledge, eating in the temple of an idol, might they not, since their conscience is weak, be encouraged to the point of eating food sacrificed to idols? So by your knowledge those weak believers for whom Christ died are destroyed.[45]

Exhibiting regard for the weak—the overly scrupulous—is an expression of love. Religious and similar communities can encourage weakness of the kind with which Saint Paul is concerned. Strength—an appreciation for one's own freedom and that of others—is a natural result of understanding the wide range of choices consistent with a creational love ethic in most situations but also of recognizing our own limitations and the value of an ecosystem conducive to moral experimentation. Care for the weak means being sensitive to the possibility that they might injure themselves by choosing against their own convictions, though it also means helping them to expand their horizons; it doesn't mean allowing them an across-the-board veto over the choices of the strong.

The Persistence of Weakness

Religious communities not infrequently leave people burdened with unwarranted worries that lead to scrupulosity, to an obsession with minor or, indeed, unreal moral requirements. (This isn't a comment on any particular community: the kind of moralistic attitude I have in mind is exhibited across traditional religious communities as well as various ideologically shaped environments that might not appear superficially to be religious.) Thus, they foster a potentially debilitating moral paralysis: they encourage people to be weak.

Why Be Strong?

A creational love ethic involves serious moral constraints. In particular, THE PAULINE PRINCIPLE grounds a range of unqualified prohibitions. At the same time, however, this kind of ethic as I have formulated it here leaves room for a

---

45. 1 Cor 8:7b–11.

substantial diversity of practice. To adhere to RECOGNITION is to acknowledge many different human goods. Given the relative flexibility that THE GOLDEN RULE embodies and the relatively narrow range of cases in which EFFICIENCY constrains our choices, a creational love ethic makes possible the exploration of a wide array of ways of being human. One can choose to narrow one's options by making self-investing decisions that carry ongoing moral weight in virtue of COMMITMENT, but in this case one has simply set one's own priorities; one hasn't submitted to any sort of external fetter.

In addition, once we acknowledge the reality of human fallibility, ignorance, finitude, and sin, the limits on human intellection; and the constrained and mediated character of divine providence, we will also have reason to recognize our own capacities to be mistaken and the value of moral experimentation. I may conclude in a given case that whether a given normative judgment is correct is uncertain, so that ongoing investigation makes sense; I may also recognize that what may seem entirely settled to me may seem so because of a blind spot on my part. In some cases, the best way of trying to determine the truth will be experimentation of one kind or another.[46] And, even if I am confident about my own normative judgments, others may not be confident about theirs, and I can easily see that, at least sometimes, their experimentation may be valuable both to them and to others who will have the opportunity to observe their successes and failures.[47]

So, in short, (*i*) a creational love ethic offers moral space for diverse choices and ways of being human. (*ii*) While the arguments I've offered are, I hope, both correct and persuasive, someone might reasonably wonder about the merits of the understanding of love I've advanced or of any conception of the moral life and seek greater insight, some of which might come from experimentation. And (*iii*) one might have reason at least sometimes to value *others'* experiments in living even if one presumes that the views they are testing are mistaken.

Care for the Weak

One has, therefore, reason to be something like the kind of person Saint Paul describes as strong.[48] Saint Paul evidently presupposes the correctness of the

46. For a moral realist's treatment of experience as a source of new moral insight, see David McNaughton, *Moral Vision: An Introduction to Ethics* (Oxford: Blackwell 1988) 102–3.
47. See John Stuart Mill, *On Liberty* (London: Parker 1859) 103–39.
48. I do not mean that Saint Paul offers anything like my arguments here.

strong person's position. At the same time, however, he recognizes the importance of being aware of the challenges and vulnerabilities faced by the weak.

The weak person assumes that there *aren't* nearly as many ways of being flourishingly human as does the strong person. She likely also assumes that she has good reason to accept her existing beliefs as unquestionably correct, so that no testing is necessary and that others should accept the same beliefs as well. There are at least two kinds of regard it's important to show for someone who assumes these things.

(*i*) It's important to join Saint Paul in welcoming the weak as members of the Christian community, in letting them know that they are included and valued. They *can't* be told, directly or indirectly, that they don't belong or that they are second-class members.

The Christian church can and should serve as a demonstration project highlighting for some or all of the rest of the world the significance and transformative capacity of open and accepting community life. So Christians must be especially sensitive to the importance of not doing anything that excludes or subordinates. This is a consequence of THE GOLDEN RULE, since most of us would not be willing ourselves to be excluded or to see our loved ones excluded. It is a consequence of THE PAULINE PRINCIPLE when exclusion or marginalization is undertaken as a way of punishing people for their putatively retrograde views or incentivizing them to change. The exclusion or marginalization in this case can be an attack on the basic good of friendship (depending on the nature of the relationships attenuated for punitive or incentival purposes). In addition, because of the distinctive value of the church as a demonstration project, some members may—either explicitly or as a matter of developed and endorsed habit—have undertaken commitments to participate in the work of this project in particularly visible ways. If they have, COMMITMENT provides them with further reason to avoid treating the weak dismissively.

(*ii*) It's also important for the strong to avoid behaving in ways that might lead the weak to adopt some or all of the practices of the strong *for the wrong reasons* and to take themselves to have behaved wrongly for doing what the strong do. They might come to imitate the strong because they fear being ridiculed, excluded, or subordinated; they might do so out of the desire to fit in; or they might do so because they've abdicated responsibility for making moral judgments to the crowd. In any case, even though they've made what are in fact objectively correct choices, in making these choices they may well have decided unreasonably and injured aspects of their own flourishing.

Self-Injury by the Weak?

Making what one takes to be an unwarranted choice will likely underwrite a habit of disregarding the deliverances of practical wisdom and, more broadly, ignoring what one takes to be reality while instead opting to follow one's whims. Making such a choice could also injure one's self-integration, creating inner tension and impeding the consistency of one's attitudes, desires, beliefs, actions, and so forth.

The weak won't always injure themselves in this way just because they become aware of the behavior of the strong. They may refuse to follow the example of the strong. And, if they do choose to imitate the strong, they need not injure themselves *purposefully*. Someone might, that is, choose a particular good for its own sake, aware that, in choosing that good, she was at the same time disrupting her own self-integration. The disruption of her self-integration will follow from her choice to participate in the relevant good, but she need not intend the disruption *as a means* to her participation in the relevant good. As long as she doesn't, her action wouldn't be inconsistent with love in the form of THE PAULINE PRINCIPLE. Still, the injuries she undergoes could be real and significant.

The extent of the injury someone inflicts on herself by flouting a given moral conviction may depend in part on how she has arrived at the conviction. If it has not been tested through the exercise of practical wisdom, if it has been embraced unreflectively, if it is rooted in fear and taboo, violating it may not involve much self-injury. That's because, when violating it, the weak person will be choosing to do something about which she may feel guilty but not something she believes to be wrong on the basis of actual reflection or any other reliable means of belief formation. She will not be injuring her capacity for practical wisdom at all, though she may inflict an inadvertent injury on her self-integration.

An obvious example of a weak person's struggle with what seems (incorrectly) like temptation is Huckleberry Finn's puzzlement over whether to try to return his friend Jim to Jim's supposed "owner," something he believes is required by divine edict.[49] Huck finally decides he's willing to go to hell if that's the cost of being loyal to Jim.[50] His action in the face of toxically false convictions seems like an instance of heroism, one in which he responds to authentic

---

49. See Mark Twain, *The Adventures of Huckleberry Finn, Tom Sawyer's Comrade* (New York: Harper 1912) 117–21.
50. Twain 282–4.

moral reality—the reality of Jim's personhood and his moral equality with Huck, together with the claim exerted by their friendship[51]—in preference to the faux morality of his society. He seems in this case to be *growing* morally.

People who are weak in Saint Paul's sense might well grow just as Huck did if they reject taboo-rooted convictions in favor of more appropriate ones because of their, even if imperfect, apprehension of the truth. If they do this, their capacity to exercise practical wisdom might well not be injured by acting against their earlier convictions. The same could be true as regards the integration of the aspects of their personalities, their wills and desires, and so forth. This might be true because they might find themselves dis-integrated in virtue of the tension between the taboos that shape their emotional reactions and the instinct that the strong are right. They might, that is, find themselves *more* integrated if embracing the standpoint of the strong ultimately leads them to shed their previously embraced taboo morality. (This doesn't change the fact that the integration of someone's beliefs and choices would in the short term be injured by choosing as Huck did.)

Suppose the weak do injure their self-integration and their capacities to exercise practical wisdom but ultimately adopt new and, we may judge, better convictions. In this case, they might, while regretting their injuries, also welcome in retrospect not their self-injury but, nonetheless, the expansion of horizons they've undergone and the goods in which they're better able to participate. They might do so, at least if they retain their self-integration and capacity for exercising practical wisdom rather than succumbing to the temptation to give in to impulse or to allow themselves to fragment.

> I may wrongly think I have an obligation that I do not have. In the past it was widely held that my believing, even misguidedly, that I have an obligation morally obliges me to fulfill it. To many of us today, however, it seems that if a person who takes too narrow a view of her own rights rebels against a falsely assumed burden of obligations, the moral gain in throwing off some of the shackles of servility may be more important than the damage to her conscientiousness.[52]

The weak may sometimes fail to grow in understanding. Instead, they may, perhaps because of the degree to which they've embraced powerful taboos,

---

51. Thanks to Fritz Guy for this point.
52. Adams, *Finite and Infinite Goods* 247.

simply find themselves torn between impulse and conviction. They might well, therefore, continue injuring their capacities or good judgment and the coherence of their lives. And the end result could well be serious difficulties associated with exercising practical wisdom and maintaining self-integration. The strong can hardly desire that such difficulties befall the weak or be indifferent to their occurrence.

When they exercise their freedom, the strong need not intend to lead the weak to violate THE PAULINE PRINCIPLE, nor need they intend that the weak suffer any injury at all. However, the strong must still take the impact of their choices on the weak into account. Most importantly, they will need to consider THE GOLDEN RULE when asking about the injuries their choices might inflict on the weak. Considering the likelihood and severity of the possible injuries, they need to inquire whether they would be willing to accept a standard that permitted the infliction of similar injuries on themselves or on their loved ones given relevantly similar circumstances, including susceptibilities to influence. (The choices of the strong can potentially influence the weak to injure themselves only if that behavior is observed and imitated. The likelihood that the weak will become aware of the behavior of the strong is thus also among the salient factors.) They will also need to ask about any commitments—as, for instance, to inclusiveness or to special concern for the weak, in addition to the regard for the weak entailed by THE GOLDEN RULE—that might be violated by acting in ways likely to foster self-injury by those who might imitate them.

Can the Weak Veto the Choices of the Strong?

In some cases, it will be inconsistent with love—in the form of THE GOLDEN RULE and COMMITMENT—for the strong to foster self-injury by the weak and, as THE PAULINE PRINCIPLE makes clear, for them to intend injury in all cases. But the weak cannot always enjoy a veto over the actions of the strong. This is especially likely to be the case when the issue is the treatment by the strong of other people—say, a choice by the strong to be inclusive.

Suppose, for instance, that a weak person sincerely believes that God has created a requirement in virtue of which people must be separate from each other in worship on the basis of their skin colors. If a strong person who belongs to the same congregation as this weak person welcomes a member of a heretofore excluded group into the congregation, the weak person may, indeed, be shocked, insisting that the congregation continue to be segregated, that the attempt to integrate it violates God's will. The strong person, it seems to me, can in this case judge that her actions are consistent with THE GOLDEN RULE and the other specifications of love.

In the case I've imagined, the strong person is not attempting to exclude or injure the weak person. She hopes that the weak person will come authentically to see that inclusion and welcome are right and necessary. It's possible, she realizes, that the weak person may succumb to her influence and accept inclusion for the wrong reasons. Even if this happens, however, the strong person might reasonably conclude, she would be willing to accept a standard that permitted the exertion of influence like hers leading to this kind of self-injury by her loved ones (or herself) in the course of the peaceful integration of a congregation.

The weak should not enjoy a veto over the actions of the strong, especially when it would be unfair to third parties, inconsistent with THE GOLDEN RULE, to try not to offend the weak at all costs. At the same time, even when the strong judge that the weak are seriously mistaken, THE GOLDEN RULE, THE PAULINE PRINCIPLE, and sometimes also COMMITMENT give the strong good reason to welcome them—inclusion applies in their case, too. Love sometimes also gives the strong reason to avoid influencing the weak in ways likely to lead them to injure themselves by doing things they believe (albeit mistakenly) to be wrong.

Restore Transgressors

> My friends, if anyone is detected in a transgression, you who have received the Spirit should restore such a one in a spirit of gentleness. Take care that you yourselves are not tempted. Bear one another's burdens, and in this way you will fulfill the law of Christ.[53]

Saint Paul's words highlight two distinct ethical ideas: Christian congregations should seek to address conflict and misbehavior internally; and, when doing so, they should keep in mind the long-term goal of ensuring that even those who have chosen badly are, where possible, embraced within the Christian community. Injuries of multiple kinds happen within congregations and other Christian groups. It can be very reasonable for those who have been injured to seek not only emotional support but also formal assistance within the church. It's important to recognize the seriousness of some wrongs and to realize that protecting people from violence might well require the involvement of the legal

---

53. Gal 6:1–2.

system, though it's also important to act in view of the genuine limitations and deficiencies of that system.

Injury in the Church

Resolving disputes and restoring transgressors to communal engagement are vital aspects of love for Christians. They matter because, not infrequently, Christians do in fact injure other Christians.[54]

The trusting environment of a church can make it easy to lure people into a fraudulent business deal. The same woman hired because of a congregational connection may be fired not for incompetence but because her eager intelligence has embarrassed her mediocre Christian manager. A would-be Don Juan may disrupt the marriages of fellow church members with a series of affairs. A pastor with a gambling problem may find her easy access to the contents of the offering plate an irresistible temptation.

Seeking Assistance in the Church

Contemporary congregations and denominations are often sufficiently large and impersonal and, at least in the Global North, people are sufficiently private that, when a member of the church chooses in a manner inconsistent with love, most other members are none the wiser. But, in a church in which people learn that they can rely on each other, those who have been injured by fellow members may, despite the unwarranted shame that often accompanies victimization, find the courage to reach out to trustworthy, responsible people with the potential to help. Not everyone who's asked to intervene can or must do so. But THE GOLDEN RULE and COMMITMENT may render it necessary for occupants of particular congregational or ecclesial roles or people engaged in particular kinds of relationships with victims or wrongdoers to become involved.

There is no guarantee that such people will be gentle, insightful, or aptly responsive to the Spirit's promptings, and therefore ready to participate effectively in addressing bad behavior within the church. Self-knowledge may rightly lead someone, in light of THE GOLDEN RULE, to decline to confront a wrongdoer

---

54. Saint Paul does not say explicitly that the kind of transgression he's envisioning involves one church member's injuring another. There's no reason for the church to decline to become involved if a nonmember asks for help with the bad behavior of a member. But I assume that members' ill-treatment of other members is more likely to lead to church involvement, and I focus on intra-church transgressions accordingly.

in a given case. But people within a given community can often contribute with exceptional effectiveness to addressing bad behavior occurring inside that community. Personal connections and shared networks can render them more trusted, make communicating with them feel safer, with the result that they may be able to address someone's transgression more effectively than an outsider could. And their identities as Christians can be expected to begin their involvement with a desire for healing and a willingness to serve as ministers of divine grace.

Being Realistic about Wrongdoing

The desire to enact God's love and the awareness of everyone's need for this love might tempt Christian intervenors to begin with assumptions like "Everyone is partly in the right and partly in the wrong, more or less" or "There are two sides to every story." But starting from this perspective may make it hard to acknowledge the unqualified inconsistency of someone's choices with love in a given case. The intervenors' involvement may lead them to discover that what seemed like a simple, black-and-white situation is more complex than they'd initially realized. But Christians can engage in unfair or thoroughly predatory behavior in relation to other Christians, and those seeking to deal with transgressions of whatever sort within the church should be prepared to discover that what they have been asked to address is unequivocally bad behavior.

Church Intervention and the Legal System

There's an unavoidable tension connected with the kind of activity Saint Paul envisions. On the one hand, it can provide a useful alternative to the involvement of the formal state legal system. That system's stock-in-trade is the deployment of force against people's bodies and possessory claims in order to punish and deter. Retribution and deterrence are, as I have already emphasized, deeply problematic, unacceptable goals for loving action. Addressing wrongdoing within the church is a way of avoiding the pointless, unjustifiable retributive or deterrent imposition of injury by the state. This isn't a matter of offering favors to wrong-doers, of "cutting them slack." It is, rather, a matter of engaging with them in ways that don't involve subjecting them to unjust penalties—unjust not because they haven't wrongly injured others but because such penalties are not appropriate even for those who *have* wrongly injured others.

For this kind of approach to be effective, it will matter that there be, as Saint Paul envisions, gracious and graceful restoration. Such restoration can lead to long-term healing and behavior change as well as to the repair of disrupted or shattered relationships. But it is also essential that the intervenors and others in the community actively address the wrongdoer's conduct and insist that she act to correct the harm she has caused and address its underlying causes. They need to insist that she do this *both*, per THE GOLDEN RULE, as a matter of regard for the person or persons she's injured (and perhaps others she might injure in the future) *and* as a crucial means of facilitating her own reintegration into the community. So, for instance, the pilfering pastor needs to return the money she has taken, with interest; pay the reasonable costs associated with the recovery of the funds she has misappropriated; enter therapy for her gambling addiction; publicly apologize to the congregation; and agree to arrangements that will not give her unmonitored access to church funds. And so forth.

Loving means recognizing the importance of not responding unjustly or encouraging unjust responses to bad behavior. Love gives us reason to be hesitant about involving the state legal system in dealing with transgressions within the church. But that hardly means that, given the existence of that system and the absence in a given case of effective alternatives, it's inconsistent with love to ask for the system's help. After all, people may not cooperate with the corrective measures sought in and through a loving church-based intervention of the kind Saint Paul envisions. And, even if they do intend to cooperate, they may still falter or otherwise choose wrongly in a variety of ways. The Sunday School teacher who beats a partner or the churchwarden who heads a company that continues to dump toxins into a shared reservoir may simply not be responsive to the entreaties of fellow church members or supportive of the remedies they propose. When it's clear that someone's behavior will continue to be dangerous or that someone is unwilling to take responsibility for providing a remedy for injuries that have already occurred, those victimized may have no realistic option but to seek state involvement—to request police protection from the violent partner, to join in a class action tort suit against the polluting company.[55] And, when victims seek the legal system's aid in cases like this, the Christians whose help they've sought have every reason to assist them with logistical and strategic guidance, communication with relevant contacts, and so forth rather than insisting that they rely on church-based mechanisms that have proved fruitless.

55. Cp. Matt 18:17.

Love and Involving the Legal System

To proceed in this way need not be in any way inconsistent with love. Employing the legal system need not involve the choice to attack any basic aspect of the transgressor's well-being. It can be motivated, instead, by the intention to restrain bad behavior and to obtain appropriate compensation.[56] It can thus be very much in harmony with THE PAULINE PRINCIPLE.

Employing the legal system as a last resort may be an expression of the victims' love for themselves and for other potential victims. And the intervenors' assistance to the victims in drawing on the legal system's resources can embody love for the victims and for others who might be injured by the wrongdoer or people acting similarly. The choice by both victims and intervenors to involve the legal system can also be an expression of love for transgressors, who can only grow and change if they confront the reality of their behavior. Presuming that one's pursuit of legal remedies for one's own benefit or that of others is consistent with THE GOLDEN RULE and any constraints rooted in COMMITMENT, there need be no tension with love involved in seeking the aid of the state legal system.

There may be serious difficulties involved in cases in which the only realistically available state remedies are wrong in principle; in this case, pursuing them *may* sometimes be inconsistent with love. Suppose, for instance, one wishes to restrain a thief while knowing that to facilitate the thief's arrest and prosecution will mean—if she is, as she likely will be, convicted—that one of her hands will be amputated. One might intend by involving the state legal system only to facilitate her restraint; mutilation need be no part of one's intention. At the same time, one might be, quite reasonably, entirely unwilling to see oneself or one's loved ones handed over to the authorities for mutilation in similar circumstances. It might therefore clash with love in the form of THE GOLDEN RULE for one to seek the involvement of the legal system in this case.

There are few universal rules to be offered here, except that one should never will harm to any basic aspect of another's well-being. Given the often punitive and violent character of the state legal system, it may be inconsistent with THE GOLDEN RULE to seek its aid. On the other hand, it might indeed be fair to do so when there's no realistic alternative way of securely restraining a predatory person or recovering valuable stolen items. The important thing will

---

56. For a classic treatment of compensation as central to optimal legal responses to bad behavior, see, *e.g*, Randy E. Barnett, "The Justice of Restitution," *American Journal of Jurisprudence* 25.1 (1980): 117–32.

be to reflect on one's purposes, on THE GOLDEN RULE, and on one's commitments while keeping the salient facts in all their complexity in view.

None of these complications affects the basic point, emphasized in Galatians, that the gentle and spiritual should seek to restore transgressors. It may be quite consistent with or even required by love for them to continue to do so even when a transgressor is engaged with the legal system, even if imprisoned. However, they can and should seek to restore any transgressor without in any way attempting to paper over the transgressor's bad behavior. Instead, they must, precisely as an expression of love, challenge the transgressor to face reality and so, in particular, the reality of how she has injured others and of what she must do to correct what's already happened and to reorder her life as appropriate to avoid repeat performances.

Those acting on behalf of the church can and should be gentle by shunning deterrence and retribution. But their gentleness must not involve complicity in any attempt by the transgressor to avoid facing reality and so to avoid compensating victims. It must also involve working to reduce risks to potential future victims and to change the relevant situation in whatever ways might be appropriate. To help the transgressor avoid reality would be inconsistent with THE GOLDEN RULE. That this is the case reflects the potential significance of the intervenors' actions for the transgressor, the victim or victims, other members of the church, those inclined to imitate the transgressor, and others still who might be affected directly or indirectly by what the intervenors themselves do.

Remember Those Who Are Being Tortured

> Remember . . . those who are being tortured, as though you yourselves were being tortured.[57]

We love when we remember and support the tortured. Torture can be devastating, yielding broken spirits and broken bodies.

Whether engaged in to establish and express dominance, to persuade the victim to do something, to punish her, or to yield or realize some other outcome, torture involves intentionally attacking the victim's well-being: certainly her freedom from physical pain and potentially her life and bodily well-being, too. It therefore violates THE PAULINE PRINCIPLE.

---

57. Heb 13:3.

Torture will almost certainly in various ways violate love in the form of THE GOLDEN RULE as well, given that none of us would likely accept standards permitting torture of ourselves or of our loved ones and so would act unfairly by engaging in or supporting torture. Certainly, Christians who acknowledge the injunction in the Letter to the Hebrews to remember the tortured, recognizing that the tortured participate in a common humanity with them, cannot themselves enact or facilitate torture.

In light of THE GOLDEN RULE, it will likely be inconsistent with love for some people at some times to avoid providing support to the tortured, if only by emphasizing to the tortured that they are known and valued. This specification of love likely also means that some people at some times must challenge both policies and individual instances of torture through acts of writing, speaking, and protest as well as support for organized groups seeking to end some or all instances of torture.

Rejoice!

The Epistles consistently enjoin their readers to rejoice.[58] Deliberate enthusiasm for the goods in which we and others participate fosters the exhibition of appropriate regard for ourselves and others. Rejoicing involves recognizing and appreciating the aspects of reality that enrich our lives. We may rejoice at natural or artificial beauty, at friendship, at renewed health, at spiritual insight, at intellectual discovery, at stimulating play . . . In so doing, we recognize more clearly the graced quality of our existence; our unavoidable reliance on the gifts offered by other creatures and, ultimately, by God; and therefore our own identities as creatures. This means that we will more readily live in harmony with God. In addition, we will interact more aptly with others because of our appreciation for their gifts and because we more clearly recognize our own limitations as well as our own value. Given the impact of rejoicing on our ongoing practice of love, it may sometimes be inconsistent with THE GOLDEN RULE to decline opportunities to rejoice. And, for the same reason, it may sometimes make sense to commit to rejoicing regularly—whether in conversation with others; in private journaling, prayer, or reflection; in ecstatic dance; through art; or in some other way.

58. Rom 12:12, 15; Phil 2:18; 3:1; 4:4; 1 Thess 5:16.

Resist Slavery

Saying "No!" to enslavement is an expression of love for enslaved persons and others. So is declining to follow earlier Christians in treating enslavement as morally permissible or to suppose that, objectively speaking, their toleration of slavery was ever consistent with love, whatever they believed.

In this chapter, I've sought to highlight the way in which a creational love ethic can help us apply multiple moral injunctions in the New Testament. But it's also worth noting the response of such an ethic to New Testament instructions that seem at first blush to be supportive of the institution of slavery. These instructions seem to reflect a generally tolerant attitude toward this institution, one in virtue of which slaves are directed to obey their self-proclaimed owners.

With many later Christians, evidently beginning with Gregory of Nyssa, I suggest that slavery is illegitimate.[59] And, like many of the nineteenth-century abolitionists, I maintain that forcible resistance by enslaved people and those providing them with support is entirely warranted. After highlighting New Testament teaching supportive of slavery, I underscore the multiple bases on which a creational love ethic challenges this destructive institution. I hope the analysis I offer here serves to provide a clear example of love in action, to highlight love's own response to a significant feature of early Christian behavior marked by defective appreciation for love's implications, and to point toward insights that may prove relevant to thinking about other moral questions.

Instructions to Slaves

Jesus's support of inclusion, his embrace of THE GOLDEN RULE, his opposition to violence, and his belief in the preciousness of persons in God's eyes all militate against the acceptance of slavery. He relativizes the significance of enslavement by urging those who wish to be leaders to take on the submissiveness of enslaved persons.[60] And he never treats enslaved people as deficient in value or status.[61] However, he doesn't directly address the practice of enslavement in the sayings

---

59. See David Bentley Hart, "The 'Whole Humanity': Gregory of Nyssa's Critique of Slavery in Light of His Eschatology," *Scottish Journal of Theology* 54.1 (Feb. 2001): 51–69.

60. Mark 10:44; Luke 17:10.

61. He doesn't hesitate to heal a slave: Luke 7:2–10. The last healing miracle depicted by the New Testament is Jesus's restoration to its rightful owner of the ear of the high priest's slave severed by Peter's sword: Luke 22:51; cp. John 18:10.

preserved by early Christians, slave "owners" are assumed without comment to be among the members of his audience, and his parables and the words of the evangelists often take enslavement for granted.[62]

The Epistles address slavery much more directly, affirming the fundamental spiritual equality of the enslaved and the free.[63] Notably, Saint Paul encourages Philemon to recognize Onesimus as his spiritual equal and perhaps, by implication, to liberate him. And slave traders are classed among the paradigmatically immoral.[64] At the same time, though, the Epistles treat slavery as a metaphor for a spiritually flourishing state.[65] While Acts depicts slaves as recipients of the Spirit's gifts[66] and portrays Saint Paul as (grumpily) exorcising a demon from a slave,[67] it doesn't insist on or even explicitly encourage abolition. And the recognition of the spiritual equality of the enslaved and the free doesn't keep multiple early Christian writers from instructing slaves that obeying their supposed masters is a matter not just of pragmatic good judgment but also of Christian duty:

> Let all who are under the yoke of slavery regard their masters as worthy of all honor, so that the name of God and the teaching may not be blasphemed.[68]

> Slaves, accept the authority of your masters with all deference, not only those who are kind and gentle but also those who are harsh. For it is a credit to you if, being aware of God, you endure pain while suffering unjustly. If you endure when you are beaten for doing wrong, what credit is that? But if you endure when you do right and suffer for it, you have God's approval. For to this you have been called, because Christ also suffered for you, leaving you an example, so that you should follow in his steps.

> "He committed no sin,
>   and no deceit was found in his mouth."

62. Luke 17:7–10.
63. 1 Cor 12:13; Gal 3:28; Col 3:11.
64. 1 Tim 1:10.
65. Rom 6:15–9; 7:6, 25; 1 Cor 7:22; 9:19; Gal 5:13. In Rom 8:15, however, Saint Paul clearly contrasts spiritual freedom with spiritual enslavement. And in 2 Cor 11:20, he implicitly urges his readers to resist such enslavement, as he does explicitly in Gal 5:1.
66. Acts 2:18; cp. Joel 2:29.
67. Acts 16:18.
68. 1 Tim 6:1.

When he was abused, he did not return abuse; when he suffered, he did not threaten; but he entrusted himself to the one who judges justly. He himself bore our sins in his body on the cross, so that, free from sins, we might live for righteousness; by his wounds you have been healed. For you were going astray like sheep, but now you have returned to the shepherd and guardian of your souls.[69]

Slaves, obey your earthly masters in everything, not only while being watched and in order to please them, but wholeheartedly, fearing the Lord. Whatever your task, put yourselves into it, as done for the Lord and not for your masters, since you know that from the Lord you will receive the inheritance as your reward; you serve the Lord Christ.[70]

Slaves, obey your earthly masters with fear and trembling, in singleness of heart, as you obey Christ; not only while being watched, and in order to please them, but as slaves of Christ, doing the will of God from the heart. Render service with enthusiasm, as to the Lord and not to men and women, knowing that whatever good we do, we will receive the same again from the Lord, whether we are slaves or free.[71]

Tell slaves to be submissive to their masters and to give satisfaction in every respect; they are not to talk back, not to pilfer, but to show complete and perfect fidelity, so that in everything they may be an ornament to the doctrine of God our Savior.[72]

At least in these passages, the Epistles treat slavery as a source of genuine moral obligations on the part of enslaved persons to their purported owners.

---

69. 1 Pet 2:18–25.

70. Col 3:22–4. Christian "owners" are subsequently encouraged (Col 4:1) to treat slaves well, but there is no suggestion that enslavement itself is unjust.

71. Eph 6:5–8. The subsequent affirmation that "owners," too, are subjects of Christ (Eph 6:9) can have been a source of at most limited relief to those enslaved.

72. Titus 2:9–10. If enslavement is unjust, then taking something from one's "owner" might seem to be a way of engaging in self-help designed to secure partial compensation for one's unjust forcible subjection to another.

Critiquing Enslavement

A creational love ethic offers multiple reasons to reject and resist slavery.

(*i*) The basic illegitimacy of enslavement is evident in light of THE GOLDEN RULE. This specification of love presupposes the moral equality of persons. So enslavement could be justified only if, *despite* the equality of persons, some could legitimately claim the submission of others without their consent and use force to compel this submission. If I am unwilling to endorse a standard in virtue of which, say, my loved ones or I could be enslaved, it is inconsistent with love for me to enslave anyone.

(*ii*) Many acts in which slave "owners" or those working at their direction engage to maintain systems of enslavement or to keep currently enslaved persons subordinated violate THE PAULINE PRINCIPLE, especially because they involve attacks on the bodies of enslaved persons. It is clearly wrong to injure someone's body in order to punish her for failing to follow the orders of her self-proclaimed "owner," because it's wrong to engage in retributive or deterrent punishment and so to use force to punish. In addition, because the claimed authority-relationship between the enslaved person and the "owner" itself isn't justified, the enslaved person hasn't done anything that could merit punishment even if, as I deny, retributive or deterrent punishment is permissible. It is also wrong to use force against someone's body to ensure that she obeys one's instructions in the future, since the use of force to incentivize someone to do something always violates THE PAULINE PRINCIPLE: it involves injuring to bring about some (putative) good. Because the use of force to punish retributively or deterrently is essentially inconsistent with love, key practices needed to maintain enslavement are always wrong.

(*iii*) Slave "owners" can use violence not only to punish enslaved persons or to compel their compliance with directives but also to prevent them from seeking to escape enslavement or to recapture them if they do so. But a person may use force justly in order to defend her own body or justly acquired possessions or the body or justly acquired possessions of someone else against unjust force. Escaping from enslavement or refusing to obey the commands of a slave "owner" doesn't as such pose a threat to anyone's body. In light of THE GOLDEN RULE, there is, as I've just emphasized, good reason to see the assertion by the putative "owner" that the enslaved person is a justly acquired possession as unwarranted. And, if it isn't justified, it is the case not only that the use of force to restrain an escaping or otherwise disobedient enslaved person is wrong but also that the enslaved person is entirely justified in using force in self-defense against an overseer or slave catcher.

(*iv*) Enslavement involves the assertion of the control of the "owner" over the enslaved person's judgment. This may not happen all the time, but it's always a live possibility. That's part of the meaning of enslavement: the "owner" expects to be obeyed without question when giving an order, as if the enslaved person were a mechanical device rather than a moral agent. The goal of the "owner" is to bypass the enslaved person's own critical judgment. And this means that the practice of enslavement involves purposeful attacks on the good of practical wisdom—or, at minimum, the intent to effect such attacks.

Recall that practical wisdom involves making judgments regarding choices. It can involve choices of goods to realize or pursue and ways of realizing or pursuing these goods. It thus involves determining whether a potential goal is itself an aspect of well-being or a means to the realization or production of such an aspect. It also involves whether a potential way of realizing or pursuing a goal is consistent with the various specifications of love.[73]

The slave "owner" intends, when doing so is consistent with her objectives, to bypass enslaved people's use of practical wisdom. She does not do so not by *persuading* enslaved people to make her goals and choices regarding the pursuit or realization of these goals their own, as in a business transaction. If she intended to persuade—to foster the formation or fulfillment of a contract, say—she wouldn't be acting as a slave "owner." As a slave "owner," she is prepared *both* to assert nonconsensual *authority* over the enslaved people, insisting that they are obligated to obey her despite their lack of consent, *and* to use actual or threatened physical *force* to compel them to do her will, whatever their own practical judgments. And whenever she seeks deliberately to cancel or override the practical wisdom of enslaved persons, she attacks a basic aspect of well-being and therefore violates THE PAULINE PRINCIPLE.

(*v*) Most people are, in general, better at assessing their circumstances and fostering their own welfare than others are, particularly given that different people assign different priorities to different aspects of their own flourishing. Enslavement thus unfairly deprives people of opportunities not only for self-direction but also for self-care and self-protection. If I am unwilling to accept a standard that denies me or my loved ones these opportunities, it is inconsistent with love in the form of THE GOLDEN RULE for me to deny them to anyone else.

(*vi*) Enslavement dramatically narrows the range of a person's choices—in the limit case, to zero. But everyone benefits, as a general matter, from other

---

73. A utilitarian might ask whether they're efficient, using whatever metric she treats as appropriate.

people's opportunities for creativity and experimentation, not only because creativity and experimentation can make possible the emergence of new goods but also because they can foster learning. Someone's experimentation can put otherwise unimagined and unexplored possibilities on display for others to assess—whether with the result that they emulate the displayed behavior or with the result that they gladly avoid copying it. Enslavement denies everyone the benefits that might otherwise flow from large- or small-scale experimentation by those who, because they are enslaved, are unable to experiment. This provides a further reason, in light of THE GOLDEN RULE, to reject it.

(*vii*) Maintaining a system of enslavement necessarily involves substantial scrutiny of and interference with the interactions and transactions that make up ordinary life. Slave "owners" and those actors in the legal system who do their bidding will regularly seek to determine whether people who might be enslaved are, in fact, enslaved. When slavery is racialized, this means that non-enslaved members of an ethnic group many of whose members are enslaved will consistently be harassed and may be subject to enslavement themselves with little recourse. Slave "owners" and their legal proxies will similarly seek to determine whether people who appear to be "owners" are in fact allies helping enslaved persons to escape slavery or to resist it. Recognizing the vigorous opposition that the practice of enslavement provokes, they will also be inclined to interfere forcibly with actual and potential expressions of dissent. And resources will be redirected to the maintenance of institutions designed to keep enslaved people from escaping or revolting. A system of enslavement in a given society thus imposes unjustly not only on enslaved persons themselves but on many others as well. Someone who would not be willing to accept a standard allowing the widespread impositions to which a system of slavery predictably leads when the burden of such impositions falls on her or her loved ones acts in a manner inconsistent with love if she supports arrangements in virtue of which they fall on others.

The practice of enslavement clashes with love in the forms of THE GOLDEN RULE and THE PAULINE PRINCIPLE at multiple points. The affirmation of enslaved persons' obedience to their putative masters at multiple points by first-century Christians is a disappointing feature of the development of Christianity. A creational love ethic does, in any case, provide one way of grounding the convictions of many later Christians—now almost all—that enslavement is thoroughly inconsistent with the Gospel.

The recognition that the practice of enslaving others is without moral justification is only one of many developments in Christian moral thinking during the past two millennia. One influential advance—building on the moral teachings of the New Testament while seeking to systematize and clarify those teachings—was the exploration of the "seven deadly sins" and the seven central Christian virtues as important windows on the moral life. In chapter 8, I consider these sins and virtues from the standpoint of a creational love ethic.

8

Creational Love, Sin, and Virtue

Over many centuries, Christians have not infrequently organized their treatments of the moral life as much around the three "theological" and four "cardinal" virtues and the "seven deadly sins" as around the Decalogue and the specific teaching of the New Testament. In this chapter, I want to show what these virtues and sins look like when viewed through the lens of love conceived of in creational terms. I seek to make clear how the sins can be understood as contrary to love and the virtues as instances of or ways of supporting this kind of love.

After an all-too-brief reflection on sin in general, I highlight the ways in which lust, greed, gluttony, sloth, anger, envy, and arrogance all involve choices that run directly counter to a creational love ethic. Then, rejecting the notion of virtue as infused, I examine prudence, temperance, fortitude, and justice before turning to faith, hope, and love.

The relationship between sin and virtue, on the one hand, and, on the other, choice is complex. We can use the language of sin and virtue to talk about dispositions to choose in particular ways. At the same time, choosing in particular ways can create or reinforce—cultivate or help to cultivate—the dispositions we talk about as sins and virtues. We can also use the language of sin to talk about particular choices directly. In addition, sinful dispositions can reinforce other sinful dispositions and so the choices flowing from them, while virtues can nourish other virtues and so the choices flowing from them. In most cases, choosing in accordance with a virtuous disposition or an interlocking set of such dispositions is primarily a way of choosing directly to love. However, the virtues of faith and hope are perhaps best seen primarily as providing crucial *support* for loving dispositions and choices. In all of these cases, however, love can offer an illuminating perspective on these central features of the moral life.

Creational Love, Sin, and the Seven Deadly Sins

A creational love ethic can helpfully ground talk about the seven deadly sins—seven pervasive disruptors of our lives.[1]

Understanding Sin

"Sin" in the singular is often used to label the underlying feature of the human condition that accounts for both inner moral turmoil and outer bad behavior. Sin in this sense is the denial that we are parts of God's good creation. Out of fear, anxiety, doubt about our own value, and self-loathing, we may refuse to see that we are parts of God's *good* creation, rejecting our own worth. Out of overweening confidence and the conviction that the world revolves around us, we may deny that we are *parts* of God's good *creation*, rejecting our own finitude. (In each case, the rejection is practical whether or not theoretical.)

Sin is sometimes spoken of as a condition of alienation from God. Denying that we are parts of the *good* creation means failing to see God's goodness; denying that we are *parts* of God's good *creation* means failing to see that God is Creator. In addition, while nothing can separate us from God's love, if we're aware of the presence of sin in our lives, we may fear that God is judging and rejecting us and thus *feel* separated from God.[2] While we can't actually injure God, when we injure ourselves or injure others, these injuries are taken up into the divine life. If all of creation is in a sense within God, we subject God to attack when we attack ourselves or our fellow sentients.

Because it involves rejecting our status as parts of God's good creation, coming to expression in our acts of injuring ourselves and others, sin is contrary to love. Sins are, in turn, habitual inclinations to choose particular kinds of injuries contrary to love. They are also individual choices that injure ourselves and others in specific varieties of ways that are inconsistent with love. It is these individual choices for which we are morally responsible. But making these choices also reinforces sins as tendencies, which can in turn lead to further choices inconsistent with love.

---

1. Henry Fairlie, *The Seven Deadly Sins Today* (Washington, DC: New Republic 1978), first introduced me (probably in 1995) to the notion that the seven deadly sins could be understood as inconsistent with love.
2. Cp. Rom 8:38–9.

We're not culpable for *experiencing* particular feelings, dispositions, thoughts, and so forth that present sin as appealing. Moral responsibility is a matter of our *choices*. But choosing to engage in particular sins is contrary to love not only because the sins themselves are contrary to love but also because engaging in them can fortify these feelings (or thoughts, or . . .) and thus lead to further choices contrary to love.

We can also, though we need not, act contrary to love when we attend internally to these feelings in ways that in fact nourish them. For instance, we can act contrary to love when, whatever our intentions, we choose in ways that in fact do nurture these feelings: we act contrary to love if choosing in ways that nurture these feelings is inconsistent with our commitments or (given the likely consequences of reinforcing them) with THE GOLDEN RULE. (Thinking obsessively about an injury, for instance, might breed resentment and prepare one for the very real possibility of engaging in revenge.) We also act contrary to love by choosing in ways that nurture feelings which encourage sin, and we choose in this way *for the purpose* of preparing ourselves to act wrongly in the public world, perhaps by suppressing feelings of guilt or remorse. In this case, we act in a manner that's contrary to love in the form of THE PAULINE PRINCIPLE.

Lust

Lust is the disposition to let the desire for erotic pleasure trump love. A lustful choice gives priority to the pursuit of this kind of pleasure in preference to love.

Erotic pleasure is a genuine good, a valuable divine gift. It's an aspect of well-being that's worth realizing in one's own life and fostering in the lives of others. But, just like the other aspects of sensory pleasure and just like each of the other basic goods and the various aspects of each good, it's not the only good. Pursuing it doesn't justify attacking other goods or disregarding the specifications of love.

If, out of lust, I break or encourage someone else to break a promise, I'm ignoring THE GOLDEN RULE. If I lie (as, say, about my marital status or long-term intentions) to secure someone's consent to engage erotically, I'm ignoring THE GOLDEN RULE and quite possibly THE PAULINE PRINCIPLE. If I cause or attempt to cause or willingly risk causing an injury for the purpose of overwhelming or bypassing consent to an erotic interaction, I'm disregarding THE PAULINE PRINCIPLE; using force to compel someone to engage erotically despite the absence of consent is also inconsistent with THE GOLDEN RULE. If I proceed with a given erotic interaction despite what I believe are negative consequences for a prospective erotic partner I wouldn't be willing to accept myself or see imposed on a loved one, I'm disregarding THE GOLDEN RULE. And, if I ignore a resolution to invest myself in a particular way, I'm ignoring COMMITMENT.

To love is to keep promises and help others to do so, to refuse to lie in order to bring about an erotic interaction, to decline to use or threaten violence to bully one's way into an erotic encounter, to take consequences seriously and choose those consequences in light of THE GOLDEN RULE, and to adhere to one's own commitments in the context of erotic interactions as in other settings.

Greed

Greed is the disposition to let the desire for money or material goods trump love. A greedy choice gives priority to the pursuit of money or material goods in preference to love.

While money and material goods are not *basic* goods, they *are* real goods, which enable us and others directly or indirectly to participate in the basic goods in multiple ways. They are thus worth seeking for others and for ourselves, as long as we remember their subsidiary relationship to the basic goods in which they can help people to participate and as long as we pursue them in ways consistent with love. But pursuing them doesn't justify attacking other goods or disregarding the specifications of love.

If, because I'm focused on making money, I disconnect from my loved ones, I'm disregarding THE GOLDEN RULE and, likely, COMMITMENT. If I lie or defraud to obtain money, I'm ignoring THE GOLDEN RULE and, quite possibly, THE PAULINE PRINCIPLE. If I unjustifiably disregard a promise to someone as a way of making money, I'm ignoring THE GOLDEN RULE and, potentially, if I've sought to support my promise with a resolution, COMMITMENT. If I choose to impose the costs of my actions on others in order to make more money—as, for instance, by pumping carcinogenic pollutants into a body of water from which others draw what they drink—I ignore THE GOLDEN RULE. If I use political connections to put an otherwise viable competitor out of business—thus causing unnecessary losses to her and allowing me to charge consumers more than I could if she were in business—I violate THE GOLDEN RULE. If I ignore my responsibility to support good causes, I turn my back on THE GOLDEN RULE. If I disregard my choice to invest in a particular good cause, I flout COMMITMENT. And there are lots of other examples we might imagine.

To love is to keep one's promises and commitments rather than letting the quest for gain sideline them, to refuse to lie or manipulate others deceptively to acquire wealth, to honor the trust of transaction partners, to bear the costs of one's own choices, to avoid using political mischief to disadvantage consumers and competitors, and to give in support of people and good causes.[3]

Gluttony

Gluttony is the disposition to let the desire for gustatory pleasure or other putative goods flowing from eating and drinking trump love. A gluttonous choice gives priority to participation in these goods in preference to love.

Gustatory pleasure is a genuine aspect of well-being; so are other related goods, psychoactive and otherwise, that flow from eating and drinking. But none of these goods is the only aspect of well-being. Pursuing these goods doesn't justify attacking other goods or disregarding the specifications of love.

If, out of gluttony, I fail to complete a serious plan to undertake a demanding task, I ignore COMMITMENT. If I find myself hospitalized and then unemployed because of the damage I've done to my health, placing unexpected stress on loved ones—both because of financial vulnerabilities and because of the threat my potential death poses to valued relationships—I almost certainly ignore THE GOLDEN RULE and, as regards my relationships with loved ones, quite possibly COMMITMENT. If I miss an important work-related meeting because I'm drunk or arrive while thoroughly inebriated, I'm likely disregarding THE GOLDEN RULE and, depending on my self-investment in my workplace and my own plans, perhaps COMMITMENT. If I drive a potential lover away because of the impact of eating and drinking on my life, I'm potentially violating COMMITMENT. The same is true if my eating and drinking impede my achievement of other goals; doing so might also implicate EFFICIENCY. And, if I eat or drink in order to injure myself—to hasten my own death, say, or to attack a body that disgusts me—I violate THE PAULINE PRINCIPLE.

To love is to choose promise keeping over eating and drinking; to take account, given one's promises and fairness more generally, of the impact of one's eating and drinking on others and, given one's commitments, of their effect on others and oneself; and to avoid consuming food or drink in order to harm oneself.

---

3. On giving, see, *e.g*, O'Neill, *Towards Justice and Virtue* 195–200; Scanlon, *What We Owe* 224; Johnson, *Sharing Possessions* 132–9; Finnis, *Law* 173–7; Schmidtz, "Separateness" 145–64; and Murphy, *Moral Demands*.

Sloth

Sloth is the disposition to let the desire for rest or relaxation or surrender to feelings of ineffectuality trump love. A slothful choice gives priority to resting, relaxing, or surrendering to ineffectuality in preference to love. (Sloth shouldn't be confused with depression. Submersion in a debilitating depression, lying outside one's control, is another matter entirely.)

Rest and relaxation are genuine instrumental goods. They're practically useful for our bodies and minds; freedom from the demands of work and of domestic and other responsibilities can facilitate participation in the basic goods of play, imaginative immersion, friendship . . . But, just like every instrumental and even every basic good, rest and relaxation aren't the only goods. Pursuing them doesn't justify attacking other goods or otherwise disregarding the specifications of love.

Ordinarily, the feeling of ineffectuality doesn't disclose reality. The sense that "there's nothing I can do" or "there's no point" is, at least often, a denial of one's own capacity to accomplish the tasks one confronts. (If one has actually taken on a responsibility that it's genuinely unreasonable to expect oneself to fulfill, that's another matter, but the existence of this possibility shouldn't be used as an excuse for giving up without appropriate self-scrutiny.) So embracing, with futility, the delusory sense of one's own ineffectuality is definitely not a reason to disregard the specifications of love.

Whatever the roots of sloth in my life, if, out of sloth, I fail to keep a promise, I've likely violated THE GOLDEN RULE. If I don't follow through on a serious resolution, I'm ignoring COMMITMENT. If just because I want to relax and disengage I refuse to help someone—a friend or a stranger—who asks for my assistance, I will in some cases likely be ignoring THE GOLDEN RULE. Out of sloth, I may choose to undertake a project in a wasteful way (I may not want to invest energy up front to organize the project sensibly), thus ignoring EFFICIENCY.

To love is to honor promises, even when doing so requires tedious exertions; to follow through on commitments, even when one can do so only by working hard; to help at inconvenient times when not doing so would be unfair or inconsistent with serious plans; and to plan projects to the degree necessary to avoid the pointless waste of time, effort, or resources.

Anger

While the sins I've examined so far typically involve the pursuit of actual goods, anger does not. Anger is characteristically a reaction to (often unacknowledged) fear. But, while fear can, of course, focus on the potential loss of or on possible damage to real goods, anger is not a wise response to fear. It is the disposition to let the desire for retribution or retaliation trump love *or* the choice to engage in retribution or retaliation in preference to the choice to love. Retribution and retaliation aren't real goods. They pointlessly add to the destruction and loss in the world. Anger can provide fuel for good work, but it's not *necessary* fuel: the desires to protect, help, save, and escape can also do the job. Pursuing the faux goods of retribution and retaliation certainly doesn't justify disregarding or attacking other goods or, therefore, ignoring love.

If I act out of anger, I'm acting for an unreal good, so I'm violating RECOGNI-TION. By seeking to injure as a matter of retribution or retaliation, I'm violating THE PAULINE PRINCIPLE and likely (because I wouldn't be willing to be, or to see my loved ones, injured under similar circumstances) THE GOLDEN RULE. I may, in particular cases, also disregard COMMITMENT when I choose angrily, depending on who my anger targets and how it's expressed, among other things. And anger can lead me to act wastefully and so to disregard EFFICIENCY.

The Epistle to the Ephesians notes, in effect, that the initial welling up of anger may be a natural process: "Be angry but do not sin; do not let the sun go down on your anger, and do not make room for the devil."[4] The onrush of anger may be something that happens to us. The point is not to condemn ourselves for *feeling the instinct* to retaliate. At the beginning of the week during which I drafted this section of *Loving Creation*, my family's home was robbed, and a number of irreplaceable items were taken. I was angry, and I certainly understand the appeal of anger at such times. But, having felt angry, we can go on either to *refuse* to treat anger as a basis for action or to embrace it as the inspiration for a program of revenge. The latter choice is inconsistent with love.

To love is to shun anger, to seek to rectify and protect without intending injury to anyone, to avoid causing anger-induced injury, to keep commitments that further restrain one's indulgence in and expression of anger, and to let oneself be energized by loyalty and concern rather than hostility.

4. Eph 4:26–27; cp. Jas 1:19–20.

Envy

Envy is the disposition to let the desire for what others have trump love. Envy in this sense may be the inclination to seek to obtain what others have in a manner inconsistent with love. It may also be the inclination—driven by irrational resentment that one's desire is unfulfilled—to deprive others of what they have whether one thereby obtains it or not. An envious choice involves attempting to acquire what others have in a way that's at odds with love or to take it spitefully away.

What one seeks when one envies might be others' status, achievements, relationships, or possessions. Obtaining something otherwise valuable (whether basically or instrumentally) because someone else possesses or has possessed it is not itself a genuine good of any sort. If I act for this imagined good, I violate RECOGNITION. If I deprive the possessor of something simply in order to deprive her—in search of some imagined equalization—I am not pursuing a real good and am therefore, again, violating RECOGNITION. In addition, if I attack a basic aspect of the possessor's well-being, I am violating THE PAULINE PRINCIPLE. If I attack something that isn't a basic aspect of her well-being with the intent to injure a basic aspect of her well-being indirectly, I also violate THE PAULINE PRINCIPLE. And seeking out of hostility to injure something that's not a basic aspect of her well-being seems likely to be at odds with love in the form of THE GOLDEN RULE.

Envy may also drive me to dispossess someone, or to seek to do so, in a manner inconsistent with THE GOLDEN RULE. In some cases, I may violate COMMITMENT at one or more points. And the attempt to possess the nongood of something-possessed-by-someone-else or the antigood of ensuring-that-something-is-taken-away-from-someone-else might well prove a wasteful way of realizing or promoting any real good involved and might thus violate EFFICIENCY.

To love is to welcome others' achievements and enjoyments, to seek authentic goods, and to resist the temptation to seek a particular good just because it's another's or to deprive another of something in order to remedy one's own insecurities.

Arrogance

Arrogance is the disposition to ignore or deny one's own vulnerability and dependence and to regard oneself as entitled to subordinate others and treat them with contempt. An arrogant choice gives priority to seeking and preserving superiority and invulnerability in preference to love. Arrogance can focus on one's physical or intellectual abilities, social skills or prominence, beauty, wealth, power, or spiritual growth (and no doubt other features, capacities, or circumstances).

The arrogant person is mistaken that any kind of excellence on her part entitles her to treat others poorly. The various ways of loving apply whatever she has done or can do and whoever she is. She wouldn't be willing to accept a norm that allowed others to demean her, so it's not consistent with love for her to treat others with scorn or condescension.

The arrogant person doesn't have a clear sense of herself as a creature. She wouldn't likely tell herself or anyone else explicitly that she was the Creator rather than a creature. But her basic attitude toward herself is one of unqualified entitlement. In effect, she declines to acknowledge her own finitude imaginatively and emotionally, even if she does so abstractly.

It's entirely consistent with love for oneself and others to want to achieve, experience, or exhibit real excellence and to be aware of and pleased by whatever excellences are evident in one's life. Others' recognition of this excellence might be validating and confirmatory and might lead in various ways to improved relationships with others, whether instrumentally or intrinsically valuable, and to other attendant opportunities to participate in real goods. But the arrogant person is likely mistaken about the empirical question of her own excellence. The odds are good that she has exaggerated it to boost her sense of her own importance. However, whether or not she has, she chooses in a way that's inconsistent with love by viewing and treating others as she does.

Arrogance as such is concerned with one's imagined superiority and invulnerability rather than on any actual excellences. It involves a misapprehension of what excellence entitles one to think or feel or do, together with the related inclinations to mistreat others and to deceive oneself. The arrogant person embraces as goods things that aren't good at all—entitlement, dismissiveness—and thus consistently violates RECOGNITION. As I suggested earlier, her treatment of others likely violates THE GOLDEN RULE. And her self-misunderstanding attacks the goods of harmony, knowledge, and practical wisdom. If she attempts purposefully to avoid recognizing the truth about herself or actively to distort her awareness of it, she attacks the basic goods of knowledge, practical wisdom, and self-integration and thus violates THE PAULINE PRINCIPLE. Even if she engages in no purposeful attack on these goods, she certainly injures them—emotionally, existentially—by denying her creatureliness. And, in treating others with contempt, she embraces a hostility that is, at any rate, hard to square with THE GOLDEN RULE and that for similar reasons, and insofar as it involves any will to injure a basic aspect of another's well-being, could lead to choices inconsistent with THE PAULINE PRINCIPLE.

To love is to accept oneself as a creature, a part of God's good creation; to be open to the truth about oneself; and to value the personhood of others and recognize their essential moral and social equality with oneself.

Creational Love and the Seven Virtues

Christians have often organized their positive understanding of the moral life around a familiar set of seven virtues. I begin with the four primary virtues of the classical world: prudence, temperance, fortitude, and justice. Then, I consider the three virtues highlighted in 1 Corinthians 13: faith, hope, and love.

These virtues both support and express love. Not only is love the pinnacle virtue of this traditional list, but, as Saint Augustine explicitly affirmed, the four cardinal virtues can be understood as forms of love.[5] Augustine's focus is on the way in which the cardinal virtues can be understood as rightly shaping our love for God. But they can also be understood as concerned with creation, as can the three "theological" virtues. They reflect and facilitate the ways of loving I have sought to elaborate here as elements of a creational love ethic.

In what follows, I explain why I believe we should look critically at the notion that virtue might be "infused" miraculously. Then, I highlight the connections of particular virtues with the specifications of love and ways in which we can see enacting the virtues as both an expression of and a source of support for love; I conclude by reflecting on love itself in light of Saint Paul's peroration in 1 Corinthians 13.

---

5. "The fourfold division of virtue I regard as taken from four forms of love." *On the Morals of the Catholic Church*, trans. Richard Stothert, *A Select Library of the Nicene and Post-Nicene Fathers of the Christian Church*, ed. Philip Schaff, ser. 1 (Buffalo, NY: Christian Literature 1887) 4: 48 (ch. 15, §25) <https://holybooks-lichtenbergpress.netdna-ssl.com/wp-content/uploads/VOL-4-Nicene -and-post-Nicene-fathers-of-the-Christian-church.pdf>. Cp. Ramsey, *Basic Christian Ethics* 210–1 (paraphrasing Augustine).

Creational Love and Infused Virtue

An important strand of Christian thinking characterizes the "theological" virtues—faith, hope, and love—as *infused* by grace, as miraculously imparted.

The understanding of particular divine action I have offered here helps us to think clearly about this account of the acquisition of the virtues.[6] We have good reason to see God as touching the world in ways that are constrained by the freedom of creatures and the integrity of natural processes. To grant the possibility of virtue imparted by miracle is to prompt obvious questions. If the theological virtues can be infused, why not the cardinal virtues as well? Why bother with a world in which they are developed through experience, exposure, and practice? If God is prepared to bypass natural processes here, why does God not do so elsewhere, perhaps frequently?

Given what we can conclude about divine action in light of the reality of evil, it makes the most sense to say that God can and does help us to acquire virtue but that God doesn't do so by imparting virtue miraculously. On PROVIDENCE, God couldn't be expected to impart a virtue miraculously. But we should not expect God to do this even on PROVIDENCE-PLUS: even if God acts miraculously in the world, to impart a quality of character to someone miraculously would be to risk disrupting the continuity of the recipient's life and so of her identity.

We need not view any of the virtues as infused. At the same time, we can acknowledge that all virtues result from grace. Consider a perfectly ordinary story about the acquisition of a virtue—as partly a matter of heredity, partly a result of instruction (both arm's-length teaching and nurturant engagement), partly a matter of imitation, and partly a matter of response to various social norms, prompts, and pressures. Such a story can make sense as far as it goes. But we can grant its relative satisfactoriness even while noting that more needs to be said.

Persuasive divine action can be at work in a person's psyche, nudging and luring her to respond positively to the prompts she receives from genes, instructors, spiritual directors, therapists, imitable others, and socially mediated incentives. At the same time, divine persuasion will also be affecting the behavior of the people who are influencing her. The structure and dynamics of creation itself—from the existence and operation of a regular, predictably physical environment to the influence of heredity to the dynamics of each person's biological

---

6. Ramsey (*Basic Christian Ethics* 213–9) offers a critical perspective on the idea of infused virtue.

and psychological development—can lay the groundwork for the acquisition of virtue and dispose people to become more virtuous. And the implicit or explicit communication of the gospel, rooted in divine action and divinely fostered awareness of that action, can itself help to shape people's attitudes and behaviors. That's because knowing oneself embraced by divine love can be empowering and healing in ways that lead to the development of character traits more open and attentive to reality, more grace filled, more confident, more anchored.

On this model, in no case is virtue imparted "from the outside" in ways that bypass human free choice and the natural processes of human growth and influence. At the same time, however, in no case does virtue emerge apart from grace. As Creator, Word, and Spirit, God underlies and informs every instance of the acquisition of virtue.

We can, at the same time, recognize that at least two of the theological virtues are interestingly *different* from the cardinal virtues in ways that might help to explain why someone might think of them as infused. Faith and hope can be experienced as, for instance, attitudes that *happen* to us. (Some aspects of love might seem to happen to us, too, but not, I think, love as appropriate regard for well-being, which clearly presents itself as a possible object of choice.) The sense that each is a gift can no doubt prompt the idea of supernatural infusion.

I think we can take the phenomenology of faith and hope seriously, however, without regarding them as products of unmediated divine action. We can do so by recognizing the degree to which important aspects of these virtues arise because of providential action through a broad range of creaturely realities. Sometimes, that action may lead to someone's being born with faith, hope, or both. But faith as basic trust can also grow out of family relationships; bonds with friends, coworkers, and others; and the experience of the world as both orderly and fruitful. And hope as a general and persistent attitude can develop in and through those experiences that give rise to basic trust but also through any experience in which individual hopes are not disappointed. We can perhaps *choose* to trust in any given case, and to hope. But general dispositions to trust and to exhibit hope at least often seem to come into being slowly and imperceptibly, as God works through diverse elements of experience.

Prudence

Prudence is the capacity and disposition to exercise—to participate in the good of—practical wisdom. A prudent choice is a choice in accordance with practical wisdom.

Prudence supports love by helping one identify whom to love and how to do so in particular cases. It can be seen as involving a willingness to learn, appropriate awareness of risk, comprehension of relevant norms, foresight, knowledge, rapidity of judgment, and the capacity to analyze and evaluate.[7]

The development of this virtue helps to ensure that one will exhibit appropriate regard for others and for oneself—that one will love. When a decision concerns the well-being of others, exercising prudence will often be a requirement flowing from THE GOLDEN RULE. If I would not be willing to accept a standard that permitted others to be imprudent in a given way when making decisions affecting *my* well-being in circumstances of a particular sort, then it will not be consistent with love for me to be imprudent in this way in comparable circumstances. The requirement of prudence also flows from EFFICIENCY, which mandates suitable sensitivity to likely outcomes and risks.

And prudence must be cultivated by anyone who wishes to undertake and fulfill serious resolutions, so it is, effectively, a presupposition of COMMITMENT. To the extent that assessing the merits of options requires awareness of genuine goods, prudence also flows from RECOGNITION. And, when assaying options involves determining whether a particular choice might be a choice to execute a purposeful or instrumental attack on well-being, prudence requires respect for, as its evident value is supported by, THE PAULINE PRINCIPLE. Prudence as a disposition sustains love; prudent choices express love.

Temperance

Temperance is the capacity and disposition to manage one's desires, to resist the tug of desire, in order to love oneself and others appropriately. A temperate choice is a choice to pursue an authentic good or set of goods in ways that are consistent with love, potentially in the face of contrary desires.

Desire is entirely appropriate: there are real goods, and their *being* real goods means that desiring them is evidence that our psyches are, at least to some extent, healthy. We are finite; there is always room for us to grow and to flourish in new ways. So temperance is not about resisting or suppressing desire. The recognition of its importance is not premised on the assumption that our desires are for illusory goods. Nor is temperance moderation for moderation's sake, much less asceticism. It is, rather, the capacity to avoid being overmastered by

---

7. See, *e.g.*, Thomas Aquinas, *Summa Theologiae*, trans. Fathers of the English Dominican Province (London: Burns 1920) II-II, q49 <https://www.newadvent.org/summa/3049.htm>.

our desires when they might seem likely to impede one's appropriate responsiveness to any and all of love's specifications, including the fulfillment of plans to which one has committed oneself. Food and drink and eros are obvious examples, but one's capacity to choose lovingly may be overwhelmed by the failure to manage desires for all sorts of goods.

Temperance supports love by helping us avoid being distracted from appropriate objects of love and ways of loving. Intemperate behavior is inconsistent with THE GOLDEN RULE when it involves being carried away by our cravings in ways that involve arbitrarily mistreating or disregarding others. It is inconsistent with COMMITMENT insofar as it involves abandoning our firm plans in favor of the goods—potentially quite real, valuable ones—that immediate desire proposes we pursue. It is inconsistent with EFFICIENCY insofar as it involves thoughtless wastefulness driven by desire. It is inconsistent with THE PAULINE PRINCIPLE insofar as it involves choosing to attack some aspect of well-being in response to longing—from using violence to eliminate a rival for an erotic relationship to lying to speed up one's access to a select bottle of champagne. It is important to nourish the habit of temperance, then, if one wants to be able to count on oneself consistently to embody the specifications of love in the face of the appeal of alluringly attractive goods. It may make perfect sense to participate in these goods, but it makes no sense to be dominated by them; temperance helps to maintain one's freedom to love.

Fortitude

Fortitude is the capacity and disposition to persevere in meeting one's obligations and enacting one's commitments despite inner turmoil or the risk of harm to aspects of one's well-being, notably physical danger. A fortitudinous choice is a choice to persist in doing one's duty or pursuing one's goals in the face of emotional resistance or external threat.

Fortitude is a crucial source of support for COMMITMENT, since we will not infrequently be prompted to avoid fulfilling our serious plans because of fear. Fortitude is also a support for love in the form of adherence to THE GOLDEN RULE. Our faithfulness to our promises will sometimes be impeded by fear of outward loss or inner upset. Because fear can also prompt one to tell lies and to avoid accepting responsibilities for protecting or promoting the well-being of others that flow from THE GOLDEN RULE, fortitude supports adherence to this requirement of love in other ways, too. To the extent that lying clashes with love in the form of THE PAULINE PRINCIPLE and that various kinds of purposeful or instrumental attacks on well-being might come as responses to anxiety or terror at the prospect of physical risk, fortitude supports constancy in living out this specification of love, too. Unreasonable anxiety might prompt one to waste resources and opportunities; fortitude can thus also serve as a support for EFFICIENCY. Embracing these aspects of love thus means seeking to cultivate and exhibit fortitude.

Justice

Justice is the disposition to acknowledge and fulfill serious obligations to others.[8] A just choice is a choice to meet such obligations.[9]

Justice as disposition and justice in choice help us love who and how we should in a wide range of important instances. Our most significant responsibilities to others flow primarily from THE GOLDEN RULE and THE PAULINE PRINCIPLE. The contents of the serious obligations with which justice is concerned are given by these specifications of love. Justice is on display when we discern what these obligations are, when we assess the particulars of each situation in the ways needed to love in that situation, and when we choose to act accordingly.[10]

Justice may involve choosing, or the disposition to choose, in accordance with the other specifications of love. When we act for an organization, an institution, or a group of some other sort, we may need to take EFFICIENCY into account when deciding how to deploy the group's resources. In some cases, too, RECOGNITION will also affect our obligations to others because showing appropriate regard for their well-being will mean seeking to promote, respect, protect, or realize genuine rather than illusory goods. However, one's obligation in

8. People sometimes speak of institutions rather than actions as just. An institution can be described as just if choices made within and on behalf of the institution are characteristically just and if the choices made in establishing it were and those made in maintaining it are characteristically just. For a related, even if not identical, account, see Jonathan Crowe, "The Idea of Small Justice," *Ratio Juris* 34.3 (Sep. 2021): 224–43. It's not entirely unidiomatic to speak of being just to ourselves, but I'll focus on justice as interpersonal obligation.

9. People sometimes use "obligations" to refer to duties arising specifically from promises or similar voluntary undertakings. Here, I have in mind a more general sense of the term in which "obligations" and "duties" are synonymous (and in which duties, in turn, need not be role- or function-dependent).

10. Wolterstorff, *Justice in Love*, affirms (summarizing what he takes plausibly to be an understanding of the Levitical injunction to love one's neighbor as oneself) that "doing justice is an example of love" (84). Of course I would agree, adding only that fulfilling *any* moral requirement is, I think, an example of love.

such cases still flows primarily from THE GOLDEN RULE, which stipulates that one good turn deserves another. One could hardly embrace this way of loving while returning an unreal good for a real one; RECOGNITION simply serves to fill out the content of one's obligation.[11]

While it is relevant to interpersonal obligation, COMMITMENT does not involve or ground duties *to* others, though our commitments may involve or ground duties *with respect to* others. So, as I've noted, in addition to making promises intended to create a marriage, someone may *also* commit to being loyal to her spouse. But the requirement that she adhere to her resolutions is not a matter of justice, since the duties grounded in these resolutions are not claimable by her spouse, who may not even be aware of them.

The virtue of justice supports and embodies most of the specifications of love.

Faith

Faith is not a disposition to accept propositions or to submit to authority. It is *trust* and, perhaps most importantly, *basic* trust, the disposition to regard the universe as having a friendly face, to regard God, if we are aware of the reality of God, as trustworthy, as love. A choice to exercise faith is a choice to rely on God as loving.[12]

The disposition to embrace basic trust and the choice to do so in particular circumstances can support love by freeing me from inner bonds that lead predictably to predation or withdrawal rather than love. When we become aware of the reality of God, basic trust can rightly take God as its object, and we can understand God as grounding and justifying it. And the thoroughgoing affirmation of the reality of God can reshape our perceptions and deepen our capacity and inclination to experience basic trust.[13] But the attitude of basic trust can

11. This doesn't mean that one need return an instance of some *basic* good for an instance of this or some other basic good; instrumental goods of all sorts can help others realize basic goods in their own lives.

12. On basic trust, see, *e.g.,* Pannenberg, *Anthropology* 220–42; Hans Küng, *Does God Exist? An Answer for Today* (New York: Vintage-Random 1981) 442–77; Jack W. Provonsha, *You Can Go Home Again: An Untheology of the Atonement* (Washington, DC: Review 1982) (my source for the friendly face metaphor); and Nicholas Lash, *Easter in Ordinary: Reflections on Human Experience and the Knowledge of God* (Notre Dame, IN: University of Notre Dame Press 1988) 202.

13. For this phrase, see Fritz Guy, "Affirming the Reality of God," *The Stature of Christ: Essays in Honor of Edward Heppenstall,* ed. Vern Carner and Gary Stanhiser (Loma Linda, CA: n.p. 1970) 13–22.

be evoked by what we experience and how we are formed whether or not we consciously apprehend the reality of God.

To exercise the virtue of faith in this sense is an expression of love for oneself because it opens one to participation in the good of harmony and helps to ground one's sense of the meaning and value of one's existence, a sense that is a crucial prerequisite to effective judgment, choice, and action in other contexts. This virtue supports a life embodying love in the form of all of its specifications because of the role played by anxiety, fear, and insecurity in so much self- and other-destructive behavior that violates THE PAULINE PRINCIPLE and THE GOLDEN RULE in particular. I may tend to dominate, dismiss, or devastate others because I feel I need to do so to establish my own secure sense of identity; or because I fear that, if I don't, others won't give me the respect I crave; or because I simply take myself too seriously—as, perhaps, the only possible source of meaning for my own life.

Failing to trust, I may find it hard not to pursue valuable ends using means inconsistent with love, convinced that, if I fail, goods about which I care will not survive. I may impatiently seek make-believe goods in preference to real ones just because the make-believe ones are ready to hand: I may lack confidence that the real goods will be accessible, that I will be able to participate in them, in the future. (For instance, I may be unwilling to connect deeply and vulnerably with anyone because I fear that the risks associated with doing so won't prove worthwhile, that I will always be disappointed, so I may choose unreal or superficial relationships in place of the good of friendship.) I may opt against investing myself deeply, and so adhering to my commitments, out of fear that the universe is the kind of place in which I can expect to experience only disappointment.

To embrace the virtue of faith, then, is to move beyond these limits and to find myself liberated to love. Cultivating this is thus a way of supporting my choices to love.

Hope

Hope as a virtue is not the irrationally optimistic delusion that everything in our lives will always turn out well. Instead, hope is the reasonable disposition to keep going, the willingness to pursue our goals and to remain open to surprises. A hopeful choice, therefore, confronts doubt and despair and moves forward.

Hope supports love by grounding constancy and commitment when we're tempted to stop loving. Enacting this virtue expresses and supports love for oneself and others. (*i*) Hope is creative. If we hope that transformation is possible, we are sometimes capable (frequently along with other agents) of *making* it happen. Hope equips us to continue seeking, engaging, working. Without it, we are likely to give up; and, giving up, we can only succeed by blind luck. (*ii*) Divine providence is always at work in every district of creation, and this means that God's influence is fostering liberation and transformation. While creatures too often say "No!" to God, divine activity gives us reason to expect that things might, indeed, change for the better. (*iii*) Secure in God's love, we can be confident (here the overlap with faith is evident) that the meaning and value of the life of each one of us can't be shaken by the vicissitudes of history. (*iv*) More than that, to hope for life in God beyond death is to anticipate transformation and reconciliation even after what may seem like definitive defeat in history. The prospect of life beyond death means we can take risks we might otherwise be unwilling to embrace. And it can inspire us not to give up or to choose against love in the face of threats that can't actually touch our lives beyond death.

Hope can help to empower us to continue seeking to protect, promote, respect, and realize love in the world even when despair might seem like the most rational option. If we wish to choose in accordance with the specifications of love, then, we will seek to embrace and foster hope.

Love

Love as a virtue is the disposition to show appropriate regard for the well-being of others for one's own. Love as a choice is to treat others and oneself with such regard, enacting RECOGNITION, THE GOLDEN RULE, THE PAULINE PRINCIPLE, COMMITMENT, and EFFICIENCY.

To understand the importance of the various aspects of well-being and of what love looks like in practice is to see why the virtue of love, which undergirds and finds expression in the other virtues and which is counter to all sins, deadly and otherwise, is well worth embracing. The idea and experience of virtue are intimately linked with love along multiple dimensions. The same is true of other aspects of the Christian moral tradition and of our lives, as we have already seen. Love is the capstone of personal existence because so much that we want to say and do is inextricable from it.

The "theological" virtues—faith, hope, and love—are, of course, drawn from Saint Paul's poetic celebration of love in 1 Corinthians 13, which remains an evocative portrayal of the heart of the Christian life and of Christian ethics:

If I speak in the tongues of mortals and of angels, but do not have love, I am a noisy gong or a clanging cymbal. And if I have prophetic powers, and understand all mysteries and all knowledge, and if I have all faith, so as to remove mountains, but do not have love, I am nothing. If I give away all my possessions, and if I hand over my body so that I may boast, but do not have love, I gain nothing.

Love is patient; love is kind; love is not envious or boastful or arrogant or rude. It does not insist on its own way; it is not irritable or resentful; it does not rejoice in wrongdoing, but rejoices in the truth. It bears all things, believes all things, hopes all things, endures all things.

Love never ends. But as for prophecies, they will come to an end; as for tongues, they will cease; as for knowledge, it will come to an end. For we know only in part, and we prophesy only in part; but when the complete comes, the partial will come to an end. When I was a child, I spoke like a child, I thought like a child, I reasoned like a child; when I became an adult, I put an end to childish ways. For now we see in a mirror, dimly, but then we will see face to face. Now I know only in part; then I will know fully, even as I have been fully known. And now faith, hope, and love abide, these three; and the greatest of these is love.[14]

Saint Paul is surely right: What, finally, is the point of communication, even of communication across barriers within humanity and between humanity and any nonhuman realm, in the absence of full-blown, authentic love? If our communication does not aim at what is good for ourselves and others, it seems meaningless, irrational. If it is an expression of hostility to any sentient God has made, it is a denial of what is genuinely valuable. If it ignores the importance of diving deep, of focused self-investment, it embodies a superficiality that is less, perhaps much less, than love can be. If it fails to count the cost of action, it runs the risk of wasting other opportunities to enrich the life of the agent and of others. And, if it discriminates arbitrarily, it reveals itself as motivated at root by regard not for each irreplaceable creature of God as such but, rather, for its own preferences. It may make a great show, a loud noise, but it's finally insufficient, empty.

Being a proudly accomplished spiritual athlete may seem like reason to cheer. But spiritual athleticism need not be a product of genuine love. Acquiring preternatural abilities, depth of understanding, and even the ability to perform what

14. 1 Cor 13.

seem like miracles on the basis of the powerful confidence that God will do what one desires can hardly qualify as satisfactory if, again, one is unconcerned with actual flourishing or is concerned with it in the wrong way. Prophecy can easily prove to be a means of self-righteous self-promotion or dominance. I can seek understanding not because of my genuine curiosity, my appreciation for the inherent value of knowledge for myself or others, or my wish to learn things that can lead to benefits for myself and others but in order to dominate others, perhaps to discover techniques of control.

Genuine faith—basic trust, confidence that the universe has a friendly face—is hardly a spur to or support for unloving behavior. Indeed, it will undermine insecurities that make unloving behavior likely. But bare confidence in a God of pure power can easily lead to a domineering, self-promoting style of engagement with the world, a style quite incompatible with love.

I can give prodigally without giving generously. For I may give out of a desire for spiritual dominance or superiority, out of a desire to manipulate, out of a sense of distaste for God's good creation or my own existence, or out of a desire to placate a frightening divine judge. I may yield my body to jailers or torturers not because I refuse to give up on love—not because, say, I'm not willing to reveal the location of hidden dissidents—but because, even if my actions *appear* worth crowing about, I have no genuine concern for those I appear to want to protect or, even worse, because I've given up on life as valueless. I may even be violating THE PAULINE PRINCIPLE by *trying* to punish my body (in the case of the discarded possessions) or by actually *seeking* death (in the case of the surrendered body).

To love is to avoid giving up because others are counting on one's persistence (THE GOLDEN RULE) and because one understands the value of deep self-investment (COMMITMENT). To love is to be kind because the attempt to wound another's mental health or disrupt her relationships would be inconsistent with THE PAULINE PRINCIPLE; because to attack her, betray her, or treat her dismissively would be inconsistent with THE GOLDEN RULE; and because to ignore one's self-chosen investment in her growth would be inconsistent with COMMITMENT. To love is to avoid envy because RECOGNITION matters: that someone else happens to have something is no reason to want it; that one doesn't have something oneself is no reason to try to take it away from someone who does have it.

To love is to recognize the importance of avoiding lies and the value of communicating truths in ways that don't leave others feeling diminished. To love is to avoid being arrogant because one acknowledges the preciousness of each irreplaceable other and so refuses to erect one's own sense of self on the domination or dismissal of any sentient. To love is to avoid being rude because of the importance, in light of THE GOLDEN RULE, of being sensitive to others' time, to their commitments, to the fact that they are not one's servants or creditors and that they are, indeed, irreplaceably precious. Expressing oneself to others is a way of giving them the gift of otherness. But to love is to avoid bullying, to let go of the illusion that one's perspective is always correct, one's own preferred way of doing things is superior to all the others, both because one wants others to be able to express themselves and realize their goals and because one loves oneself too much to embrace the illusion that one doesn't need to learn and grow in response to others' insights and perspectives.

To love is to shun irritation and resentment out of love for oneself and others. Dwelling on the negative thoughts that birth these negative attitudes means pursuing what are very much not authentic goods. Poisoning one's own mind distracts one from participating in genuine goods alone or with others and from assisting others in participating in the real goods they choose. Worse than that, it can prompt one to act—contrary to THE GOLDEN RULE and RECOGNITION and perhaps to THE PAULINE PRINCIPLE—in not only petty but also punitive ways.

To love is to decline to rejoice in wrongdoing because one recognizes that rightness and wrongness are not arbitrary creations of a God who is pure will but, rather, reflections of what *love means*, of what appropriate regard for well-being involves. And to love is to cheer for the truth both because knowledge is a basic aspect of well-being, and so worth discovering and transmitting, and because an important truth is, precisely, that what matters is love, that doing evil, attacking love, is finally out of sync with reality.

To love is to bear, to endure everything—not out of a holy masochism but rather out of an awareness that giving up accomplishes nothing, a love for oneself and others that welcomes and looks forward to future opportunities for flourishing, and a hope in virtue of which one refuses to believe that defeat won't have the last word. Hope helps to sustain love—not only hope in God beyond death but also hope in what God is doing in the world and in the possibility of beginning again after tragedy and loss, recognizing that believing that a new start is possible can help to *make* a new start possible. And love is sustained by trust in the God whose goodness lies at the root of all things, trust that recognizes the essential friendliness of the world God has made and refuses, therefore, to give in to despair.

Our necessarily limited attempts to grasp reality continually run up against our own inadequacies, our ignorance, our finitude. That's true of our attempts to understand scientifically, historically, logically, poetically. It's true, therefore, of attempts to gain and offer spiritual insight as well. None of us knows what God knows, and our attempts to pretend otherwise will, we can only hope, end as we come to a clearer apprehension—ultimately in God's future, beyond death—of what our creatureliness involves and of who God is. But our love for ourselves and others will still matter whatever our limitations. It *won't* come to an end. We will always be parts of God's good creation, always both loving and beloved, and love will always be the right response to those God has made.

God will always love and invite us to love, and love will always be central to our own flourishing. We know and understand so little about a dizzyingly complex universe, about our place in it, and about its place in the divine life. We will always have more to learn; but we look forward to continued growth in understanding beyond our present reality. We know that we will continue to understand more about what it is to love—to exhibit appropriate regard for the well-being of—those God has made. As we grow, in this life and beyond, trust and hope will sustain us. And God's good creation, including us as well as every other sentient God has made, will continue rightly to evoke our love.

Conclusion

Loving creation—exhibiting love to those God has created—is the task of the moral life. The creation within which we are called to love is itself a loving creation, a creation characterized at its best by loving interchange, a kind of interchange we have good reason to help foster. God's own creative activity has been and continues to be a matter of loving creation, of creativity exercised lovingly. God is engaged in loving creation, in bestowing love on those God has made. And our individual moral acts should be instances of loving creation—of creativity exercised with love, of bringing new situations into being lovingly, in our own lives and those of others.

If God is love and calls us to love, a common Christian view in accordance with which moral requirements are created by God and then announced to us in unambiguous terms is implausible.

Theistic voluntarism suggests that God, having created moral agents, might then choose to create a range of moral requirements to be imposed on those God has created. But this way of thinking is difficult to square with the idea of divine love, not least because it risks rendering such love meaningless. (If God creates norms, then anything God does is loving.) God determines what is good and right by creating a certain kind of world, not through any sort of separate, contingent creation of moral requirements. A voluntarist conception of vocation is no easier to sustain than any other voluntarist account of obligation. And, while the language of vocation captures something important about the moral life, the best way (as it seems to me) of making sense of it doesn't lead us to posit the kind of *requirement* vocation is often thought to involve.

If God is love, then divine action in the world must be at least primarily persuasive. This means that, while God is constantly communicating with humans, divine communication takes place in and through the actions of fallible, ignorant, sinful creatures. God's action in the world thus doesn't provide a royal road to truth that bypasses the need for careful reflection and inquiry.

Reflection and inquiry prompt us to see that love is appropriate regard for the welfare (or fulfillment or well-being or flourishing or self-realization) of creatures. A creational love ethic is a pure ethic of love,[1] featuring no requirement that is not a specification of love.[2] But such an ethic must refer to *more* than love because love must be concerned with the well-being of the one loved.

Well-being is not an undifferentiated blob. There are many different ways in which someone's life can go well. They include aesthetic experience, avoidance of physical pain, friendship, harmony with reality, imaginative immersion, knowledge, life, play, practical wisdom, self-integration, sensory pleasure, and skillful performance. We recognize these diverse aspects of flourishing because we cannot love without knowing what love involves, without knowing something about the well-being for which love means showing appropriate regard.

While there are no ethical elements of a creational love ethic apart from love itself, this doesn't mean that we can't or shouldn't reason about what it means to love, about how we can be consistent in our choices to love, and so forth. Accepting a creational love ethic is perfectly compatible with "admit[ting] no rules or principles other than the 'law of love' itself" and with denying "that there are any 'perceptual intuitions' about what is right or wrong in particular situations independently of the dictates of love."[3] But we can grant this without confusing love with unstructured goodwill, undifferentiated benevolence. Rather, we can and should seek to understand what love means, what it looks like; we can recognize that it is *structured*, that it is specified in ways that give it form.

Reflecting on love's inner dynamics, on what love wants and is, we can see that loving well means exhibiting appropriate concern for authentic elements of well-being. Love must be anchored ultimately in a recognition of the sheer beauty of being and so with the irreplaceable preciousness of each sentient existence, so that it must decline to make arbitrary distinctions and instead treat all those God has made as worthy of moral standing. Love must refuse to deny the genuine worth of any aspect of any sentient's well-being, and thus to attack any good in the purported interest of any other—the agent's, the target's, or any other sentient's. Love sees that a powerful way of loving is diving

---

1. Cp. Frankena, "Love and Principle" 224–30.
2. For another take on the relationship between love and natural law, see Charles Pinches and David Matzko McCarthy, "Natural Law and the Language of Love," *Journal of Moral Theology* 1.2 (2012): 116–46.
3. Frankena, "Love and Principle" 211.

deep, focusing, investing, even when doing so is challenging and unrewarding. And love means caring enough about our ability to protect, promote, respect, and realize well-being to acknowledge the actual consequences of choices and decline to expend resources pointlessly when they could instead benefit the agent or others.

The various specifications of love don't add to love or constrain it. They don't provide us with reasons to make essentially unloving choices. Choosing well doesn't mean following general rules even when doing so isn't loving or isn't required by love. No: RECOGNITION, THE GOLDEN RULE, THE PAULINE PRINCIPLE, COMMITMENT, and EFFICIENCY are *ways of loving* that apply universally, that apply to all our choices with respect to others and ourselves. We couldn't ignore them and still choose lovingly.

We love everyone by always adhering to THE PAULINE PRINCIPLE: we never make injury to anyone's good, our own or someone else's, our *purpose*—our goal or a means to the achievement of our goal. We also love everyone by always following THE GOLDEN RULE: no one gets arbitrarily excluded, ignored, or treated differently.

While at the ground level, as it were, THE GOLDEN RULE rules out refusing inconsistently to take anyone into account, it also provides reasons to focus on particular people and activities, reasons including promises, explicitly or implicitly invited reliance, immediate vulnerability . . . And COMMITMENT also helps to determine who and how we will love. We choose to invest in particular projects, particular people and relationships, particular organizations or groups. We establish priorities. When we commit to doing so, we've moved beyond the possibility of making choices simply in light of our whims. We've chosen to dive deep, to care in ways that, again, give our love focus.

In addition, RECOGNITION is a matter of loving: we love by showing appropriate regard for actual well-being. Similarly, we love by adhering to EFFICIENCY because doing so enables us to plan wisely, to take real consequences for ourselves and others into account, to love using our time and energy and money without wasting them.

In addition, we can see that some aspects of well-being themselves give specificity to love by necessarily channeling love toward particular people: you can't participate in the good of friendship without focusing on friends or participate in the good of play without focusing on those with whom one plays. And realizing other goods will often naturally, even if not necessarily, mean focusing on particular relationships: with teachers, say, when one seeks speculative knowledge; with pastors and fellow congregants when one seeks harmony with reality through worship and study; with erotic partners when one seeks some varieties of sensory pleasure.

To embrace a creational love ethic is to enact love in the form it is given by the various aspects of well-being and by the specifications. Such an ethic can inform economic life, politics, or the arts. I've chosen here to illustrate it in several ways, initially by highlighting its relevance to our choices about the use of force and our erotic interactions.

Love rigidly, robustly constrains the use of force. But using force is still potentially consistent with love because, rightly undertaken, it can qualify as a way of loving by stopping unjust violence. As with force, so with eros: we don't need any sort of special subset of moral norms for this aspect of our lives. A recognition of the immense array of human goods implicated by eros and of the relevance of THE GOLDEN RULE to our efforts to participate in these goods should be sufficient to guide our loving action in the erotic arena. We do not love each other if we distort our erotic interactions by lying, using or threatening violence, or breaking promises; nor do we do so if we disregard one another's vulnerability. But we can love erotically—seeking real goods, avoiding purposeful and instrumental attacks on anyone's well-being, adhering to THE GOLDEN RULE—in a range of relational forms, from the casual to the comprehensive and lifelong, and whatever the sexes or genders of our partners. One important way in which we can do so is by offering the liberating security that comes from bringing into being a marital *we* with the simple promise "I will never leave you."

Love has repeatedly been discerned at the root of the Christian moral tradition. We can understand a creational love ethic more clearly by seeing how key elements of that tradition can be applied when treated as expressions of love. In turn, we may be able to see these elements more clearly if we ponder them in love's light. Reflecting on the Ten Commandments, multiple New Testament texts, and the classic virtues and sins Christians have highlighted can all prompt fruitful deliberation, growth, and action.

A creational love ethic is a pure love ethic. Its imperatives flow not from natural tendencies or structures but from love. It is a love ethic because it involves no injunction that is not a specification of love. At the same time, it is a creational ethic because love *presupposes* creation. Love presupposes, is about, flourishing, and flourishing is rooted in creation. And what we examine to determine the shape of flourishing is the work of the Creator; the Spirit blows over it; and the *Logos* is the light that enlightens every creature within it. So, for instance, marriage as understood by a creational love ethic is not a matter of following a purported biological imperative to engage in reproduction. Rather, marriage as

I am concerned with it here is an expression of love that acknowledges the full range of created potentialities that actually constitutes each partner.[4]

"To the Christian faith," Emil Brunner asserts, "the *lex*, even the *lex creatoris*, is never the final principle. . . . It is qualified by two concepts: by the sovereignty of God, which also stands above His Law, and by the Love of God which administers the law, and at the same time overcomes it."[5] But to frame things in this way is to assume that the *lex creatoris* is somehow a direct product of the divine will rather than simply what it is for the creation to flourish. It is also to fail to see that the *lex creatoris* is, precisely, the law of love, not only because God the Creator *is* love, but also because the law of creation is the law of love, love for those God has made. There is and could be no divine love that was inconsistent with the love embodied in the *lex creatoris*, the law of love for creatures like us.

It is perhaps because he still was tempted to see a creational ethic as "independent" that Paul Ramsey could write to Joseph Fletcher, "My quarrel with Paul Lehmann is not over any natural law norm of truth-telling, but over what faithfulness, agape, covenant, require in this regard."[6] It is precisely with this sort of contrast that I want to take issue. A "natural law norm of truth-telling" might be worked in a number of different ways. But, whether as a matter of (*i*) fairness or of (*ii*) respect for the reasoning capacities of those with whom we communicate or of (*iii*) regard for the self-integration of those who communicate, such a norm can be understood as embodying love. It is a matter of love for the other, love for the agent, love for both, love for their relationship, understood, in any case, in light of what makes for our well-being in light of how God has made us. There is no warrant for separating love and creation. It makes no sense, therefore, to say that love is primary, justice derivative.[7] Justice is, precisely, a vital aspect of what it means to love well—to choose with appropriate regard for well-being in accordance with key specifications of love, THE GOLDEN RULE and THE PAULINE PRINCIPLE.

An ethic of love is a creational ethic. To love well is to choose with appropriate regard for well-being. And well-being, in turn, is a function of who we are, and so of how we have been and are being made by God.

4. Cp. Long, *Tragedy, Tradition, Transformism* 78.
5. Emil Brunner, *The Divine Imperative: A Study in Christian Ethics*, trans. Olive Wyon (Philadelphia: Fortress 1947) 449–50.
6. Paul Ramsey, letter to Joseph Fletcher, June 29, 1965, box 8, "Correspondence Series, ca. 1939–1982 and Undated," Paul Ramsey Papers, David M. Rubenstein Rare Book and Manuscript Library, Duke University, qtd. Hollowell, *Power and Purpose* 102.
7. Cp. Hollowell, *Power and Purpose* 197.

Index

About the Author

Gary Chartier is Distinguished Professor of Law and Business Ethics and associate dean of the Tom and Vi Zapara School of Business at La Sierra University in Riverside, California. A theologian, philosopher, legal scholar, and political theorist, he is the author, coauthor, editor, or coeditor of twenty current or forthcoming books, including *Understanding Friendship: On the Moral, Political, and Spiritual Nature of Love* (Fortress 2022), *Public Practice, Private Law: An Essay on Love, Marriage, and the State* (Cambridge University Press 2016), and *The Analogy of Love: Divine and Human Love at the Center of Christian Theology* (2d ed., Griffin 2017). His byline has appeared over forty times in journals including *Religious Studies*, the *Anglican Theological Review*, and the *Heythrop Journal*.

After qualifying for a BA in history and political science from La Sierra (1987, magna cum laude), he earned a PhD in the Faculty of Divinity at the University of Cambridge (1991), exploring philosophical and theological ethics, theology, the philosophy of religion, political theory, and Christian origins. He graduated with a JD (2001, Order of the Coif) from UCLA, where he studied legal philosophy and public law and received the Judge Jerry Pacht Memorial Award in Constitutional Law. The University of Cambridge presented him with an earned higher doctorate, an LLD, in 2015 for his work in legal philosophy.

A proud Southern California native who wishes he had attended UC Sunnydale, he shares a slowly improving 1920 home in Riverside with his wife, Alicia Homer; Willow Rosenberg the Kitty; and Rupert Giles Feline. His hobbies include long-arc television, biography, genre and philosophical fiction, spicy food, politics, human psychic and social dynamics, interminable conversation, and the esoteric, the quirky, and the arcane. A passionate friend, he embraces E. M. Forster's "Only connect" as both an invitation and a personal motto. Visit him online at <http://www.garychartier.net>.